an unorthodox faith

an unorthodox faith

a new reformation for a postmodern world

Kurt Struckmeyer

RESOURCE *Publications* • Eugene, Oregon

AN UNORTHODOX FAITH
A New Reformation for a Postmodern World

Copyright © 2017 Kurt Struckmeyer. All rights reserved. Except for brief quotations in critical publications or reviews, no part of this book may be reproduced in any manner without prior written permission from the publisher. Write: Permissions, Wipf and Stock Publishers, 199 W. 8th Ave., Suite 3, Eugene, OR 97401.

Wipf & Stock
An Imprint of Wipf and Stock Publishers
199 W. 8th Ave., Suite 3
Eugene, OR 97401

www.wipfandstock.com

PAPERBACK ISBN: 978-1-4982-3452-8
HARDCOVER ISBN: 978-1-4982-3454-2
EBOOK ISBN: 978-1-4982-3453-5

Manufactured in the U.S.A.   FEBRUARY 7, 2017

Biblical quotations are primarily from the New Revised Standard Version Bible, copyright © 1989, Division of Christian Education of the National Council of the Churches of Christ in the United States of America. Used by permission. All rights reserved.

Also by Kurt Struckmeyer:

A Conspiracy of Love: Following Jesus in a Postmodern World

To my grandchildren
Henry, Eleanor, Wyatt, and Phoebe

May you work toward a better world
where children no longer weep from poverty and hunger,
where they no longer live in fear from violence,
and where they are taught kindness, compassion, and love.
Love freely.
Act compassionately.
Live justly.
Seek peace.

contents

acknowledgments | ix
preface: a dissenting opinion | xi

   introduction: a new reformation | 1

part 1: the great detour
   chapter 1   losing our way | 19
   chapter 2   the two gospels | 40

part 2: deconstruction
   chapter 3   deconstructing god | 49
   chapter 4   the god of the cosmos | 73
   chapter 5   the god who intervenes | 86
   chapter 6   the apocalyptic christ | 102
   chapter 7   sin and atonement | 122
   chapter 8   heaven and hell | 131
   chapter 9   resurrection and eternal life | 142

part 3: reformation
   chapter 10   a god of love | 163
   chapter 11   a prophetic jesus | 180
   chapter 12   a holy spirit | 195

part 4: a new path
   chapter 13   a theology of weakness | 201
   chapter 14   a religionless christianity | 215
   chapter 15   the way of love | 220
   chapter 16   a conspiracy of love | 233

bibliography | 251

acknowledgments

I'd like to offer my deep gratitude to Jean Struckmeyer, my best friend, life partner, lover, and proofreader, for her ongoing support and encouragement. She is my role model for faithful living and my inspiration for compassionate service and justice. Her passionate life and loving relationships are visible expressions of her theology.

preface
a dissenting opinion

Just when we think that all the ladders between heaven and earth have fallen down we discover that our own heart, all along, has been the source of our greatest insights. That's where all the ladders begin.[1]

—RICHARD HOLLOWAY (B. 1933)

This book is a minority report. For centuries, we have witnessed what the majority of Christians have professed about the fundamentals of their religious faith. Today, even people who have not been raised in the church are exposed to the predominant ideas of Christian theology. Christian orthodoxy (from the Greek for "correct thinking") began in 325 CE when the Roman emperor Constantine (272–337) invited the leaders of the early church to assist him in unifying an empire. Unity—as is often the case—was defined by conformity. Prior to that date, Christians exhibited a broad range of controversial and contending ideas about Jesus and his relationship to God. At the Council of Nicaea (May–June 325), Constantine pressured church leaders to fall in line around an approved set of theological principles. He literally would not let them out of the room until they agreed. The result was the emergence of a set of orthodox creeds and dogmas that defined the acceptable limits of Christian belief and practice. Those who saw things differently were known as heretics.

1. Holloway, *Doubts and Loves*, 44.

A heretic—from the Greek word *hairesis* (*hah'-ee-res-is*) meaning "that which is chosen"—is one who chooses to think or believe in ways other than a ruling majority expects or demands. The heretics of the past were often silenced by the institutional church if they expressed an alternative viewpoint that challenged the boundaries of acceptable belief. Heretics were ordered to recant their ideas, they were forbidden to teach, their writings were banned, and their lives were often at risk if they refused to conform.

Fortunately, the church has stopped burning heretics. The eclectic variety of the approximately 41,000 Christian denominations and sects that arose after the Protestant Reformation is testimony to a significant breakdown in uniformity of belief. After centuries of schisms over what some might see as theological nuances over "correct thinking," we are now entering a period of increasing denominational fellowship and cooperation based on an affirmation of the fundamental ideas that lie at the heart of Christianity. Still, creeds and doctrines continue to define acceptable boundaries within many churches. In spite of this, heretics are found in nearly every congregation—people who pick and choose what to believe based on what makes sense to them, what inspires them, and what gives purpose to their lives.

In and out of the church, people are increasingly choosing different ways of understanding God, the Bible, and a life of faith. They are challenging traditional church teachings and practices while looking for a faith that combines intelligence and passion. In the process, heretics are crafting wholly personal faiths that are meaningful and believable. This is a life-long process. As we grow and change, our ideas evolve and expand. The Apostle Paul (c. 5–67 CE) wrote, "When I was a child, I spoke like a child, I thought like a child, I reasoned like a child; when I became an adult, I put an end to childish ways."[2] Some observers have commented that too many people in the church lack an adult faith. Childhood ideas and images persist. One cannot mature in faith without embracing our many questions, doubts, and skepticism as part of the process. What follows is one person's version of a maturing faith.

Many of the heretics who remain in the institutional church do so because they are comfortable with the fellowship in their local religious communities and find solace in familiar rites and rituals, even if they are often uneasy with the theological baggage that accompanies them. To avoid discord and disruption, they tend to keep their ideas about religious belief and practice to themselves. They become "closet heretics" who mouth the creeds in public worship but no longer truly accept them in private. For those lucky few who are part of progressive congregations, theological questions are

---

2. 1 Corinthians 13:11

encouraged and unorthodox ideas are openly discussed. However, for many others, the church remains much too restrictive—intolerant and afraid of serious doubt or dissent. And so, many of those who cannot conform to intellectual suppression have left the church because they find that an unquestioning acceptance of fourth-century doctrines no longer makes sense in a postmodern world. Bishop John Shelby Spong (b. 1931) refers to those who have left as "the church alumni association."

This book is for the heretics among us, whether they dwell in the midst of the church, linger at the margins, or reside outside its walls. In these pages, I offer a dissenting theological opinion. I will call into question many accepted doctrines of the church, but will often do so on the basis of the Bible itself, demonstrating that many of the most cherished Christian beliefs are extra-biblical, meaning that they are not found in the biblical texts themselves but are derived from outside influences, especially from Greek philosophers. Traditional Christian dogma was formulated by leaders of an imperial church who were centuries removed from the life and teachings of Jesus, and who considered ideas *about* Jesus to be more important than the ideas *of* Jesus.[3]

Any religion is really an evolving conversation, sometimes transpiring over many centuries. More specifically, it is a cluster of conversations by people in a given community who have developed a shared vocabulary and image system about the divine and the meaning of life. These conversations are impacted by history, cultural developments, and social change. As a result, a living religion evolves and grows. When the conversation is suppressed and concepts become frozen in time, a religion begins to die. With each new generation in an ever-changing world, an unchanging religion has less and less meaning for young people. For Christianity to survive and thrive, conversations must be opened up and encouraged. A healthy church nurtures continual questioning, deconstruction, and reformation.

But the intent of this book is not to harm the church or to threaten the orthodox beliefs of the average churchgoer. It is simply to say that there are many different ways of thinking about God, Jesus, and the Christian life. Much of what I have to say is not new. Many of the ideas I express are hundreds of years old, though they are rarely discussed by educated clergy with Christian laypeople. These are simply the ideas and beliefs I have gravitated toward and settled on after many years of searching and questioning. Unlike orthodoxy, I do not propose a new "correct way of thinking," nor do I insist that you agree with me. I am simply stating what I believe to be

3. Note that both the Apostle's Creed and the Nicene Creed have nothing to say about the content of Jesus' ministry. They were only concerned about his birth, death, and resurrection as events pointing to his divinity.

true. However, I will be the first to say that my ideas may be wrong. I am convinced that five years from now, some of my ideas will have evolved and changed, at least to some degree. Even though theology is often stated as fact, it is always simply an opinion. This is a minority opinion. I only ask you to listen, to think, to decide for yourself, and to form your own opinions about the substance of your faith.

INTRODUCTION

a new reformation

*There is a time to break down, and a time to build up . . .
a time to keep and a time to throw away.*[1]

—QOHELETH, THE TEACHER OF ECCLESIASTES (C. 250 BCE)

The church is Plan B.[2]

—JOHN CAPUTO (B. 1940)

On Halloween night in 2017—along with the appearance of small beggars roaming the streets in the form of ghosts and goblins, pirates and princesses, superheroes and stormtroopers—the world will briefly pause to note the 500th anniversary of the Protestant Reformation. Five centuries ago, this event helped to usher in the early modern age, giving birth to the spirit of democracy, the rise of secular humanism, and a plethora of Christian denominations.

On October 31, 1517, Martin Luther (1483–1546), a thirty-three-year-old Augustinian monk, priest, and professor of theology, nailed a list of ninety-five debating points to the door of All Saints church (*Allerheiligenkirche*), often called the Castle Church (*Schlosskirche*), in the university town of Wittenberg, the seat of the medieval duchy of Sachsen-Wittenberg in the Holy Roman Empire of the German Nation. Whether Luther actually nailed his "ninety-five theses" to the church door is debatable, but he did

---

1. Ecclesiastes 3:3, 6
2. Caputo, *What Would Jesus Deconstruct?*, 35.

include them in a letter on that date to his Roman Catholic bishop detailing his concerns over a church practice of selling personalized certificates called "indulgences" to raise funds for the building of St. Peter's basilica in Rome. Similar to a "get out of jail, free" card, these indulgences were offered as a way to reduce the extent of temporal and eternal punishment one has to undergo for sins—both in acts of penance while living and for time spent in purgatory after death. Purgatory is a medieval theological proposition that immediately after death sinners are required to suffer punishment for their sins as a kind of purification to achieve the degree of holiness needed to enter heaven. Unlike the Monopoly card, indulgences were not free.

Luther was angered by the deceptive practices of a religious marketer and peddler, Johann Tetzel (1465–1519), a Dominican monk who had been appointed by Pope Leo X (1475–1521) as Grand Commissioner for indulgences in the German lands. Luther charged that Tetzel claimed "As soon as the coin in the coffer rings, the soul from purgatory springs."[3] Not only could indulgences be purchased for one's self, but also for one's deceased relatives. Fees varied according to sins. For instance, eight ducats would gain forgiveness for murder, six ducats for polygamy, and two ducats for witchcraft. A monetary donation was considered a valid substitute for confession and contrition. Luther believed that God alone could forgive sins, and that salvation could not be purchased for any amount of money. For Luther, the grace that redeems us from sin is a free gift of God. And so, Luther protested.

Unfortunately, by refuting the validity of indulgences and the theology behind them, Luther was also challenging the authority of the pope who authorized their sale. In 1518, Vatican officials ordered him to report to Rome to answer for heresy. Without the intercession of Frederick the Wise (1463–1525), the prince-elector of Saxony, Luther might have been quickly silenced and forgotten. Frederick refused to let Luther be tried in Rome and instead moved the trial to the imperial diet (the general assembly of German prince-electors) that was scheduled to meet in the Bavarian town of Augsburg. Luther remained adamant during the trial that unless he could be convinced by scripture that his ideas were wrong, he would not admit to error. Cardinal Thomas Cajetan (1469–1534), the papal legate who questioned Luther for four days, found him guilty of heresy and demanded that the civil authorities send him to Rome for punishment or banish him from their protection. Instead, Frederick allowed Luther slip away by night to Wittenberg where he continued to teach and write. Three years later, in

---

3. The couplet also rhymes in German: *Wenn das Geld im Kasten klingt, die Seele aus dem Feuer springt.*

May 1521, Luther was called to a meeting of the imperial diet in the city of Worms, where the emperor gave him a final chance to recant his writings. Just months earlier, Luther had been excommunicated by the pope. Now he was called to answer to civil authorities who could impose a secular punishment for his offenses. Luther refused to recant on the basis of both scripture and conscience and was declared an outlaw by the emperor. As Luther left Worms, Frederick had him kidnapped and taken to safety at Wartburg Castle in the town of Eisenach. While in protective exile—as he translated the New Testament from Greek into German—the whirlwind of reform that Luther had ignited was beginning to spin out of control throughout the empire. Luther secretly returned to Wittenberg in 1522, but while focused on theological and ecclesial reforms, more radical reformers were inspired to foment peasant rebellions that demanded political and economic reforms from the German princes. Around 250,000 peasants were killed in the Great Peasants' Revolt (1524–1525), the greatest popular uprising in Europe until the French Revolution.

Luther's battle was theological, not temporal. He saw the church standing in the way of salvation. He believed, as Jesus did, in an unmediated religion. For Jesus, no brokers could stand between each individual and God. The priesthood and the temple were unnecessary to faith. Luther realized that the sacramental system of the church—by which the church claimed the authority to save some people and to damn others—was contrary to scripture. For Luther, each believer is a priest and needs no one other than Jesus Christ as a channel to God and God's forgiveness. The pope, the bishops, the priests—the entire institutional structure of the church—was more of a roadblock than a pathway. Luther proposed that the death and resurrection of Christ had guaranteed free access of all believers to God. The freedom from the guilt and penalty of sin—that Luther associated with the Apostle Paul's term "justification"—came only through belief, not through baptism, nor the eucharist, nor through any other sacrament, and certainly not through good works. It was *sola scriptura*—the Bible alone that was important. According to Luther, a single Christian with a Bible was superior to any clerical authority, religious doctrine, spiritual practice, or church tradition that lacked biblical foundation. Thanks to Gutenberg's printing press, Luther's ideas were widely disseminated, the foundations of the church were shaken, and the world was dramatically altered. The priesthood of all believers eventually became the framework for the rise of modern political democracy—the equality of all people before God and the law. It was the beginning of the end for aristocratic monarchies, both ecclesiastical and civil. Little did Luther know in October 1517 what was to come from his relatively narrow theological dispute over a minor church practice. He did

introduction

not establish the massive change that followed; he simply liberated a pent-up power that was seeking expression.

a great rummage sale

In *The Great Emergence*, Phyllis Tickle (1934-2015) refers to a comment by Episcopal bishop Mark Dyer (1930-2014) that "about every five hundred years the church feels compelled to hold a giant rummage sale." Dyer was referring to those rare events when the church cleans out old forms of religious beliefs and practices, and replaces them with new ones. Each upheaval disrupts the dominant expression of Christianity but also brings about a new and more vital form.

Certainly, the decline of institutional Christianity in the twenty-first century and the birthing of some new religious or spiritual form in our day constitutes a five-hundred year span from the Reformation in the sixteenth century—and that is the key point that Dyer and Tickle are making—but going back chronologically from 1500 CE to 1000, and then back to 500, presents a bit of a problem for this metaphor. Tickle tried to flesh it out by pointing backward to two defining events in church history: the Great Schism in 1054 between western Christianity (based in Rome) and eastern Christianity (centered in Constantinople), and then further back to the papacy of Gregory the Great (540-604) who was known as "the father of Christian worship" because of his efforts in revising the Roman worship of his day. But in neither case did the church truly discard old forms and ideas. Gregory made some liturgical reforms and the great schism simply confirmed an ongoing struggle for power between the two main branches of Christianity. But the most significant defining event in the transformation of Christianity was the creation of an imperial orthodoxy under the Roman emperor Constantine at the Council of Nicaea in 325 that gave the church its first universal creed. Perhaps, if one had to pick another key event at the end of the first millennium—one could point to the reign of Charlemagne (c. 747-815) who, as the first secular emperor crowned by a pope (on Christmas day in 800), inaugurated a new era in church and state relations and converted the Saxon tribes at the point of a sword. Unfortunately, each of these events spoils the timing of the metaphor by occurring two centuries too early. But you get the essential idea. Every once in a great while, the church occasionally reforms itself as new ideas emerge and significant transformation is called for.

Tickle was right in one respect—something dramatic is happening to Christianity in our day. Something new is emerging while old forms are dying. The church was born in a pre-modern age where religion was believed to hold all the answers to the important questions in life. The modern era, marked by the spirit of skeptical inquiry, has explained the world around us through science and reason. We are now entering a postmodern world where younger people believe that both religion and science have failed to adequately address the problems facing us. Neither path has offered a remedy for widespread poverty, environmental devastation, and unending military conflict. The Christian church is rapidly expanding in the Global South where a pre-modern worldview of patriarchy, homophobia, and supernatural belief holds sway—a perfect birthing ground for traditional Christianity. But in the developed countries of the Global North—particularly in Western Europe and North America—the church is not faring well.

Postmodern people are engaged in a great spiritual journey. Many of us began life with an inherited religious tradition—a hand-me-down faith of prepackaged ideas. As we matured, some of us began to question whether those theological ideas still made sense and we initiated a process of picking and choosing religious teachings, or in some cases discarding them altogether. Even though increasing numbers of younger generations are turning their backs on the traditional faith of their childhood, some are now trying to piece together a more meaningful faith based on their own experience of reality. The great spiritual movement of the postmodern age is the democratization of theology. The brokers of religion are fading in importance. We are all becoming theologians who redefine the essence of faith in our specific context. To a great extent, the postmodern theology of the laity is becoming simpler, less doctrinal, and more personal.

This development is uncomfortable for those who guide the institutional church. The virtue of orthodoxy has always been its ability to preserve discipline, stability, order, and continuity. When people become their own spiritual guides, heaven only knows where they may wind up—which is why orthodox religions build walls around traditionally acceptable doctrine and approved conduct, separating truth from error. But Jesus himself had a problem with the doctrinal gatekeepers of his day who separated the world into holy and profane, sacred and secular, clean and unclean, and who maintained borders between righteous and sinful people with a detailed law code and a rigid morality. Jesus incurred the wrath of the religious authorities of his day by challenging their assumptions about God and humanity and messing up their tidy world of pat religious answers. He compared the inbreaking kingdom of God to a man who tossed a handful of tiny mustard seeds into a well-tended kitchen garden. The result was an infestation of pungent weeds—the uncontrollable spread of mustard plants—that brought chaos to well-planned order. For the traditional church in our day, the postmodern world has become a distressing mustard seed dilemma. Change is in the air, and for many churches it is troubling.

calls for reformation

Seismic shifts are not always apparent. Yet a half-century ago, some observers saw that church must change to respond to the social and spiritual revolutions occurring in the modern world. In calling for the Second Vatican Council (1962–1965), Pope John XXIII (1881–1963) said that it was time to open the windows of the church to let in some fresh air. The major result was a modernization of the language of the mass, but it provided hope to many that more change might be possible. In the Roman Catholic Church, the hope for greater change was shattered by the reactionary papacies of John Paul II (1920–2005) and Benedict XVI (b. 1927). But in the Protestant world, starting in the 1970s, a handful of liberal Protestant churches broke the age-old barrier of gender discrimination by ordaining women as pastors. More recently, barriers to sexual orientation have begun to fall in an even smaller number of progressive denominations as LGBT (Lesbian, Gay, Bisexual, and Transgender) members are being accepted into membership and more importantly, into pastoral and denominational leadership. Both of these changes emerged over significant opposition from theological conservatives within these denominations because they challenged a rigid interpretation of the Bible and its authority.

In recent years, new worship styles have emerged, pioneered by theologically conservative churches. Increasing numbers of Protestant congregations—both evangelical and mainline—have tried to attract and hold younger members by employing technological enhancements including amplified bands, lively praise music, digital media projection systems, dramatic stage lighting, and even fog machines. In the "lattes and liturgy" movement pioneered by non-denominational megachurches, commercial Christian music is offered as a new hymnody—a contemporary style with an upbeat rhythm (sometimes called "happy clappy" music) combined with lyrics rooted in the conservative theology favored by Christian radio. The intent is to make worship casual, comfortable, entertaining, inspirational, and highly emotional, but not particularly challenging. The lyrics frequently praise God and thank Jesus, but rarely promote the call to service and justice. Church growth, not personal or social transformation, is the primary goal of this movement. Smaller churches that seek to emulate megachurch practices are enamored by their wealth and success. Being part of a large, successful, and non-demanding church is appealing to many Christians, but

Jesus does not call us to comfort or success. Jesus calls us to put our lives on the line to change the world.

In spite of all of these institutional and liturgical changes—some major and some minor—traditional Christian beliefs and practices have remained largely the same as they were in the sixteenth century, and not much different from the imperial foundations of the fourth-century church. Many churches and denominations find renewal acceptable only if it is a subtle course correction, but their worst fear is a dramatic turning point. The postmodern revolution calls for much more than inclusive leadership and entertaining worship. It requires a major upheaval in church doctrine and teaching—a new reformation of substance, not just style. In 1965, Anglican bishop John A. T. Robinson (1919–1983) wrote:

> *The second reformation, if it comes, will be distinguished from the first by the fact that it is a time of reticence, of stripping down, of travelling light. The church will go through its baggage and discover how much in can do better without, alike in doctrine and organization.*[4]

Robinson believed that a deeper renewal and more profound change are required. He drew upon the words of German pastor and theologian Dietrich Bonhoeffer (1906–1945) who wrote from a Nazi prison cell about the possibility of a "religionless Christianity."

> *What is bothering me incessantly is the question what Christianity really is, for us today.*
>
> *We are moving towards a completely religionless time; people as they are now simply cannot be religious anymore. Even those who honestly describe themselves as "religious" do not in the least act up to it, and so they presumably mean something quite different by "religious" . . .*
>
> *And if therefore man becomes radically religionless—and I think that is already more or less the case (else, how is it, for example, that this war, in contrast to all previous ones, is not calling forth any "religious" reaction?)—what does that mean for "Christianity"?*
>
> *Are there religionless Christians? If religion is only a garment of Christianity—and even this garment has looked very different at different times—then what is a religionless Christianity?*[5]

---

4. Robinson, *The New Reformation?*, 20.
5. Bonhoeffer, *Letters and Papers*, 279–280.

These words from 1945 found resonance among those who tried to introduce needed reforms in the church beginning in the 1960s and 1970s. Yet the trajectory of the church in the postmodern world is toward collapse, not renewal. Seventy years later, it seems that the time has come to fully address Bonhoeffer's questions and challenge the doctrinal assumptions of a church that is mired in imperial and medieval theology. Over the last two decades, voices calling for a new theological reformation have included progressive scholars, theologians, bishops, and priests including Robert Funk, John Shelby Spong, Don Cupitt, and Matthew Fox.

Robert Funk (1926–2005) was a biblical scholar and co-founder of the controversial Jesus Seminar. In his book *Honest to Jesus* (1996), Funk attempted to recover the essential elements of the religion *of* Jesus in contrast to the church's dogmatic religion *about* Jesus. In the book's epilogue, Funk shared twenty-one theses for the future of our understanding of Jesus in a new age.[6]

John Shelby Spong (b. 1931) is a retired Episcopal bishop and prolific writer. In his book *Why Christianity Must Change or Die* (1998), Spong called for a new reformation of the church's faith and practice. Soon after the book's release, Spong published a brief article titled "A Call for a New Reformation" in which he listed twelve theses disputing orthodox teachings.[7]

Don Cupitt (b. 1934) is an English philosopher and theologian. In his book *Reforming Christianity* (2001), Cupitt proposes a way of living that is "post-dogmatic" because he believes that "historic orthodox Christianity was based upon an almost outrageously bad interpretation of the meaning and message of the original Jesus."[8] His many books indicate that his aim has been not a reformation of doctrine but a wholesale re-formulation of Christianity into what he calls the "kingdom religion" of Jesus that is fully at home in the present-day secular world.

Matthew Fox (b. 1940) is a priest and theologian who was expelled by the Dominican order of the Roman Catholic Church in 1993 and is now a member of the Episcopal Church. In 1988, Fox wrote a public letter to Cardinal Joseph Ratzinger (b. 1927)—later to become Pope Benedict XVI—entitled "Is the Catholic Church Today a Dysfunctional Family?" He was subsequently expelled from his order and was no longer allowed to teach in Roman Catholic universities. The Episcopal Church received him as a priest in 1994. In his book *A New Reformation* (2006), Fox proposes ninety-five theses or articles of faith for Christianity in the third millennium reflecting

---

6. Funk, *Honest to Jesus*, 297–314.
7. Spong, "Twelve Theses," 4.
8. Cupitt, *Reforming Christianity*, 3.

his theology of Creation Spirituality.[9] These are not so much a refutation of current doctrine as they are an addition of newer ideas.

Some of these reforming voices call for a renewed Christianity in a postmodern world by discarding the pre-modern cosmology of the Bible, outdated fourth-century creedal concepts, unquestioned ecclesiastical authority, and uncritical belief in supernatural beings. They vary widely in their depth and scope, but a few fundamental ideas are held in common. This can be made clear by contrasting their proposals with the traditional creeds of the church.

The Apostle's Creed states the following theological principles:

> *I believe in God, the Father almighty, creator of heaven and earth.*
>
> *I believe in Jesus Christ, God's only Son, our Lord, who was conceived by the Holy Spirit, born of the Virgin Mary, suffered under Pontius Pilate, was crucified, died, and was buried; he descended into hell. On the third day he rose again; he ascended into heaven, he is seated at the right hand of the Father, and he will come to judge the living and the dead.*
>
> *I believe in the Holy Spirit, the holy catholic Church, the communion of saints, the forgiveness of sins, the resurrection of the body, and the life everlasting.*
>
> *Amen.*[10]

Creeds are intended to draw a line in the sand. They separate believers from nonbelievers. Personally, I now find thirteen statements in the Apostle's Creed that I can no longer accept as part of my evolving faith. Likewise, what I *truly* believe in—the core of my faith—is entirely missing from the historic creeds. Between brief references to his miraculous birth and his sacrificial death, nothing is said regarding the life of Jesus in these statements of faith. His teachings about love, compassion, generosity, forgiveness, and inclusion are completely missing—as if they are unimportant and inconsequential details. Yet those are the things that I believe in, that I trust in, that I have faith in, and that I would stake my life on. Whenever I stand in silence as other worshipers recite the creed, my very silence proclaims me as an outsider who does not subscribe to the core doctrines of my faith

---

9. Fox, *A New Reformation*, 60–108.

10. The Apostle's Creed was not authored by the disciples of Jesus, later called apostles (meaning *messengers*). The creed was most probably shaped about the same time as the Nicene Creed and originated as a statement of belief called the Old Roman Creed, first referred to in a letter dating from 390 CE. The current form of the creed was refined and finalized sometime after the death of Charlemagne (814) in the early ninth century.

community. If the creeds are a litmus test of who belongs and who doesn't, I have failed. And so have many others.

Shanta Premawardhana (b. 1952), president of the Seminary Consortium for Urban Pastoral Education (SCUPE), recently commented on this dynamic:

> *Those who accept this set of beliefs are in, and those who deviate from it are out. As with any theology imposed from above, the problem with this "received" theology (teachings that come from church tradition) is that it is rigid, unbendable, and unforgiving. Throughout history numerous people were executed or exiled as heretics if they deviated even slightly from the creedal assertions. This is because deviations posed a direct threat to ecclesial authority and thereby to the political power structure.*
>
> *Received theology therefore, creates a natural limitation for deep and genuine expressions of love, acceptance, welcome, and hospitality, values which Jesus Christ himself espoused, lived-out, and encouraged in his disciples to follow.*[11]

And so, in the twenty-first century, a few theological voices are calling for a new way of being true to the spirit of Jesus without retaining conventional doctrines. In reaction to the orthodoxy of the creeds, reformers such as Funk and Spong have challenged the following contentions of traditional Christianity:

- A supernatural theistic God that is transcendent over nature and humanity
- God as the creator of the universe
- God as an interventionist in human history
- The special creation of the human species
- The doctrine of original sin
- The virgin birth of Jesus
- Jesus as a divine figure—the Son of God, the Son of Man, the Logos of creation, and the incarnation of God
- The miracle stories of the New Testament
- The crucifixion of Jesus as a sacrificial atonement for humanity's sins
- The bodily resurrection of Jesus and the resurrection of Christian believers

11. Premawardhana, "A Demonstration of Contextual Theology."

- The ascension of Jesus into heaven
- The return of Jesus as a judge of the living and the dead
- Eternal life after death in a heavenly realm
- The Holy Spirit as a supernatural being
- A triune God—Father, Son, and Holy Spirit
- Prayer as requests to a God who will supernaturally intervene
- Ethics as absolute rules of moral behavior for all time

At this point, I'm sure that many readers are either running for the hills or circling the wagons. These challenges to orthodoxy threaten the fundamental content of traditional Christian belief and practice. Yet, perhaps the time has come for many of these ideas to be put to rest so we can get on with the more important task of following Jesus in transforming our common life on earth. Discarding this traditional baggage, stripping down to essentials, and traveling more lightly may be the answer to Bonhoeffer's question about what a "religionless Christianity" might look like as we enter the postmodern world.

the postmodern era

A great cultural shift—a new historical epoch—is unfolding before our eyes. It began about the middle of the twentieth century and is continuing to develop today. The postmodern worldview is the successor of modernity and stands in reaction to it. We are not sure how it will play out in the long term, but some initial observations are being made about its nature. The term *postmodernism* has been applied to a number of late twentieth-century movements, mainly in art, architecture, music, and literature that developed in response to modernism. But that may be the only unifying characteristic that they share. New forms of creative expression such as performance art, conceptual art, and installation art became part of these postmodern movements. In this sense, postmodernism has to do with a variety of new styles and new definitions of what constitutes art. I use the term *postmodern* not in reference to any style of artistic endeavor, but instead to indicate a vast cultural sea change in the secular societies of the Global North—especially in Europe and North America.

The pre-modern worldview—or what comparative religion scholar Huston Smith (b. 1919) calls the traditional worldview—developed during the time of the ancient temple-state, in which an alliance of the ruling class and the priestly class closely intertwined religion and political power.

Religion's role was to legitimize the king's rule by providing a moral and religious authority for his decrees. The king was viewed as God's representative on earth. He was sometimes spoken of as the "Son of God" (as was ancient Israel's King David), and was sometimes seen as divine himself. For these ancient societies, the ruler and the social order reflected the will of their god. The pre-modern worldview was essentially the only worldview from ancient times through the Middle Ages. The ancient traditional worldview is characterized by an unquestioning acceptance of authority and a belief in absolute truths. Pre-modern people generally believe what they are told by authority figures, both religious and secular. They trust religion to provide the answers to life's mysteries. A half-century ago, in 1960, about 82 percent of the adult American population said just that to pollsters.

The Bible is a product of two pre-modern societies—the scribes of ancient Israel who produced the Hebrew Bible, also known as the Old Testament, and the Hellenistic evangelists of the early Christian communities who produced the New Testament.[12] The pre-modern view of the world represented in these documents was accepted without question by the audiences to which they were written. A pre-modern culture was the context in which Jesus lived and died.

The modern worldview had its roots in the Renaissance of the sixteenth century, but began to bloom and flourish in the Enlightenment of the eighteenth century—at least among the literate. Modernity was founded on the pursuit of objective knowledge and the use of the scientific method. It is characterized by a questioning of authority and the pursuit of truth over tradition. Modernity believes that truth is based on facts. In the modern worldview, people believe only what they can observe. Modernity trusts the power of reason and critical thinking to solve the world's problems. It looks to science, not to religion, to provide the answers to life's mysteries.

In the early eighteenth century, some notable Enlightenment thinkers—including Thomas Jefferson (1743–1826)—felt empowered by scientific inquiry and the new rationalism to re-read the Bible. They began to question the literal truth of biblical miracles, the virgin birth, and even the divinity and resurrection of Jesus. In the universities of Germany, biblical scholars began to use the tools of historical research and textual analysis—usually called "higher criticism"—to separate the Bible's historic elements from what they perceived as later legendary additions. They began to look beyond the Christ of doctrinal faith to the earlier Jesus of history who they

---

12. Hellenism is a term used to describe the influence of Greek thought and culture on the peoples of the Greek and Roman Empires. Hellenism had a great influence on the developing ideas of early Christianity. Greek philosophy shaped Christian theology for many centuries.

believed had been obscured by layers of Christian preaching and teaching, including the accounts found in the gospels. Then, in 1859, Charles Darwin (1809-1882), who studied to be a deacon in the Church of England, published *On the Origin of Species*, introducing radically new ideas about the evolutionary nature of life that challenged conventional Christian belief in the literal truth of the biblical creation story.

By the end of the nineteenth century, the findings of Darwin and the higher biblical critics had been embraced by many educated Christians and by influential figures in the media, universities, and seminaries. The largely upper-class and urban people who accepted the new learning became known as modernists or liberals. Many of them developed an optimistic faith in the gradual progress of humanity through knowledge, scientific inquiry, innovation, invention, and rational thought. Much of that optimism was lost after the horrors of World War I.

The rise of modernity led to the rise of secularism; the two go hand in hand. Secularism is defined as a system of ideas or practices that rejects the primacy of religion in society. In its hard form, secularism is atheistic—it denies the reality of God. But in its softer, more widespread form, secularism accepts God's reality but rejects religious institutions like the church, synagogue, or mosque as controlling forces in the life of the national community. When the United States Constitution declared a separation of church and state, it was in response to and a rejection of the state-sponsored religion of many northern European nations. The major Protestant faiths of the newly-formed United States supported the legal separation because each denomination feared that another might achieve favored status over them. In effect, the modern secularism of America's founders encouraged the growth of a plurality of religious expressions in America not seen anywhere else.

The liberal and moderate mainline Protestant churches in the United States slowly adapted to modernity. They embraced higher criticism in their seminaries and adopted the principles of the social gospel that sought to eradicate the evils of poverty and ignorance. But, millions of other Americans saw their historic faith threatened by the spread of these ideas and began to engage in a great cultural war with modernity and the movement toward secular humanism. Two key groups—evangelicals and fundamentalists—have led the battle against the modern secular worldview.

Postmodernism is a different reaction to modernity. Postmodern people are essentially disenchanted modernists. But they are not trying to go back to a pre-modern worldview. They are convinced that human reason and cleverness cannot achieve the happiness we seek. They have witnessed the environmental ravages of the industrial revolution, the bloody history of competing twentieth-century nations, and continued misery, poverty, and hunger around the globe. None of these problems have been solved by scientific knowledge or reason. To the contrary, the by-products of science and the industrial revolution have exacerbated many of our human problems. Science has provided cures to disease, but it has also created the threat of global warming and nuclear annihilation. If any event can be said to inaugurate the postmodern age, it was the bombing of Hiroshima and Nagasaki in August 1945 and the resulting nuclear arms race. This may have been the spark that marked the demise of modernity and ignited the rapid rise of a global postmodern culture.

The movement from modernity to postmodernity in America began with the Baby Boomers, born between 1946 and 1964. This was the first generation raised under the threat of nuclear weapons. Boomers knew in their guts that science had created a demon that could destroy the world. The postmodern movement has accelerated as younger cohorts—Generation X (1965-1981) and the Millennial generation (1982-2000)—have reached adulthood.

Postmodern people reject the notion of absolute truth. They no longer trust authority and they reject any institution that claims to have a claim on the truth. They have become highly suspicious of facts. They believe that all truth, even to some extent scientific knowledge, is subjective, biased, and socially constructed. Truth depends on what one's culture regards as truth. Therefore the truth is not really true.

deconstruction

In addition to this major cultural shift, the term *postmodernism* is also used to describe a late-twentieth-century philosophical movement that arose in post-war Europe, especially in France. I will not pretend to understand the theoretical arguments of postmodern philosophy that deal with language, knowledge, and truth, but I will shamelessly borrow its use of the term *deconstruction*. French philosopher Jacques Derrida (1930-2004) used the term while exploring how language and language symbols influence meaning. The deconstructive strategy is to reveal how conventional ways of thinking, and the categories and labels we create, construct limits to the expression of new ideas and opportunities. Deconstruction—as opposed to destruction—is a process of taking things apart carefully and purposefully so that they can be discarded or reconstructed in new ways. It dismantles the constraints of past thinking in order to move forward with greater freedom.

In clear uncomplicated language, this book will challenge many traditional teachings of the church by deconstructing such concepts as God as a transcendent omnipotent creator of the world; Jesus as the divine Christ, Messiah, Son of God, and apocalyptic Son of Man; the virgin birth and bodily resurrection of Jesus; the Holy Spirit as a person-like being; the doctrine of original sin; the kingdom of God as an apolitical post-apocalyptic event; the cross as a symbol of sacrificial atonement; and eternal life as an everlasting heavenly existence.

Alternatively, this book will present a simple postmodern theology that presents God as a symbolic personification of human love; Jesus as a teacher of radical compassion and an outspoken agent of social justice; the kingdom of God as a "conspiracy of love" that challenges the unjust systems of the world; the Way of Jesus as a journey of transformation from cultural captivity to a counter-cultural life of activism and service; the cross as a symbol of the consequences of defying the authority and power of the domination system; and the resurrection of Jesus as the epiphany of his ongoing spirit and presence in a vision, in a voice, or in the face of a stranger.

What many people do not realize is that the church with its structures, dogmas, and doctrines is Plan B. Jesus did not seek to found a new religion centered on rites, rituals, buildings, and clergy. Instead, he proclaimed the inbreaking kingdom of God, the reign of God here on earth—a vision of the way the world would be if a God of love governed our common life. Moreover, he taught a way of living consistent with that vision—focused on love, compassion, generosity, and forgiveness. To be faithful followers of Jesus is to return to Plan A.

PART 1
the great detour

CHAPTER 1

losing our way

Jesus came preaching the kingdom, and what arrived was the church.[1]
—ALFRED LOISY (1857–1940)

Around 6 BCE (Before the Common Era), a child was born to a peasant family in Galilee, a region of the Roman province of Palestine. His parents named him *Yehoshu'a (yeh-ho-shoo'-ah)*—Joshua in English. He was often called *Yeshu'a (yeh-shoo'-ah)* or *Yeshu (yeh-shoo')* for short. We know him today as Jesus of Nazareth.

During his life, Yeshu attracted attention in Galilee as a healer and teacher of uncommon wisdom. More importantly, he was a prophet, a radical social critic, and a voice for change. He challenged the conventional social and religious wisdom of his day and confronted the prevailing politics and economics of domination that brought increasing poverty to the weakest members of his peasant class. He taught an alternative wisdom and encouraged a distinct way of living with love, compassion, and generosity.

a revolutionary vision

Yeshu announced good news to the poor. He said that those who were destitute, hungry, and weeping were blessed by God—an amazing statement in any age. For Yeshu envisioned the creation of a radically different kind of society in which there would no longer be a great divide between the incredibly wealthy

---

1. Although frequently quoted, no citation is given. Some sources date the quote to 1902, the year he published *The Gospel and the Church*.

and the abject poor. He called this transformed community the "kingdom of God." We might call it the "reign of God," the "rule of God," or the "governance of God." It was an ambitious vision of a compassionate human social order modeled as if God, not Caesar or Herod, was in charge. Yeshu dreamed of a society that would elevate the lowly status of the poor and the outcast, the sick and the suffering, the hungry and the homeless. He sought a politics of compassion in which God's protection of widows, orphans, and immigrants would be extended to all in need. His was a vision of a renewed humanity where people who had nothing would receive a fair share with those who had everything; where lost wealth, homes, and land would be restored; where debts would be forgiven; and where lives that had been wasted or stolen would be redeemed. For Yeshu, a time was coming when God's reign would bring forth equality, justice, and peace, and those who worked to make this a reality would be known as the children of God.

Yeshu invited the rich to sell their excess possessions and share the proceeds with the poor. In particular, he called for the redistribution of wealth, which in an agricultural economy meant the reallocation of land accumulated by the economic elites through foreclosure on the debt of peasant farmers. Yeshu declared that the year of Jubilee had arrived, an ancient Hebrew tradition of forgiveness of debts and return of land from the rich to the dispossessed. In Yeshu's vision, the low would be raised up and the high brought low to meet at a common level. He knew that when the spirit of generosity motivated people, there was enough to go around for everyone. Rather than a mad accumulation of wealth to provide security for an uncertain future, Yeshu taught his followers to trust God, to create a compassionate community to provide for each other's needs, and to respond when called upon to care for and share their resources with their brothers and sisters. He taught his followers to reject self-centered affluence and to pray for sufficiency—just enough for tomorrow, "our daily bread." Yeshu's image of this mutually supportive lifestyle was a lavish wedding banquet in which everyone would feast abundantly and celebrate as a community of equals.

This simple vision was a threat to the status quo of the conservative and comfortable economic elites in his society. They refused to give up their power and privilege and to share their abundance with the poor. As a result, the wealthy and powerful people of his society, in collusion with the Roman authorities, executed Yeshu as a social insurrectionist—a dangerous disturber of the peace. The Roman method of capital punishment for a member of the peasant class who dared to challenge the governing authority was crucifixion—a slow and painful death of asphyxiation on a cross that was fashioned from wooden beams. It was intended to be public, painful, and humiliating. The naked corpse was typically left on the cross to decay and be scavenged by carrion birds and dogs.

a compassionate community

After Yeshu's death, a small movement in Palestine carried on his ideas. His followers claimed that his spirit had not died, but instead remained alive and permeated their lives, empowering them to live without fear of repressive authorities or the threat of death. These men and women were filled with the spirit of Yeshu, the spirit of God, a holy spirit. And this renewed spirit gave them the passion, zeal, and courage to carry on the vision of Yeshu, whom we call Jesus.

Biblical scholar Burton Mack (b. 1931) believes that much of what is commonly called the resurrection of Jesus was really a process of remembering and retelling the life and message of Jesus—a process that kept him alive within and among the people of the movement that he created.

> *Jesus' life did not end with his death. That, of course, is the message of Easter. In these early communities of Jesus' followers, his life continued in his ideas and teachings. The resurrection occurred in the activity of a group who sought to understand and then live out the message of Jesus. The spirit of his teachings was kept alive, but, as with all life, these teachings grew and changed with time.*[2]

Clarence Jordan (1912–1969), a New Testament scholar and translator of *The Cotton Patch Gospels* once wrote that the proof of the resurrection was a transformed and spirit-filled community of his followers.

> *The proof that God raised Jesus from the dead is not the empty tomb, but the full hearts of his transformed disciples. The crowning evidence that he lives is not a vacant grave, but a spirit-filled fellowship; not a rolled-away stone, but a carried-away church.*[3]

The followers of Jesus began to live out his vision of a compassionate community, committed to the welfare of one another. Widows, orphans, the sick, the destitute, and the disabled were cared for. Shared community meals insured that no one would go hungry. Financial resources were pooled and distributed. This was a model of God's radical new society based on Yeshu's vision.

---

2. Mack, original source not found.
3. Jordan and Lee, *The Substance of Faith*, 29.

I give you a new commandment, that you love one another. Just as I have loved you, you also should love one another. By this everyone will know that you are my disciples, if you have love for one another.[4]

contrasting worldviews

The people to whom Jesus spoke were trying to survive in what biblical scholar Walter Wink (1935–2012) has called the ancient "domination system," a society characterized by unjust economic relations, oppressive political relations, and patriarchal gender relations. At the heart of any domination system, then or now, is a fundamental view of reality. It is a mental model of how the world works. In this paradigm, the ultimate reality of the universe is indifferent to human needs. People perceive the world as a cruel place, and realize that in a largely selfish world, others will be unconcerned and unmoved by a desire for mutual welfare—the common good of a society. As humans, we all tend to become anxious about the future, which fills our hearts with worry, insecurity, and self-concern. By and large, many of us find we cannot trust God or others to care for us and realize that we are ultimately alone and on our own in an uncaring and hostile dog-eat-dog world. At the root of this paradigm is the belief that we are ultimately separate from one another. If we see ourselves as mutually-exclusive beings, we must then prioritize self-reliance and self-sufficiency. In a world of scarce resources, we become competitors and ultimately become enemies. As a result, we must care for ourselves first and provide for our future security. We grasp what we can get and hoard it for tomorrow. We look to wealth, possessions, status, pleasure, power, and dominion over others to make ourselves feel better. But it does not work because it never works, and it's never enough. Our greed, selfishness, and indifference to the needs of others simply confirm and perpetuate this paradigm. The perception becomes reality and is transmitted through domination system cultures from generation to generation.

Jesus offered a different paradigm, a different worldview, a different perception of reality. He believed that the ultimate reality of the universe is a God of love. For Jesus, it was important that our lives and relationships reflect God's love. He taught that God's love reigns within the lives of caring individuals who extend themselves for others and within a compassionate community that concerns itself with the welfare of all. The essential nature

---

4. John 13:34–35

of love calls forth responses of empathy and compassion, generosity and forgiveness, inclusion and acceptance. In a community based on love and compassion, the basic needs of all are satisfied.

> *He said to his disciples, "Therefore I tell you, do not worry about your life, what you will eat, or about your body, what you will wear. For life is more than food, and the body more than clothing."*[5]

If one is able to trust in the generosity of God's spirit in others, one no longer has to trust in oneself alone. Communities of compassion can alleviate fear and insecurity about the future. Indeed, they are the only thing that can. This assurance frees us to share our resources with others in mutuality and partnership. Loving, caring relationships give our lives a meaning and satisfaction that reliance on power, wealth, and status cannot provide. This is the fundamental paradigm of the reign of God that Jesus proclaimed. It stands in sharp contrast to the domination system of individual self-concern and the politics of selfishness that governs most societies.

But because the paradigm of the domination system is so pervasive, it takes an act of radical faith to believe in Jesus' contrasting vision. We cannot enter this new paradigm if we do not learn to trust the spirit of God in others. We must learn to trust the love and compassion that dwells deep within the hearts of others and is expressed when they are no longer governed by fear.

Trust has to do with the future, but is based on the past. For instance, I can trust you only if you have a proven track record of trustworthiness in relation to me. Trust is based solely on a mutual relationship. Trusting others is a sometimes daring and risky venture. It requires the commitment of a faithful relationship and the sustaining courage of hope. But this was the risk taken by Jesus' followers. He called them to live in a way that does not make sense if trust in others is absent. He asked them to live recklessly, but not without the safety net of a community. He invited them to share their resources generously with others, even with strangers, trusting that this generosity would be shown to them in return. The followers of Jesus could do this because they were surrounded by a new family of brothers and sisters who would willingly support them in difficult times. The paradigm of Jesus only works within the context of community.

---

5. Luke 12:22–23

the community in Jerusalem

A glimpse of the early Jesus movement is found in the New Testament book called the *Acts of the Apostles*, or more simply as *Acts*. It describes the community of Jesus' followers in the city of Jerusalem in the weeks and months after his death. The term "apostles" in this text, refers to the disciples of Jesus after the Resurrection. Before his death, they were disciples—students and followers of Jesus. Now they have become his apostles—messengers of his vision.

> *Awe came upon everyone, because many wonders and signs were being done by the apostles. All who believed were together and had all things in common; they would sell their possessions and goods and distribute the proceeds to all, as any had need. Day by day, as they spent much time together in the temple, they broke bread at home and ate their food with glad and generous hearts, praising God and having the goodwill of all the people. And day by day the Lord added to their number those who were being saved.*[6]

> *Now the whole group of those who believed were of one heart and soul, and no one claimed private ownership of any possessions, but everything they owned was held in common. With great power the apostles gave their testimony to the resurrection of the Lord Jesus, and great grace was upon them all. There was not a needy person among them, for as many as owned lands or houses sold them and brought the proceeds of what was sold. They laid it at the apostles' feet, and it was distributed to each as any had need. There was a Levite, a native of Cyprus, Joseph, to whom the apostles gave the name Barnabas (which means "son of encouragement"). He sold a field that belonged to him, then brought the money, and laid it at the apostles' feet.*[7]

Jesus had taught his disciples that their example would be like a tiny pinch of yeast in a large amount of bread dough. Though small, insignificant, and nearly invisible, their counter-cultural lifestyle would become a sign of hope for all human life. Theirs was a new community of compassion and generosity. They were manifesting the revolutionary reign of God as an alternative reality in the midst of a domination system.

Jesus saw that the lifestyle he envisioned would not appeal to large numbers of people. His followers would always be a small contrast community within larger society.

6. Acts 2:43–47
7. Acts 4:32–37

> *Do not be afraid, little flock, for it is your Father's good pleasure to give you the reign of God.*[8]

the Jesus movement in Palestine

For nearly four decades after the death of Jesus, this was the form of the Jesus movement in Roman Palestine. These followers of Jesus did not see themselves as anything other than observant Jews inspired by a new way of living. Some scholars refer to the movement as Jesus Judaism to differentiate it from Pharisaic Judaism, but it was fully a part of the Jewish religious tradition, inspired by Jesus' interpretation of the Torah covenant and the social message of the ancient prophets. The term "Christian" had not yet been applied to them. Instead, they were "followers of the Way"—agents of the social agenda that Jesus had preached.[9] Then, in 70 CE (the Common Era), the Jerusalem community came to a sudden end when Jewish insurrections against oppressive social conditions brought ranks of Roman armies into the city, leaving widespread destruction in their wake. The followers of the Way living in Jerusalem abandoned the city and fled to the countryside for safety. The massive temple complex in Jerusalem was destroyed and every Jewish sect was shaken to its foundation. The members of the Jerusalem community were never heard from again.

Prior to the destruction of Jerusalem, other small communities of the way had developed in the rural areas and small towns of Roman Palestine, especially in Galilee, the center of Jesus' activity. All of these groups were invested in the concept of the kingdom of God as articulated in Jesus' teaching. Each small group or network of groups began to work out the details of how to live together in a new way. According to scholar Burton Mack (b. 1931), they had three things in common. The first was the notion of a more perfect human society conceptualized as a realm in which a God of love ruled. It was to be a society in which self-giving love overcomes human selfishness. The second was the idea that any individual, no matter of what extraction, status, or innate capacity, was fit for and would be fully accepted as a member of this inclusive society. The third concept was the novel notion that a mixture of people was exactly what the kingdom of God should look like.[10]

---

8. Luke 12:32
9. See references to "the Way" in Acts 9:2, 19:9, 19:23, 22:4, 24:14, and 24:22.
10. Mack, *Who Wrote the New Testament?*, 43.

The earliest communities of the Jesus movement shared stories and teachings about Jesus orally, retelling them in ever more encapsulated forms that biblical scholars today call aphorisms—short, pithy nuggets that are easy to memorize and repeat. Later, they were crafted into written collections that included the Sayings Gospel Q and the Gospel of Thomas, and also into various miracle and pronouncement stories which would later be used as sources for the gospel of Mark, the earliest story of Jesus.

Burton Mack believes that for these early followers, the teachings of Jesus were more important than his life story. The first followers of Jesus were not interested in preserving accurate memories of the historical Jesus. They found his teachings—a subversive wisdom of personal and social transformation—to be much more important. As a result they left us no record of his appearance and few details of his life.

Many different ideas about Jesus' identity, mission, and message were developing within the diverse communities of his followers. Who was Jesus really? They knew he was a teacher of profound wisdom and an advocate of the poor, but did he have a larger role to play in Jewish history? Was he a new prophetic voice like the Hebrew prophets of old who spoke truth to power with a message from God? Was he a new Moses, presenting people with a new law—an ethic of love and forgiveness? Was he the long-awaited Messiah, anointed to restore the greatness of the Hebrew people? Was he the first of the martyrs to be raised in the coming resurrection of the dead? Many very different ideas about Jesus emerged within these communities.

the Christ cult

In some Hellenistic cities of the Roman Empire outside of Palestine, a dramatic transformation of Jesus began within a few years after his crucifixion. Greek-speaking Jewish communities of the Jesus movement began shifting their attention away from the teachings of Jesus and focused instead on the significance of his death. Spreading quickly through the Mediterranean trading cities of the empire among Jews and Gentiles who were attracted to Judaism, this Hellenistic Christ cult soon became the predominant form of the growing faith.

Beginning just a few years after the death of Jesus—most likely in Antioch in northern Syria—a religious cult began to develop around the figure of Jesus as "the Christ." The book of Acts records:

> It was in Antioch that the disciples were first called "Christians."[11]

---

11. Acts 11:26

The term *Christ* comes from the Greek *christos* (*khris-tos'*) which means *anointed*. The English word *messiah*, from the Hebrew word *mashiach* (*mah-shee'-akh*), means the same thing. In Jewish history, this was term for a person who was anointed to perform a special office, originally a king or a high priest. Later the term was used for prophets who spoke about the restoration of a just society. But as Hellenistic Christianity developed, the term *Christ* took on new dimensions. These communities were convinced that Jesus had been transformed at death into a divine spiritual presence. The Greek-speaking followers of the way developed rudimentary theological formulas, rituals, prayers, and hymns that they shared when they gathered together in the name of Jesus, the Christ.

In the Greco-Roman city of Damascus in the southern part of Syria, a young Hellenistic Jew named Saul of Tarsus—soon to be known as the Apostle Paul (c. 5–67 CE)—was introduced to this strain of Christianity. He later shared what he had learned from these communities in his letter to the small house church at Corinth in Greece:

> *For I handed on to you as of first importance what I in turn had received: that Christ died for our sins in accordance with the scriptures, and that he was buried, and that he was raised on the third day in accordance with the scriptures, and that he appeared to Cephas* [Peter], *then to the twelve. Then he appeared to more than five hundred brothers and sisters at one time, most of whom are still alive, though some have fallen asleep. Then he appeared to James* [the brother of Jesus], *then to all the apostles. Last of all, as to someone untimely born, he appeared also to me.*[12]

(Scholars are uncertain as to which passages in the Hebrew Bible Paul was referencing when he mentioned Christ having "died for our sins in accordance with the scriptures" and being "raised on the third day in accordance with the scriptures." Possible passages are extremely obscure, but this formula of "accordance with the scriptures" was part of the tradition that was handed on to Paul and clearly accepted by him.)

The Jewish followers of the Way in Palestine had focused on remembering the teachings of Jesus and applying them to their lives, but the Hellenistic Christians began to praise Jesus in worship. It was here that the first creed, "Jesus is Lord" was proclaimed—a counter-cultural and insurrectionist statement within the Roman Empire where all citizens were required to confess that "Caesar is Lord."[13] As a result, these Hellenistic Christian

---

12. 1 Corinthians 15:3–8

13. In Greek, "Jesus is lord" is *Iésous kurios* (*ee-ay-sooce' koo'-ree-os*). "Caesar is lord" is *Kaisar kurios* (*kah'-ee-sar koo'-ree-os*). In antiquity, the term "lord" (*kurios*) was

communities were viewed with suspicion as atheists and traitors by Roman authorities. For the high priest in Jerusalem—a Roman political appointee—the Hellenistic leaders of the Way needed to be weeded out in order to suppress potential rebellion and keep the peace. Saul had been one of those appointed to the task of arresting the ringleaders. Instead, he became fascinated by possibilities of their faith, especially their image of a dying and rising messiah.

Paul spent three years immersed in learning and contemplating the ideas of this cult, both in Damascus and in the Arabian Desert. During this period, he reflected on the implications of the spiritual Christ in the context of the popular Greek mystery religions that attracted many people throughout the Roman Empire. They included cults from Greece, Asia Minor, Egypt, and Persia that focused on the death and rebirth myths of Demeter, Orpheus, Dionysus, Adonis, Cybele, Osiris, and Mithras. Central to each of these mystery religions was a symbolic reenactment of the natural cycle of growth, death, decay, and rebirth, experienced when plant life dies every fall and is renewed every spring. Each cult was centered in a similar myth in which a deity returns to life after death or descends to the underworld and returns with the arrival of the vernal equinox. They were called "mystery" religions because they involved clandestine ceremonies, often in connection with an initiation rite that imparted secret knowledge. Only initiates were allowed to observe and participate in rituals. The rites were structured to lead worshippers toward heightened feelings and emotions, sometimes guiding them to a religious ecstasy that expressed the beginning of a new life through the mystical experience of dying and being reborn with the deity. More importantly, the mystery religions offered some kind of redemption or salvation in the present life and the promise of immortality in an afterlife.

Paul was a product of two contrasting cultures—the ancient Hebraic tradition of Israel and the Hellenistic civilization of the Roman Empire that had far greater dominion, power, and importance. He spent his adult life trying to find a way to bring these different traditions together in some new fashion. Judaism held an ethical appeal for many Gentile pagans, known as "God fearers," who were attracted to Jewish synagogues. It was a faith that drew people in, yet held them apart with requirements of strict dietary laws and male circumcision. Paul envisioned a religion that could bridge these biblically-mandated ethnic and cultural divisions, creating a unified community for the future of humanity. But first, the Torah requirements would have to be abandoned. In the dying and rising of the Christ, Paul found a

---

a courtesy title for social superiors, but its root meaning was "ruler." Claiming that "Jesus is lord" is a rebellious statement of political allegiance.

metaphor for dying to his old life centered in the Hebrew law and rising to a new life in a radically new community no longer based on racial heritage or religious tradition, but simply on love and compassion for one another. Paul believed that the Hebrew Torah was now replaced by love.

> *For the whole law is summed up in a single commandment, "You shall love your neighbor as yourself."*[14]

> *Owe no one anything, except to love one another; for the one who loves another has fulfilled the law. The commandments, "You shall not commit adultery; You shall not murder; You shall not steal; You shall not covet;" and any other commandment, are summed up in this word, "Love your neighbor as yourself." Love does no wrong to a neighbor; therefore, love is the fulfilling of the law.*[15]

For Paul, love for one another replaced the restrictive dietary requirements and genital mutilation of the Torah as signs of common group identity. He believed that the crucifixion and resurrection of the Christ changed the ancient religious rules and "justified" (meaning vindicated and validated) their life together as a multi-cultural community in spite of Jewish law codes. The old law of the Hebrew Bible was fulfilled and supplanted by concrete acts of love. The artificial barriers of the past were torn down and replaced by a new community centered in mutual love.

> *There is no longer Jew or Greek, there is no longer slave or free, there is no longer male and female; for all of you are one in Christ Jesus.*[16]

For Paul—a Pharisee—the resurrection of Jesus also meant that the general resurrection of the dead was about to commence. Jesus had simply been the first of many martyrs that the Pharisees believed would be restored from death to a renewed life among the living. The faithful dead would soon be raised from their graves and would be judged on the quality of their lives and sacrifices. In the new Pauline community, this promise of restoration would be available to everyone. Paul believed that the future was rapidly heading toward an end point when the Christ—an apocalyptic judge—would return to vindicate his death by crucifixion, reward the faithful martyrs, punish their oppressors, and set things right in the world. The resurrection anticipated by Paul was never about a heavenly afterlife, but was instead focused on the transformation of life on earth into a new reality.

14. Galatians 5:14
15. Romans 13:8–10
16. Galatians 3:28

an apocalyptic mystery religion

Through Paul's evangelistic efforts over the next three decades, the emerging Christ cult that he encountered in Damascus and embellished with his own ideas began to spread throughout the major trading cities of Asia Minor, Greece, and Rome. As the Christ cult grew and spread, the Palestinian-centered communities of the Way declined as the primary form of the faith. Thus the Hellenistic apocalyptic mystery religion developed and proclaimed by Paul became the foundation of orthodox Christianity. Soon, these ideas began to dominate, obscuring the kingdom of God at the heart of Jesus' message and mission, and transforming his identity with mythological images.

For the next century in the emerging Christ cult, Greek concepts about the dualism of body and soul as distinct entities eventually replaced the Jewish idea of an integrated, inseparable personhood that ended at death. The Pharisaic belief in an earthly resurrection of the dead became incorporated with the Greek idea of an eternal soul existing beyond death. The combination of the two eventually became a belief in an afterlife in heaven—something which would have been very foreign and strange to Jesus and probably to Paul as well.

The story of Jesus as a martyr who was raised by God from the dead had resonance with the popular pagan mystery religions of a dying and rising god. Like these mystery religions, a rite of initiation (in this case, baptism) became part of the Christ-cult observances. The shared common meal of the early Christian communities soon became a distinctly ritual meal, the eucharist—from the Greek *eucharistia* (*yoo-khar-is-tee'-ah*), which means "thanksgiving"—a meal that commemorated the death of Jesus and recalled his last supper with the disciples. Pagan spiritual practices like ecstatic speech (speaking in tongues) were sometimes incorporated. The trappings of a real Greco-Roman religion began to develop around the cult of the mystical Christ.

As time went on, mythical stories grew up around Jesus. He was known in Palestine as a healer and exorcist, but new stories gave Jesus miraculous power over the elements of nature. For a century after the death of Jesus, his teachings were blended with Jewish apocalyptic and Greek Gnostic thought. Words that Jesus never spoke were attributed to him by later generations seeking his word for their social context and life situation.[17] He was rapidly

---

17. Biblical scholars have written scores of volumes that demonstrate that the gospel writers were second or third generation Christians who combined and edited previous materials and traditions of their communities in ways to present a distinctive story of Jesus. Mark presents Jesus as a wide-eyed apocalyptic preacher. Matthew views

transformed from a teacher of wisdom, a radical social critic, and a voice for justice into an apocalyptic preacher who proclaimed the end times. His obvious failure as a militaristic and nationalist messiah was corrected by the claim that he would soon return in great power and authority to rid the earth of evil and violently destroy the persecutors of the new faith. The nonviolent prophet was transformed into an avenging warrior king.

communities of compassion

Yet, even in these early beginnings of the church, a commitment to nonviolence, the sharing of goods, a radical social equality, and the welfare of the destitute set Christian communities apart for several hundred years after the death of Jesus. From the first small peasant communities in rural Galilee and urban Jerusalem to the rapidly spreading house-church communities of Paul in the trading towns of the Mediterranean and Aegean seas, the early churches were distinctly counter-cultural groups that stood in opposition to the prevailing domination systems of the Roman Empire that catered to people of privilege and wealth, and that violently suppressed any call for social and economic reform.

These Christian communities existed on the margins of society. In the beginning, they were composed of marginalized people—tenant farmers, fishermen, day laborers, slaves, and outcasts—although they soon attracted artisans, merchants, and a few wealthy elites to their ranks. They became communities of radical equality that cut across class differences, economic status, ethnic backgrounds, and gender roles, although this was sometimes difficult for the wealthiest members who were culturally conditioned to consider themselves superior to common people. These communities developed a lifestyle outside of accepted Roman norms that offered their members security in an insecure world without social safety nets. Each tight-knit community of compassion provided its members with food, shelter, and support when necessary.

Jesus as a new Moses who gives a new law on a mountain. Luke sees Jesus as a prophet like Elijah concerned about the sick and the poor. It is likely that Matthew and Luke shared a document of Jesus' teachings now known as the "Q Sayings Gospel." But each of these creative editors amplified these words with other messages that spoke to their present circumstances half a century or more after Jesus' death. John's gospel reflects a sophisticated Greek theology that presents Jesus as a manifestation of the *logos*, the word or creative intelligence of God that was spoken at creation. The further the distance from the time that Jesus lived, the more the authors promoted their evolving ideas about Jesus over the authentic words of Jesus. These writers and their communities saw revelation as an ongoing process and they freely put words into the mouth of Jesus that spoke to their current situation in life (*Sitz im Leben*).

Early Christian communities varied in the nature of their gatherings and worship, but a shared weekly meal seems to be a common element. The second-century Christian writer and theologian Quintus Septimius Florens Tertullianus, known as Tertullian (160–220), writing from Carthage in North Africa, described their weekly gathering.

> *We are a body knit together as such by a common religious profession, by unity of discipline, and by the bond of a common hope . . . We assemble to read our sacred writings, if any peculiarity of the times makes either forewarning or reminiscence needful . . . Our feast explains itself by its name. The Greeks call it* agapē *(ag-ah'-pay). Whatever it costs, our outlay in the name of piety is gain, since with the good things of the feast we benefit the needy . . . As it is with God himself, a peculiar respect is shown to the lowly . . . The participants, before reclining, taste first of prayer to God. As much is eaten as satisfies the cravings of hunger; as much is drunk as befits the chaste. After manual ablution [washing of hands], and the bringing in of lights, each is asked to stand forth and sing, as he can, a hymn to God, either one from the holy scriptures or one of his own composing . . . As the feast commenced with prayer, so with prayer it is closed.*[18]

These *agape* feasts, or love feasts, seemed to be a way for Christian communities to ensure that at least once a week the poorer members shared a good meal in mutual fellowship. Sometimes—but not always—a ritual Eucharist was celebrated as part of the meal or after the communal dinner had ended.

The Eucharistic words of institution, used in contemporary Christian liturgies, derive from Paul's letter to the community at Corinth. It alludes to the last supper of Jesus in which the breaking of bread came *before* and the drinking of wine came *after* a shared meal.

> *For I received from the Lord what I also handed on to you, that the Lord Jesus on the night when he was betrayed took a loaf of bread, and when he had given thanks, he broke it and said, "This is my body that is [broken] for you. Do this in remembrance of me." In the same way he took the cup also, after supper, saying, "This cup is the new covenant in my blood. Do this, as often as you drink it, in remembrance of me." For as often as you eat this bread and drink the cup, you proclaim the Lord's death until he comes.*[19]

---

18. Tertullian, *Apologeticus*, Chapter XXXIX.

19. 1 Corinthians 11:23–26. The word "broken" does not appear in many ancient texts.

The practice of these love feasts probably derives from a common practice of religious fellowship meals on the weekly sabbath and periodic festival days among first-century Jews. Similar social gatherings occurred in the larger Greco-Roman world among pagans. In Judaism, small groups of friends would gather weekly in a home, or another suitable gathering place, before sundown. The host, giving thanks to God, would break a loaf of bread, and distribute it among the participants. This marked the beginning of the meal. Mealtime would often be a festive occasion. As darkness set in, lamps were lighted, and thanks was given to God for the creation of light. When the meal was over, hands were washed, and a prayer of thanksgiving was said over a cup of wine—the cup of blessing—acknowledging God as the giver of all good gifts. The singing of a Psalm concluded the meal. This tradition spread across the Mediterranean world in Jewish communities and was continued as the early Christian communities with Jewish heritages took root in new locations.[20]

In addition to sharing food, Tertullian explains that members of early Christian communities contributed to a common fund to aid their work with the poor in their town or city.

> *On the monthly day, if he likes, each puts in a small donation; but only if it be his pleasure, and only if he be able: for there is no compulsion; all is voluntary. These gifts are, as it were, piety's deposit fund. For they are not taken thence and spent on feasts, and drinking-bouts, and eating-houses, but to support and bury poor people, to supply the wants of boys and girls destitute of means and parents, and of old persons confined now to the house; such, too, as have suffered shipwreck; and if there happen to be any in the mines, or banished to the islands, or shut up in the prisons . . . One in mind and soul, we do not hesitate to share our earthly goods with one another.*[21]

People were more attracted to the early churches for how they lived than for what they preached. It was service, not theology that mattered. Tertullian, wrote,

> *What marks us in the eyes of our enemies is our loving kindness. "Only look," they say, "look how they love one another."*[22]

That became the hallmark of the early Christian communities. For over 300 years, these radically inclusive and egalitarian small groups, based on

20. Gloer, "Love Feast."
21. Tertullian, *Apologeticus*, Chapter XXXIX.
22. Ibid.

the teachings of Jesus, remained as distinctive communities of justice, nonviolence, generosity, and hope in an oppressive world. Then, in the fourth century, the Roman emperor Constantine invited the church to participate in the power of global empire and everything changed.

the Constantinian shift

Constantine (272–337) became emperor of the western half of the Roman Empire upon his father's death in 306 CE. In 312, he began suppressing challenges to his authority and sought to gain control of the eastern half of the empire as well. While preparing for a battle near Rome against a superior force, Constantine reportedly saw a vision of a flaming cross in the sky inscribed with the Latin words, "*In hoc signo vinces*" (*in hohk sin'-nyoh vin'-chees*)—"*In this sign, you shall conquer.*" He led his troops into battle bearing a cross-like standard fashioned from a gold-encrusted spear with the monogram of the Greek word *christos*—the Greek letters *chi* and *rho* superimposed in a gold wreath. He was victorious. By 324 CE, Constantine finally achieved full control over an undivided empire. In 330 he relocated the imperial headquarters from Rome to the eastern capital of Byzantium, and changed the name of the city to Constantinople.

Constantine recognized the strength of Christianity, and saw that even while it was a prohibited religion—because Christians refused to make offerings to the Roman gods—it was growing increasingly popular. In the major cities of the empire, unemployment and dissension among the poor was a growing social and political problem. Constantine found that the Christian bishops who had initiated feeding programs for hungry people were gaining the trust and respect of the lower classes. This was a religion that could help him maintain his rule and keep the masses under control. Constantine believed he could harness the power of its God and the compassionate practices of its adherents for the benefit of the state.

As early as 313, he issued the Edict of Milan which established toleration of Christian worship throughout the empire. The edict made Christianity a lawful religion but did not make it the official state religion. Constantine continued to tolerate paganism and encourage the imperial cult begun three centuries earlier in the time of Augustus (63 BCE–14 CE). At the same time, however, he endeavored to unify and strengthen Christianity.

In 314, Constantine convened a meeting of church leaders at Arles (in modern France) to regulate the church in the western part of the empire centered in Rome, and in 325 he convened and presided over a council in the eastern part at his palace in Nicaea (in modern Turkey) to arbitrate theological disputes about the nature of Jesus. The resulting Nicene Creed and related doctrines established the first official orthodoxy of the imperial church.

Under Constantine's leadership, the church was carefully and craftily co-opted by the state. Christianity moved from a position of state persecution to state protection. Five decades later, in 380, the emperor Theodosius (347–395) declared Christianity as the official religion of the empire, replacing the cult of the emperor. As state support for the old pantheon of Roman gods declined, they dwindled in importance. The small autonomous Christian communities throughout the empire were soon organized into a clerical hierarchy based on the structure of Roman government. The church as a powerful, centralized institution rapidly took form.

The success of the imperial church was also its eventual undoing, although that would not become apparent for nearly 1600 years. In the early days of the Christ cult, membership in a community followed a period of preparatory training in which catechumens were taught the subversive wisdom of Jesus—limitless love and compassion, boundless forgiveness and generosity, and radical sharing of worldly goods in mutual support. Now, as an imperial church, the net was cast much wider to bring in as many people as possible. As a result, people were admitted to membership first and were later instructed in the faith. And the essential part of the faith now concentrated on creedal statements, not on a counterworld lifestyle. From the fourth century onward, becoming a Christian became an increasingly popular trend within the empire. As the upper classes entered the church, the church became progressively more wealthy and powerful. But wealth and numbers transformed the original forms of the church, comprised of closely-knit communities of life and goods. The very communal life that distinguished early Christianity began to gradually disappear. The extreme differences between social strata made that increasingly impossible.

French philosopher and theologian Jacques Ellul (1912–1994) proposed that as the church grew, the previous forms of small, intimate communities became gradually unworkable.

> *Success and the alliance with social categories of power initiated a process whereby the church became an affair of the masses. Jesus told his disciples that they were a little flock. All his comparisons tend to show that the disciples will necessarily be small in number and weak: the leaven in the dough, the salt in the soup, the sheep among wolves, and many other metaphors. Jesus does not seem to have had a vision of a triumphal church encircling the globe. He always depicts a secret force that modifies things from within, that*

> *acts spiritually, that shows us community, unable to be anything else but community.*
>
> *The kingdom of heaven [the kingdom of God] is the little grain, the seed buried in the soil, the treasure hidden in a field . . . But the situation is now the very opposite. It is no longer possible to live in community because of the numbers involved. How can masses of this kind conceivably be organized as a community?*[23]

Ellul further believed that the role of women in the church became degraded after Constantine. He did not think this had to do with two or three texts about the subordination of women that have been (mistakenly) attributed to Paul in Colossians and Ephesians.[24] Rather, Christianity was moving away from its compassionate beginnings to a virile lust for worldly success and political power that had no place for feminine values.

> *After a period of independence that came with the spread of Christianity, they [women] were relegated to a lower order. This is all the more interesting because the gospel and the first church were never hostile to women nor treated them as minors, and the situation of women in the Roman empire (particularly in the East) was relatively favorable. In spite of this, when Christianity became a power or authority, this worked against women. A strange perversion, yet fully understandable when we allow that women represent precisely the most innovative elements in Christianity: grace, love, charity, a concern for living creatures, nonviolence, an interest in little things, the hope of new beginnings—the very elements that Christianity was setting aside in favor of glory and success.*[25]

Seduced by wealth and power, the church willingly became the servant of the Roman Empire. Where once its role was prophetic—calling the economic elites and ruling powers to create a just society—it now became a chaplain to powerful and wealthy elites, accommodating Christian values

---

23. Ellul, *The Subversion of Christianity*, 35.

24. Parallel sayings about the required subordination of women, children, and slaves to their male husbands, fathers and masters are found in two letters formerly attributed to Paul. Known to German scholars as "haustafeln" or household codes, they are recorded in Colossians 3:18—4:1 and Ephesians 5:21—6:9, along with an additional variation of the theme in 1 Peter 2:13—3:7. Biblical scholars Marcus Borg and John Dominic Crossan dispute Colossians and Ephesians as authentic Pauline letters. They believe that the mind of Paul is more evident in Galatians 3:28: "There is no longer Jew or Greek, there is no longer slave or free, there is no longer male and female; for all of you are one in Christ Jesus." See Borg and Crossan, *The First Paul*.

25. Ellul, *The Subversion of Christianity*, 33–34.

to the needs of politics and blessing the very domination system that oppressed the poor. For the first time, Christians willingly went to war.

The church of Constantine became a wealthy institution invested in empire. To support the socially conservative politics of the emperor and the economic elites, the church became theologically conservative as well. Jesus and his teachings were spiritualized, because the political and social elements of the reign of God were too threatening to concentrated wealth and power. The creeds and the doctrine of the Holy Trinity elevated Jesus to the godhead. As his divinity increased, his humanity diminished. He became sinless and perfect, well beyond the ability of anyone to follow his lead.

With the establishment of creeds and doctrines, uniform church dogma was mandated and enforced. Those who dared to deviate were called heretics. In the centuries that followed, both books and people were burned to eliminate the threat of heresy. The church—once a victim of persecution—had now become a persecutor.

Through all of this, Jesus was efficiently and effectively domesticated. His vision of the reign of God was twisted and distorted into a harmless description of an inner personal state, a coming apocalypse, a heavenly afterlife, or even of the church itself. The revolutionary reign of God was spiritualized to the extent that it was no longer a threat to the status quo of the rich and powerful. First, the elites of the empire killed Jesus; now, the elites of the imperial church effectively killed his vision.

Throughout the Middle Ages, the church was a powerful force in international power politics and a champion for the status quo of the domination system. The Protestant Reformation of the fifteenth century created a stir in the system, but it didn't restore the counter-cultural role of the church in opposition to the state. Reformers like Martin Luther challenged the doctrines of the church, but in the end they needed the support of the princes and emperors to survive. The church continued to be the servant of the state supporting exploitation, domination, and militarism.

Then, near the end of the eighteenth century, the Constantinian church and Christendom (the wedding of church and state) began to show the first signs of disintegration. Revolutions in France and North America created nations in which the church no longer played a significant role. Anti-clericism was very strong in revolutionary France. The Bill of Rights in the United States prohibited the government from establishing a state religion.

During the early twentieth century, the role of the church as state chaplain got it into further trouble, particularly in Europe. The Protestant churches in Germany had enthusiastically supported German aggression in World War I. German soldiers wore belt buckles with the inscription

"*Gott mit uns*" (God with us). In fact, so many nations—on both sides of the war—claimed that God was on their side that the God of the Constantinian church became absurdly separated into a number of proprietary national Gods. Every side claimed God's support for their unrestrained violence. In the 1930s, when Adolf Hitler (1889–1945) united the Reformed and Lutheran churches under a state-appointed Reichsbishop and invited the German churches to play a supporting role in his proposed new world order, a majority of German pastors and bishops gladly accepted the offer. The new German Evangelical Church (*Deutsche Evangelische Kirche*) commonly known as the *Reichskirche* became a hand maiden to evil.

The situation of the German church in the first half of the twentieth century was not unique in history. Churches in the United States have had a long tradition of supporting our nation's wars, at least until they become unpopular with the general public. When the U.S. invaded Iraq in 2003, many evangelical and fundamentalist churches in America applauded the effort. Any Christian church with an American flag next to the altar is simply the latest manifestation of the state church of Constantine. The flag and the cross are competing symbols of allegiance. The presence of an American flag in the sanctuary demonstrates that the state has an equal claim to one's loyalty as does the reign of God. And for some Christians the two are indistinguishable.

Many people think of Christianity as a religion of peace. But our history belies that claim. Since the time of Constantine, Christians have regularly gone to war, endorsed slavery, tortured and burned heretics, and committed unspeakable acts of terror upon those they deemed enemies of Christ. These were not the acts of a small number of fundamentalist religious fanatics. They were fully supported by church leaders of mainstream churches. To be sure, some Christians protested the rampant violence of church and society, but they have always been in the minority.

an irrelevant faith

Today, throughout Europe, the church is increasingly seen as an irrelevant force. On both sides of the Atlantic, churches have repeatedly failed to oppose evil in the political realm and have instead focused their message on a condemnation of personal immorality, frequently confined to the private realm of sexual behavior. Increasingly, people are demonstrating no real need of the church unless they experience trouble in life. With each new generation, more and more people relate to the church only at significant events in life's journey: birth, marriage and death; or as some clerics say:

"hatching, matching and dispatching." But that too is diminishing. I've recently heard the comment that many younger people no longer attend church because they believe that nothing of importance will happen there on Sunday morning. The church of Jesus has become irrelevant to younger generations because it is intent on maintaining its own comfort and security and not on changing the world through a counter-cultural community with a radical ethic and vision.

Over the centuries, Christianity has become radically removed from the life and teachings of the Palestinian peasant who is the object of its devotion. Jesus the Christ has become an object of worship for millions of people. In his honor, Christians have created monumental architecture, majestic music, and inspiring paintings. In his name, they have also committed horrendous crimes of hatred, persecution, and violence. For the last 1700 years, the followers of Jesus have lost their way. *We* as followers of Jesus have lost *our* way.

Many people believe that the Christian church was founded by Jesus. Still others see the Apostle Paul as the originator of the faith. Neither of these ideas is true. The real creator of Christianity as we know it today was the Roman emperor Constantine. And the faith he brought into being is now falling apart.

CHAPTER 2

the two gospels

They have taken away my Lord, and I do not know where they have laid him.[1]

—MARY MAGDALENE

In the twenty-first century, we are confronted with a theological battle between two different gospel messages found in the New Testament. I first presented this material in my earlier book, *A Conspiracy of Love* (2016). For those who may not have read that volume, here is a brief summary.

In *The Heart of Christianity*, New Testament scholar Marcus Borg (1942–2015) described two very different ways of seeing what the Christian life is all about—two different visions of Christianity. Borg labeled these as an "earlier paradigm" and an "emerging paradigm."[2] Others might call them conservative Christianity and liberal Christianity, or traditional Christianity and progressive Christianity, although Borg did not prefer those terms. The earlier paradigm is still the majority voice in American Christianity today, but according to Borg, it no longer speaks to millions of Christians who are uncomfortable with its definition of the faithful life.

> *This earlier way of being Christian views the Bible as the unique revelation of God, emphasizes its literal meaning, and sees the Christian life as centered in believing now for the sake of salvation*

---

1. John 20:13
2. Borg, *Heart of Christianity*, 6–20.

> later—believing in God, the Bible, and Jesus as the way to heaven. Typically, it has also seen Christianity as the only true religion.[3]

The dominance of the earlier paradigm causes many progressive Christians to wonder if they can still call themselves Christian if they do not buy into biblical literalism, religious exclusivity, and a heavenly afterlife as the goal of the Christian life. According to Borg, an emerging alternative paradigm has been developing steadily for the last century and has become a kind of grassroots movement within the mainline denominations.

> *The emerging paradigm sees the Christian life as a life of relationship and transformation. Being Christian is not about meeting requirements for a future reward in an afterlife, and not very much about believing. Rather, the Christian life is about a relationship with God that transforms life in the present.*[4]

Borg, in his characteristically compassionate pastoral manner, was careful to say that "the issue isn't that one of these paradigms is right and the other wrong. Rather, the issue is functionality, whether a paradigm 'works' or 'gets in the way.'"

> *The earlier paradigm has nourished and continues to nourish lives of deep devotion, faith, and love. The Spirit of God can and does work through it. It has for centuries and still does. When it leads to a strong sense of the reality and grace of God, to following Jesus, and to lives filled with compassion and a passion for justice, as it sometimes does, all one can say is, "Praise the Lord."*
>
> *But for millions of others, the earlier paradigm no longer works. Unpersuasive to them, it has become a stumbling block. What is the Christian message, the Christian gospel, for people who can't be literalists or exclusivists? What do we have to say to them? In an important sense, this is an issue of evangelism. For these millions, the emerging paradigm provides a way of taking Christianity and the Christian life seriously.*[5]

conflicting gospel messages

I believe that these alternate forms of Christianity are based on two very different gospel messages found in the pages of the New Testament. The term

---

3. Ibid, xii.
4. Ibid, 14.
5. Ibid, 18.

gospel derives from an Old English word meaning *good news* or *glad tidings*. In Greek, it is *euaggelion* (*yoo-ang-ghel'-ee-on*). From this Greek word, we derive the English terms *evangelical* and *evangelism*.

As one reads the four gospels and the letters of Paul, it becomes evident that there are two distinctly different messages of good news proclaimed in these ancient writings—two contrasting narratives at the heart of Christianity. The first message of good news encountered in the New Testament is presented in the gospels of Matthew, Mark, and Luke: the good news proclaimed by Jesus. The second gospel is the good news announced by Paul in his epistles (letters) and in the gospel of John. To clarify the difference, we might say that the first is the gospel *of* Jesus, while the second is a gospel *about* Jesus.

The gospel *of* Jesus is primarily a social gospel, announcing good news to the poor. It is the proclamation of the present and future kingdom of God—a just and peaceful human society. The most authentic message proclaimed by Jesus was never about himself or his role in the salvation of the world. Those ideas were later developed by the Hellenistic church. Instead, the gospel *of* Jesus was about what he believed God desired in the world, about the radical transformation that God was seeking in human lives and social relationships. It was and is a gospel about redeeming our life together in the here and now. It seeks the common good by elevating the status of those at the bottom of the economic ladder. The gospel *of* Jesus is good news to the poor.

The gospel *about* Jesus changes all that. Paul is very clear about the gospel he is proclaiming. In a letter to the house church at Corinth, he says:

> *Now I should remind you, brothers and sisters, of the good news that I proclaimed to you . . . that Christ died for our sins in accordance with the scriptures, and that he was buried, and that he was raised on the third day in accordance with the scriptures.*[6]

The good news proclaimed by Paul puts the emphasis on Jesus himself and the salvation from sin that Paul believed resulted from the death and resurrection of the Christ. It was the messenger and not the message that ultimately dominated and shaped the history of the church. The gospel *about* Jesus is a message of good news that the death and resurrection of Jesus has changed everything for humanity in relation to a wrathful God. It is a gospel aimed at individual lives and their eternal fate. The gospel of John enhances Paul's good news *about* Jesus. In John's narrative, Jesus repeatedly

---

6. 1 Corinthians 15:1–4

speaks about himself and his close relationship to God, whom he regarded as a metaphorical father.

What is missing from the gospel *about* Jesus is the kingdom of God. Paul and John rarely refer to it. Paul, in fact, says little about the wisdom tradition of Jesus. The life and teachings of Jesus are not central to Paul's message. John's gospel includes none of Jesus' parables but instead offers us lengthy discourses like those of ancient Greek philosophers. Together, Paul and John present us with a very different figure than the Jesus of Matthew, Mark, and Luke.

Marcus Borg differentiates between the Jesus of history—a real human being who lived and taught among us—and the cosmic Christ of the Christian faith, a product of Paul and the Hellenistic Christian community who were focused on an impending event: the future appearance of the Son of Man, the resurrection of the dead, and a final judgment of humanity. Borg calls these contrasting images the pre-Easter Jesus and the post-Easter Jesus. In other words, the pre-Easter Jesus was a human teacher of love and compassion, while the post-Easter Jesus was an apocalyptic figure of judgment, reward, and punishment.

The distinction between these competing New Testament gospels and their images of Jesus is extremely important, because which message one hears and responds to will shape one's Christian faith and life. The gospel *of* Jesus focuses on personal and social transformation while the gospel *about* Jesus focuses almost exclusively on individual salvation from God's wrath. The gospel *of* Jesus is primarily a social and public gospel; the gospel *about* Jesus is an individual and private gospel.

One's orientation to the gospel *of* or *about* Jesus will determine one's central mission as a believer or a follower. The atonement gospel of Paul calls his adherents to a mission of evangelization and conversion so that others may experience a heavenly afterlife with God. The social gospel of Jesus calls his followers to transform both individual lives and social structures to deal with the pervasive issues of human suffering: poverty, hunger, shelter, education, and employment. One gospel is afterlife oriented; the other is centered in the present. It is all a question of whether one puts an emphasis on the teachings of Jesus or the teachings of Paul.

These two streams of Christianity have existed side by side since the beginning, often integrated by Jesus' followers in the early church. But today, these two competing gospels are dividing Christians around the world into irreconcilable camps. In the twentieth century, historian Martin Marty (b. 1928) saw these expressed in the United States as what he termed *Public Protestantism* and *Private Protestantism*. The Public Protestants responded to the social gospel in the Progressive Era from the 1890s to the 1920s and sought to remake American society as an expression of God's kingdom. They focused on eradicating poverty, ignorance, disease, and crime. Martin Luther King, Jr. revived the social gospel in the 1950s and 1960s. On the other hand, Private Protestants sought to keep the church solidly within the individualistic sphere, focused on the condition of the human soul. One could easily extend Marty's terminology beyond the Protestant denominations to include Roman Catholics and others with the broader terms *Social Christianity* and *Private Christianity* in the current debate over the understanding of the gospel message.

faith: living or believing

As the center of Christianity moved away from Jewish Palestine and into the Hellenistic urban centers of the Roman Empire, a transformation took place. It had to do with a shift from faith as a way of living to faith as a way of believing. This was not a sudden change or a sharp demarcation in the life of the early church. The gospel *of* Jesus began to decline in significance as the gospel *about* Jesus ascended. By the fourth century, when Christianity became the official religion of the Roman Empire, the way of belief began to dominate in the church and the unique way of life evidenced in the Jesus movement began to fade. Theologian Harvey Cox (b. 1929) has recognized this distinct shift by calling the early stage of the church the Age of Faith, and the latter stage the Age of Belief.[7] The Roman Emperor Constantine represented the demarcation between the two periods.

Understanding the difference between faith and belief is vital. Faith is essentially an act of trust, a confidence and hope that allows one to risk everything, even putting one's life on the line. Faith is evidenced by one's lifestyle and ethical behavior. Belief, on the other hand, is principally an intellectual assent to certain ideas or propositions. Faith dwells in the gut, while belief resides in the head. Faith is about loving one's enemies, sharing one's goods, and speaking truth to power. Belief is about accepting the concept that Jesus was the son of God, that he performed miracles, and that he died for our salvation. Because following Jesus requires risk, the gospel *of* Jesus requires faith; it calls for a living trust. The gospel *about* Jesus demands unqualified belief. Unfortunately, many people today use *faith* and *belief* as synonymous terms. The more faith is seen as belief, the more we miss the point.

The church's proclamation of grace can be, and often is, passively received without changing how we live. Our souls may be redeemed but our lives are not necessarily transformed. We can continue to lead self-absorbed

---

7. Cox, *Future of Faith*, 4–5.

lives ignoring the cries of the poor, and many Christians do. We often find ourselves captive to a culture dominated by selfishness, greed, and violence.

But the gospel of Jesus invites us to go beyond ourselves and live for others—feeding those in need, sheltering them, clothing them. Followers of Jesus do not undertake good works to get to heaven; they do so because charity, service, and a commitment to justice represent the faithful lifestyle that Jesus invites us to enter.

To fully understand the social gospel of Jesus and to follow the distinctly counter-cultural Way of Jesus, it is important to recover the message and mission of the kingdom of God that has been lost, hidden, or misrepresented in far too many Christian churches. The kingdom of God is not about personal redemption; it is about social transformation. It is about engaging in a conspiracy of love to change the world.

PART 2
deconstruction

CHAPTER 3

deconstructing God

Si Dieu n'existait pas, il faudrait l'inventer.
(If God did not exist, it would be necessary to invent him.)[1]

—VOLTAIRE (1694–1778)

In the 1960s, comedy writers Carl Reiner and Mel Brooks created a series of improvised comedy sketches called the "2000-Year-Old Man," with Reiner asking the old man to share his observations on historical events and the evolution of human culture. At one point, Reiner asks Brooks, "Did you always believe in God?"

> Brooks: *"No. Before there was an Almighty, we had a guy in our village named Phil, and for a time we worshiped him. Out of respect, we called him Phillip."*
>
> Reiner: *"You worshiped a guy named Phil? Why?"*
>
> Brooks: *"Because he was big and strong . . . nobody was as powerful as Phil. If he wanted to, he could kill you. He could break you in two with his bare hands!"*
>
> Reiner: *"Did you have prayers to Phil?"*
>
> Brooks: *"Yes, would you like to hear one?—'Oooh Phillip, please don't hurt us. Please don't pinch us.'"*
>
> Reiner: *"So when did you start worshiping God?"*

---

1. Arouet, François-Marie (Voltaire), "Épître à l'Auteur du Livre des Trois Impostuers" (Letter to the Author of the Book of the Three Impostors), dated 1770.

> Brooks: "Well, one day a big thunderstorm came up, and a lightning bolt hit Phil. We gathered around and saw that he was dead. All of a sudden, we looked up in the sky and said, 'There's something bigger than Phil!' From then on, we worshipped the new God who was more powerful than Phil. We called him 'Oy gevalt!' which in ancient Hebrew means, 'WOW!'"[2]

The belief that there is something bigger than us is the root of our belief in God. Most people go through life with a vague image of God, a "bigger than us" being in their heads, but rarely think too deeply about it. Some of our most cherished ideas about God are created in childhood, but as we mature, these concepts often find themselves in conflict with the scientific advances of a modern secular society or the vicissitudes of an unfair human existence in which good people suffer and bad people prosper. At times, it may seem that our image of God and how God operates in the world cannot keep up with a rapidly changing world and the ever-evolving ethical dilemmas that confront us.

Jesus clearly had a profound trust in God—a belief in an image of God that was unusual for his time and culture—and this belief formed the core of the way Jesus lived. Jesus never wrestled with the reality and existence of God. That is probably more of a modern dilemma than it was in the ancient world. For Jesus, the essential question had to do with the nature or character of God. Jesus imagined God not as an angry despot who needed to be assuaged or flattered by continual sacrifice of burnt offerings, but rather as a compassionate, caring, and forgiving parent. Like the ancient Hebrew prophets, Jesus believed that God was passionate about justice and the creation of a just society. Jesus believed that God had an abiding concern for people at the bottom of the economic ladder—destitute, hungry, and defenseless people—especially widows, orphans, and alien residents. Thus, God represented a powerful combination of love, compassion, justice, generosity, and forgiveness to a degree that was almost incomprehensible. It was these attributes—and not an image based on an enthroned supernatural being who possessed unparalleled majesty and incomparable power—that made God accessible for Jesus. A vast gulf separated a poor Mediterranean peasant from an earthly monarch, much less a divine one, but Jesus saw himself in an intimate relationship with God, as close as a son is to a loving father.

Additionally, God was an essential part of the vision he proclaimed—the coming of the kingdom of God. So in order to follow Jesus, we must take his relationship with God seriously. But images of God change with

---

2. Carl Reiner and Mel Brooks, "Phil," track 5 on "2,000 and Thirteen," audio recording, Warner Brothers, 1973.

time. What follows in the next three chapters is an attempt to understand God in the context of a postmodern world. Furthermore, it is an attempt to determine whether a postmodern image of God has any relation to the one that motivated, empowered, and infused the life of Jesus.

However, I must begin with a personal confession so that the reader understands my own position. Although Jesus has been instrumental in shaping my life of faith from an early age, a supernatural theistic God has never been a significant part of it. Since childhood, a sense of God's presence has been largely absent from my personal life. I do not mean that I was unaware of the importance of God as a part of the Christian faith; I learned all the basics about God in Lutheran catechism classes at the age of thirteen. I have participated in worship for over half a century singing hymns of praise to God and participating in liturgical prayers. But God never seemed very real. Much as I felt that I should deeply believe in the existence and presence of a supernatural God, I frankly could not, even in my teen years. It was not just a matter of believing that God existed; the psychological aspects of God as comforter and protector eluded me as much as the intellectual aspects of God as creator. As much as I tried, I simply could not find (or manufacture) the feeling that a divine presence was beside me, surrounding me with love, protection, and care. All that I truly experienced was God's absence and a vast silence in response to my prayers.

In my adult life, I have explored the Bible in depth and have examined twentieth century theological ideas about God. I have studied the biblical stories of God with thought and reason, but have not encountered a supernatural God in my personal life in any meaningful way. For the church, God is absolutely central. As a participant in the church, God cannot be avoided. But for me, the supernatural theistic God of religion has been a relatively unimportant factor in my life, and I have quietly viewed others' experiences with God with a bit of both wistfulness and skepticism. It took a long time to admit to myself that I was a Christian who could not accept the traditional God as proclaimed by the church, but that is exactly what I am. I strive to be a follower of Jesus, but I find that I cannot believe in a God as traditionally defined. So I have settled on a form of Christianity without the existence of a traditional God.

As a modern person who respects the scientific method, I essentially view anything that is of a supernatural nature with disbelief. The Bible is filled with a host of supernatural beings, including angels, archangels, seraphim, cherubim, demons, and the Devil. Do these beings truly exist, or are they merely products of an ancient human imagination? When I was a young child, the Holy Spirit was called the "Holy Ghost." Few people today believe in ghosts. Medieval images of demons and devils are slipping from our imagination. Nature miracles, the virgin birth, and a bodily resurrection after death all defy the laws of nature and human reason. Yet the idea of a supernatural God still seems to be central to religious belief. So, my fundamental question has been whether one has to accept a supernatural dimension of life to be a Christian. I often wonder if there is any room in the church for people with rational scientific minds. It seems that in many churches there is not.

Perhaps a transcendent God or a divine creative force exists beyond space and time, but I am simply lacking an adequate perception or belief in order to personally connect. I wrote the following two chapters—"the God of the cosmos" and "the God who intervenes"—in an attempt to see if I have missed anything that might convince me that a supernatural being has been an active force in the world, but has remained silent and hidden in my personal experience. In the following chapters, I will call into question many of the traditional ideas about the nature and character of God in the hope of arriving at some new understanding.

the task of theology

In *The Heart of Christianity*, Marcus Borg says:

> *At the heart of Christianity is God. Without a robust affirmation of the reality of God, Christianity makes no sense. And just as important, how we "see" God—how we think of God, God's relationship to the world, and God's character—matters greatly.*[3]

If one accepts the existence of God, or even the *possibility* of the existence of God, then one has several tasks at hand. First, one must come to grips with the nature of God—transcendent (existing outside the material world), immanent (permeating the material world), or incarnate (dwelling within humanity or a particular human). Second, if God is a being, one must define the character of this being—angry and retributive, distant and aloof, loving and compassionate, and so on. When one considers that "God" is often a symbol for ultimate reality—meaning the defining characteristic of the fundamental existence of the cosmos—one's God reveals an image of life itself as hostile, indifferent, or compassionate. The answers to these questions regarding God's nature and character will determine both the nature of one's God and the content of one's religion or one's life of faith. This is the work of theology—from *theos* (theh'-os), meaning "god," and *logia*

---

3. Borg, *The Heart of Christianity*, 61.

(*log'-ee-ah*), meaning "sayings." In other words, theology is a conversation about God, or God talk.

Frankly, the Bible is only of marginal help in our search to determine God's nature and character. Because its sixty-six books[4] were created by a multitude of ancient writers over the span of a thousand years, the Bible's answer to our questions about God's nature and character is "yes—all of the above." The Bible as a whole provides an insight into the evolving understanding of God's character by two ancient communities—the development of religious ideas among the Hebrew people for over a thousand years before the birth of Jesus and the insights of Hellenistic Christian communities for about a century after his execution. And those historic understandings are widely varied, not just between Jews and Christians, but within each of these ancient communities. However, for contemporary Christians, as we sort through these competing concepts, Jesus should be the touchstone of our understanding of the nature and character of God. His perception of God should be our guide. For followers of Jesus, all the rest of the Bible is merely a foundational prolog or an epilog of interpretation. Nevertheless, discernment of what Jesus really thought and said is often difficult because so many layers of interpretation have been included in the writings of the New Testament that they obscure the ideas of the historical Jesus. This is why a critical analysis that tries to separate the Jesus of history from the later Christ of faith is so important.

Jesus and his earliest followers lived in a pre-modern world. Our knowledge of the cosmos has radically changed over the past two thousand years. Even within the last century, dramatic new insights have arisen, including the Big Bang, quantum mechanics, string theory, and multiverses. Our view of reality is now profoundly different. So, for us, the question is not only how Jesus imagined the character of God, but more importantly, how we see God today. Separated by two millennia, the issue before us is whether these images can ever be the same, or whether they will inevitably differ. What can we say about God in a postmodern world? That is the beginning of our search as we struggle to follow in the Way of Jesus.

---

4. This represents the number of biblical books found in a Protestant version of the bible, which does not include the so-called "apocryphal" books of Roman Catholic editions.

supernatural theism

Supernatural theism is the most common view of God in the Western world and is the term that describes the traditional set of beliefs about God in the Abrahamic religions: Judaism, Christianity, and Islam.

Theism is a belief in the existence of at least one god. Theism comes from *theos* (*theh'-os*), the Greek word for divinity or god. The "*ism*" part refers to a religious or philosophical school of thought. So theism is a school of thought about divinity. Yet, theism defines the word "god" in a certain way. In most cases, especially in the Abrahamic traditions, theism conceives of a God who is a personlike being—the creator of the universe and the controller of human destiny. A theistic God is often viewed in anthropomorphic terms—envisioned with human characteristics, usually including male gender and the full range of human emotions. For at least three thousand years, this image has been the prevailing opinion about the nature of the gods in nearly every culture, both polytheistic and monotheistic.

The Abrahamic faiths also believe that the theistic God is *supernatural*, meaning something that is above, beyond, or transcendent to the natural world. Neither a part of nature itself nor dependent upon natural laws, the supernatural is greater than nature and can disregard or violate the natural order. It is also sometimes conceived of as being better, higher, or more pure than the natural world. In theistic traditions, the creation of the natural world is utterly dependent on a supernatural creator.

The term *supernatural theism* thus implies a being that exists above and beyond the natural world, separated from humanity and our earthly existence. Swiss Reformed theologian Karl Barth—pronounced *Bart*—(1886–1968), often considered the greatest theologian of the twentieth century, referred to God as the "wholly other," meaning that God is completely separate from us. Some people believe that while God is apart from humanity and our world, God is still actively involved with creation, especially with the history of humanity, orchestrating human events, great and small. Others believe that since the time of creation, God has left the world alone and no longer interferes. In either case, the God of supernatural theism is transcendent, meaning God is fully independent of and outside the material universe and is far beyond our human experience, perception, and comprehension. This supernatural transcendence allows God to be omnipresent (present everywhere at once), omniscient (knowing all things), and omnipotent (all-powerful). These are the classical characteristics of God taught to many of us in catechism classes.

biblical images of God

The ancient Jewish and Christian communities that created the writings of the Old and New Testaments of the Bible reveal many different images of God in their stories:

- a God of creation and life
- a God of destruction and global genocide
- a God of war and ethnic cleansing
- a God of laws and requirements
- a God of purity and separation
- a God of holiness and otherness
- a God of nearness and tenderness
- a God of faithfulness and patient endurance
- a God of comfort and compassion
- a God of liberation and salvation
- a God of justice and protector of the poor
- a God of condemnation and damnation
- a God of wrath and anger
- a God of vindictiveness and violent retribution
- a God of acceptance and forgiveness
- a God of graciousness and generosity
- a God of peace and love

All of these images of God are biblical. Because of this, some critics claim that God has a serious personality disorder. Of course, it is possible to view these varied images as descriptions of changing moods or varied behavior reflecting God's good and bad days. And many people excuse the drastic differences by saying that the God of the Hebrew Bible is angry and judgmental while the God of the New Testament is loving and forgiving. Yet anyone who reads the Bible with open eyes and a critical mind soon finds that these contrary images are found side-by-side in both parts of the Bible. The Hebrew Bible overwhelmingly portrays God as compassionate, merciful, and forgiving. The book of Revelation and some of Jesus' parables in Matthew's gospel imagine God as a wrathful judge and violent avenger.

The multiple personalities are not representative of two different revelations of God. They are representative of *many* different revelations of God. These diverse images represent very different perceptions of God's character by many different biblical writers at different times in history. Sometimes, the wrathful, violent, and punitive characterizations were shaped by the dominant culture of the time or were created to serve the social, religious, and political objectives of the nation's leaders. At other times, prophetic people called their nation to embrace justice and compassion in the name of a just, compassionate, and loving God.

Many Christians today—particularly the more conservative ones—believe that the Bible is the "inspired word of God"—meaning that if God did not actually pen the words, God at least inspired the writers as to what to say. In this sense, the people who wrote the texts were merely instruments, like secretaries taking dictation; God was the sole author of every word. But another—and perhaps more insightful way to view the biblical texts—is to see God as the *subject* of the Bible, not as its author. In this sense, the Bible is not the word *of* God, but is rather a collection of words *about* God. [5]

God as a human creation

I believe that the entire notion of God is a human construct. I realize that statement may anger or frighten many people, but I think that any rational and critical look at the question of God must come to that conclusion. Every idea about God, every image of the character of God, every description of God that has ever been spoken or written, has come to us through the minds and words of fellow human beings who have been speculating about the concept of God for thousands of years. At some moment during the past 2.8 million years of human evolution (beginning with the emergence of the genus *Homo*), human consciousness has conceived of powerful forces controlling the mysteries of nature and of life and death. Beginning about 200,000 years ago, the idea of supernatural beings or spirits slowly appeared in the minds of *Homo sapiens* (a term that means "wise man"). Because we continue to speculate on these unseen realities, some theologians contend

---

5. The Bible never declares itself to be the "word of God." The Gospel of John characterizes Jesus as the *logos* of God, usually translated from the Greek as the *word* of God. (John 1:1–5) John saw Jesus as the definitive "word of God" to humanity. For Christians, this should be the normative view. When the authentic words of Jesus differ from the opinions of other writers of the ancient Hebrew community and the first-century Christian community (and they often do), Jesus should be the final arbiter for his followers. For Christians, the "Word of God" (Jesus) should trump the many other words that seemingly come from God.

deconstructing god 57

that our species is more aptly called *Homo religiosus* ("religious man"), the only religious species on earth.

When I say that God is a human construct, I do not completely deny that a divine essence may be woven through the fabric of the universe. I am not smart enough to know one way or the other. A supernatural essence may somehow exist amidst the stardust from which all things come. Nonetheless, we have no tangible or verifiable evidence that there really is any mystical, spiritual, sacred power at work in the world outside of ourselves. Human beings simply have no way of knowing one way or the other if a God exists or what the true character and nature of that God is like. Instead, it is natural to gravitate toward an idea of the divine that makes sense to us, that fits our time and fills our needs, or that is appropriate to our culture and worldview. When a concept of God works, humans believe it. But, because human knowledge and understanding is constantly changing, so also our concepts of God are constantly changing. When one concept no longer works, we seek another one that does. Hence, the ongoing work of theologians.

There have traditionally been two sources for the human understanding about God—*natural theology* and *revealed theology*. Natural theology is the process of inference or deduction about God's nature that can be derived from the natural world around us and that we experience with our physical senses. Primitive societies inferred the existence of spirits in natural phenomena through this process. When dangerous thunderstorms arose, something was clearly going on in the world that was far greater than a pre-modern understanding could comprehend. Just look at how many ancient civilizations created a god who personified thunder and lightning, often elevating him—always a male—to the chief of all gods: Zeus (Greek), Jupiter (Roman), Thor (Norse), Hadad (Canaanite), Tarhun (Hittite), Perun (Slavic), Indra (Hindu), Lei Gong (Chinese), Raijin (Shinto), Xolotl (Aztec), Chaac (Mayan), Mamaragan (Australian aboriginal), among many others.

For many people, there is something inherent in our world—and in us—that suggests a divine origin to all we see and know—a god or gods of creation. From ancient times to today, this has been an enduring constant of belief. Natural reason infers or deduces the existence of God because we sense an order in creation with a level of design that speaks of a designer, and a human conscience within us that seemingly points to a divinely moral structure of the universe. Still, these remain merely inferences or deductions, not any tangible proof of God.

In contrast to natural theology, revealed theology is knowledge about God that theoretically comes from outside of our senses and our intellects, at least for those of us who are not agents of divine disclosure. Revelation tells us things about God that we could not deduce for ourselves. These divine revelations usually come through inspired individuals who have had a first-hand encounter with something beyond everyday experience. Throughout history, these people have become human mediators for God, conduits of knowledge from God, and witnesses to the reality of God's existence. They—or a community gathered around them—have created writings that record the details of their disclosures regarding God's nature, intention, or message. Revealed theology is the study of these documents, which some regard as sacred texts and thus accord reverence and authority to them. The Hebrew Bible and the Christian writings of the New Testament are examples of this revealed literature, as are the holy scriptures of many other religions and cultures like the Qur'an of Islam, the Hindu Vedas, the Tao Te Ching of Taoism, the Book of Mormon, and the Scientology writings of L. Ron Hubbard.

In actuality, there is little substantial difference between revealed theology and natural theology. They are both products of the human mind. In addition, everything we know is ultimately limited to what we can comprehend with our human senses. Obviously, nothing beyond our intellectual capability can be expressed. So, what every religion has to say about God is ultimately a human construction, a guess, a conjecture, an opinion. Our many diverse images of God are the products of the extraordinary human imagination.

In English, the word "God" (spelled with a capital "G") is commonly used as a proper name for the creator and ruler of the universe and serves to distinguish the monotheistic deity of Hebrew and Christian traditions from the polytheistic gods (with a lower case "g") of other ancient cultures. Regardless of how we spell it, the term "god" is a language symbol that stands for something, but is not the thing itself. What we refer to as god or God is like a blank canvas. (The fancy Latin term is a *tabula rasa (tah'-buh-lah rah'-sah)*—a blank slate.) People draw their own image on it. Moreover, that image will vary considerably from person to person. When the United States Senate adopted the phrase "one nation under God" into the pledge of allegiance in 1954 in the midst of widespread anticommunist hysteria, the white Christian men who proposed this language had an image of God in their heads that probably did not include Allah or Shiva. Thus, when people talk of God, they mean many different things.

It is true that nearly every culture throughout human history has had some concept of a god, or a family of gods, or good and evil spirits from another dimension of reality. These ideas arose out of a human need to explain the unexplainable, to provide an understanding of how natural events occurred, to speculate on what happens to a person's spirit when the body

deconstructing god

dies, and to grasp why suffering and evil exists. However, with the rise of modernity and scientific inquiry, many of these questions have now been answered without recourse to God as the explanation.

The first chapter of Genesis states that *Elohim* (*el-o-heem'*)—a Semitic term which means "god" or "the gods" depending on the context—created humans in the image of the divine beings that were assembled in his heavenly court.

> *Then Elohim said, "Let us make humankind in our image, according to our likeness; and let them have dominion over the fish of the sea, and over the birds of the air, and over the cattle, and over all the wild animals of the earth, and over every creeping thing that creeps upon the earth." So Elohim created humankind in his image, in the image of Elohim he created them; male and female he created them.*[6]

In spite of this parable of creation, the opposite is true. Humans have created God in *their* own image. Male and female, they have created the old gods of the past and the many competing images of God we have today, filling them with every human passion and emotion.

Some humans, including the ancient biblical writers, took their highest aspirations—goodness, compassion, peace, justice, and love—and wrote them on the blank slate that is "God." Others took elements of humanity's dark side—wrath, anger, domination, slavery, war, violence, genocide—and wrote those elements on the same slate. So what is God like? The God that is revealed in the Hebrew and Christian bibles is very much like humanity in all its manifestations. How could we conceive of anything different in a deity of our own creation?

Nearly 2,600 years ago, a wandering Greek philosopher and poet, Xenophanes of Colophon (c. 570–475 BCE), suggested that we humans always imagine a God like us. He wrote that if horses and oxen had hands and could draw pictures, their gods would look remarkably like horses and oxen.

> *But if cattle and horses and lions had hands or could paint with their hands and create works such as men do, horses like horses and cattle like cattle also would depict the gods' shapes and make their bodies of such a sort as the form they themselves have.*[7]

---

6. Genesis 1:26–27. In spite of what many conservative theologians have suggested, this reference to "us" is not an indication of the presence of the Holy Trinity at creation but rather a reference to the heavenly court of divine beings that was a part of the worldview of ancient Middle Eastern civilizations.

7. Diels, Die Fragmente der Vorsokratiker, 15–16.

The type of God we believe in will shape our lives. Likewise, the way we live and the things we want from life will often shape the type of God we believe in or, at the least, the type of God we are willing to accept. In the end, if we believe in God, we have a choice. We can choose between a God who calls us to fully realize the greatest possibilities of our human nature, or we can choose a God that serves our baser needs and desires. The choice is between a God who liberates us from self-centeredness and calls us to our better selves, or a God who justifies our worst behavior and sanctifies our domination over others, placing self-interest above the common good.

Let us briefly examine some of the different images of God that developed over the past four thousand years in the Hebrew and Christian traditions beginning with the most common perception of God today—a supernatural theistic being. Specifically, this perception is usually a transcendent, anthropomorphic, omnipotent, interventionist, creator deity. This concept of God runs throughout the Bible and has not only shaped mainstream Jewish and Christian theology, it has influenced the development of Western Civilization.

the evolution of Yahweh

The God of the Hebrew bible results from an integration of several different cultural traditions in the ancient Middle East. As the tribes of Israel established themselves as a distinct culture among the peoples of Canaan, differing images of God were eventually integrated into the oral and written traditions that shaped the Hebrew Bible.

As we just saw, the Hebrew texts often refer to God by the Canaanite term *Elohim* (el-o-heem'). It is based on the ancient Semitic root *el* (ale) meaning "strong one." This word had often been used as a generic term for god since the rise of civilization in Mesopotamia. It was the proper name of the Canaanite high god *El*, considered the father of humanity and of all creatures. El fathered the other gods (*elohim*) in the Canaanite pantheon and was the husband of *Asherah* (ash-ay-raw'), a mother goddess of Phoenician origin. In our English Bibles, both "El" and "Elohim" are translated as "God." (It is interesting to note that instead of elohim, Jesus would have used the related Aramaic term *alaha* (ahl-ah-hah') to speak of God. The Arabic *Allah* derives from the same Semitic root. Each word is rooted in the ancient Mesopotamian *el* tradition.)

As the cultures mixed in the land of Canaan, the Hebrew people overlaid the Sinai desert tradition of a tribal god named *Yahweh* onto the established agrarian tradition of El and Elohim, forming a creative combination of a deity who was not only a god of deliverance from slavery but was also the creator of the universe. Because the traditions about these two gods were somewhat similar, as the stories of the two cultures merged, the different terms and names for God became interchangeable and are found throughout the Hebrew Bible.

In written Hebrew, which has no vowels, the name Yahweh is spelled with the consonants *yod hey vav hey*. In English, it is rendered as YHWH. Because the name has no specified vowels, the exact pronunciation is unsure. Today, it is commonly pronounced as Yahweh (*yah'-way*), although in prior centuries Jehovah was the more common usage because German scholars transliterated the Hebrew as JHVH. (In German, J is pronounced like Y and V sounds like W.) The origin and meaning of the name Yahweh is disputed, but it may be associated with the Hebrew verb *hayah (haw'-yaw)*, "to be." Some scholars believe it is a shortened form of a word that means "he causes to be" or "he creates," giving Yahweh the character of a creator god.

During the Enlightenment, German biblical scholars began to detect two distinct traditions in the Hebrew Bible by separating the El/Elohim texts from the Yahweh texts. They referenced these traditions in shorthand as "E" (for Elohist) and "J" (for Jahwist or Yahwist). In these texts, the word *El* is used for God about 238 times while *Elohim* is used about 2,600 times. The personal name *Yahweh* is used far more extensively—about 6,800 times.[8]

Most of us would not know any of this because in most English translations, the name Yahweh is eliminated and is replaced with the term "the LORD" and at other times simply with "God," while Elohim is always replaced with "God." This substitution of "the LORD" for Yahweh began about 500 BCE when the people of Israel began to feel uncomfortable speaking the sacred name of God. As they read the Torah and other sacred writings, readers would substitute the Hebrew title *adonai (ad-o-noy')*, meaning *lord*, for the name Yahweh.[9] Sometimes this word would be written above or below the consonants YHWH in the Hebrew scrolls so that the reader would use the alternative word. About two centuries later, the Hebrew Bible was translated into Greek by and for the many Greek-speaking Jews who lived throughout the Greco-Roman world. The translators who created this version, known as the Septuagint (*sep'-too-a-jint*), substituted the Greek words *ho kyrios (ho koo'-ree-os)*, meaning "the lord," for the Hebrew *adonai*. Unfortunately, this practice has continued to this day in most English

---

8. "The Many Names of God," Agape Bible Study web site. No pages. Online: http://www.agapebiblestudy.com/documents/the%20many%20names%20of%20god.htm

9. Many observant Jews refer to the Hebrew YHWH simply as *Hashem* or "the Name."

translations, and for most Christians, the gods Yahweh and Elohim have vanished from the story.[10]

Originally, Yahweh had been a minor tribal god, perhaps first of the Midianite tribe (or possibly of the Kenites, which may have been a related clan) and later of the Hebrews. According to the story recounted in Exodus, Moses (in Hebrew, *Mosheh,* pronounced *mo-sheh'*)—the son of Hebrew slaves—is raised in the court of Pharaoh.[11] As a young man, he kills an Egyptian overseer who was beating a Hebrew slave and then flees to the land of Midian to avoid prosecution. The location of Midian is not known for sure, but it was most likely located near the Gulf of Aqaba, which separates the Arabian and Sinai peninsulas. There Moses meets Jethro, a man from the Kenite clan who serves as a priest in Midian.[12] Moses settles down with the Midianites, marries Jethro's daughter Zipporah, and has a son named Gershom.

We are never told which god Jethro served as a priest, but it seems likely that the Midianites and Kenites worshipped a god named Yahweh who was associated with a nearby sacred site called "the mountain of elohim" (the mountain of the gods), also identified as Mount Horeb or Mount Sinai. At this point, the writer/editor of the final version of the Exodus story tries to integrate several different traditions about the Hebrew, Canaanite, and Mesopotamian high gods into a single cohesive unity—theological syncretism at work.

While herding sheep near the mountain, Moses encounters Yahweh in a burning bush. In this account, Yahweh and Elohim are used interchangeably. When Moses asks the god's identity, Elohim responds in this way:

> Elohim said to Moses, 'I AM WHO I AM.' He said further, 'Thus you shall say to the Israelites, "I AM has sent me to you."'[13]

---

10. One of the few contemporary translations that still retains the name of Yahweh is the *New Jerusalem Bible* (1990).

11. The Hebrew name for Moses—Mosheh—was most likely derived from the Egyptian word *mose* or *mes* which means "child" or "son." Many pharaohs were considered sons of a god and their names included the suffix *mose* or *mes* attached to the name of the deity. For instance, Thutmose means the "son of Thoth." Rameses means the "son of Ra." In the Exodus account (2:1–10), the daughter of Pharaoh discovers a Hebrew infant in a small basket-like boat in the river. She names him Moses "because I drew him out of the water." The Egyptian name *Mosheh* sounds like the Hebrew verb *masheh* which means "to draw."

12. Jethro is also called Reuel in the text.

13. Exodus 3:14

The Hebrew phrase translated "I am who I am" is *ehyeh asher ehyeh* (*eh-yeh' a-sher' eh-yeh'*). It can also be translated as "I am that I am" or "I will be what I will be." Elohim continues:

> Elohim also said to Moses, 'Thus you shall say to the Israelites, "Yahweh, the God [*Elohe*] of your ancestors, the God [*Elohe*] of Abraham, the God [*Elohe*] of Isaac, and the God [*Elohe*] of Jacob, has sent me to you."'[14]

In these two verses, four different names or terms for God from four different traditions are linked: the Canaanite *Elohim*, the newly revealed *I AM WHO I AM*, the Midianite *Yahweh*, and the *Elohe* (*el-o-hay'*) of the Mesopotamian ancestors, another variation of the root *el* that is usually translated as "god."

The conversation between Moses and Yahweh / Elohim / I AM WHO I AM continues as the deity reveals that the ancient Mesopotamian patriarchs knew God by the term *El Shaddai* (*el shad-dah'-ee*).

> I revealed myself to Abraham, to Isaac, and to Jacob as El Shaddai, but was not known to them by my name, Yahweh.[15]

Some Hebrew scholars think that the term *El Shaddai* may link *El* with the Akkadian word *shadû* (*shad'-oo*), for "mountain," or *shaddû`a* (*shad-oo-ah'*), for "mountain-dweller." Derived from those words, El Shaddai would mean "god of the mountains" or "god who lives on the mountains." Other scholars believe El Shaddai is derived from the Hebrew word *shadayim* (*shad-ah-yeem'*)—a plural form of *shad*, meaning "breast." That would indicate a "god with breasts." I doubt, however, that the high god El was ever considered feminine. Yet, the use of breasts as a metaphor for mountains is possible. In Montana, the Grand Teton (French for "large breast") is the highest mountain in the Teton range. However, biblical translators usually substitute the phrase "God Almighty" for El Shaddai based on the Semitic word *shadad* (*shah-dad'*) that means "to deal violently with" or "to destroy." In that case, El Shaddai would really mean "god of destruction."

However, understanding El Shaddai as "god of the mountains" makes a great deal of sense because Yahweh, like many other ancient gods, was thought to live above the clouds and could be approached on mountaintops where the earth and the heavens met. In Greek mythology, the gods dwelled on Mount Olympus. This association of gods with mountains is why mountains were often chosen as sites for the construction of altars and temples

---

14. Exodus 3:15
15. Exodus 6:3

for worship. The elevated location helped to assure that the smell of burnt (barbecued) offerings and the voices of prayers would reach the gods' nostrils and ears. At first, Yahweh was associated with specific mountains in the region of modern Israel—Mount Horeb or Sinai (where Moses encountered Yahweh in the burning bush); Mount Ebal (where an altar was built to Yahweh by the Hebrew tribes after they crossed the Jordan into the promised land); Mount Gerizim (a holy site of the Samaritans, where after the exodus some Hebrew tribes were commanded to pronounce blessings, while on Mount Ebal across the valley other tribes were commanded to pronounce curses); and Mount Moriah or Zion in Jerusalem (where a temple was built by Solomon for Yahweh's earthly home).[16]

Some scholars believe that the biblical story of the exodus of twelve Hebrew tribes from Egypt is not an accurate historical account. Later Hebrew history shows a natural division between two groups of tribes, evidenced in the split into the northern kingdom of Israel and the southern kingdom of Judah after the reign of Solomon. A case has been made that the southern tribes of Benjamin and Judah may have been captive in Egypt, while the northern tribes probably emerged from Semitic groups already dwelling in the highlands of northern Israel at the time of the exodus. These marginal peoples gradually merged into a single culture blending their religious stories. The northern tribes had adopted the Canaanite El tradition, while the southern tribes had embraced the Yahweh tradition. Throughout the centuries these traditions were blended, but not always completely or smoothly.

Yahweh initially emerged as a tribal war god—a deity of liberation and conquest—leading the Hebrew slaves out of captivity in Egypt and enabling them to conquer the land of Canaan. As the Israelite culture became more settled over time and a broader national identity was formed with the tribes that already dwelled there, Yahweh took on additional roles—envisioned as a lawgiver, ruler, and judge over the people. Eventually, Yahweh adopted the role of the high god El and was considered superior to competing gods within the land of Israel and to the gods of surrounding nations. The early monotheism of the Hebrew people did not claim that there was only one God; rather it claimed that their God was greater and more powerful than the gods of other nations. In the newly acquired role of high god, Yahweh now became the creator of heaven and earth.

The Canaanite god El was sometimes referred to as *Toru El* (the bull god), identifying him with that ancient metaphor of strength, power,

---

16. For the significance of mounts Ebal and Gerizim that stand on either side of a valley that is now in the West Bank of Israel, see Deuteronomy 27.

and virility. The worship of a sacred bull was common in many cultures throughout the ancient world. In the book of Exodus, we are told that Aaron, the brother of Moses, fashioned a golden calf as a physical representation of Yahweh, mirroring the sacred image of El. Although the attributes of El were gradually assimilated into the traditions of the Hebrew people, the Exodus story tells of the complete rejection of any symbolic image to represent Yahweh. The first two of the Ten Commandments recognize the ongoing problem of integrating other religious traditions into the developing Hebrew story.

> *You shall have no other gods* [elohim] *before me. You shall not make for yourself an idol, whether in the form of anything that is in heaven above, or that is on the earth beneath, or that is in the water under the earth. You shall not bow down to them or worship them.*[17]

It is interesting to note that one of the chief wives of El was the Phoenician mother goddess *Asherah* (*ash-ay-raw'*), sometimes called *Elat*, the feminine form of El. Based on recent archeological discovery of figurines and inscriptions on storage jars in Israel, some scholars now believe that at one time Asherah may have similarly been worshiped as the lover and sexual companion of Yahweh and was referred to as the "Queen of Heaven," a title given to other ancient female sky gods and later to the Virgin Mary. Also associated with El were lesser gods—most often his sons—known by the title *Ba'al* (*bah'-al*) or *Baal* which means "master" or "lord." The chief among these was *Ba'al Hadad* (*bah'-al hah-dahd'*), the son of El who was lord of the sky—the god of thunder and lightning—providing rain and fertility for agriculture. He was also known as the primary god in an assembly of gods that gathered on Mount Zaphon, located near the mouth of the Orontes River on the Mediterranean Sea.[18] As one reads the Hebrew Bible, the worship of Asherah and Baal is a recurring problem in the enforcement of monotheism and the preservation of a strict Yahweh cult.[19]

---

17. Exodus 20:3–5

18. The mountain is located in modern Turkey at the border with Syria. Zaphon is mentioned in Isaiah 14:13: "You said in your heart, 'I will ascend to heaven; I will raise my throne above the stars of God; I will sit on the mount of assembly on the heights of Zaphon.'"

19. See 1 Kings, chapters 21 to 13.

a God who is like us

As we mentioned earlier, our basic introduction to Yahweh and El as two variants of a supernatural theistic God is found in the first pages of the Bible beginning with the stories of Genesis. There are two very different creation stories in the first three chapters of Genesis, although many Christians are unaware of the different tales. They come from two independent sources who were writing hundreds of years apart in ancient Israel.

The earliest story was written about 800 BCE by an anonymous Yahwist author who biblical scholars have labeled J. This tale does not deal with the creation of the universe; instead, it focuses on the creation of human beings. Starting in the second chapter of Genesis, J writes that Yahweh shaped a male human being from the clay of the earth and breathed life into his nostrils.[20] The man—*adam (aw-dawm')*, a generic term in Hebrew for a human being—is created from the earth—*adamah (ad-aw-maw')*. In English, we could think of an "earthling" being created from the "earth." Yahweh plants a garden, forms animals from the dirt, and creates a woman from the man's rib. When his creation is finished, Yahweh strolls through the garden in the evening breeze, converses with the new creatures, and gives them a few rules. Later, when Yahweh expels Adam and Eve from the garden in anger at their disobedience, Yahweh fashions clothing for them out of animal skins. This biblical God, who walks on earth, talks to his creations, and works with his hands, is clearly a human being writ large.

Anthropomorphic gods like Yahweh were the norm in the ancient world. The Greek Zeus, the Roman Jupiter, and the Norse Odin were all powerful male Gods who were pictured in human form. They were full of human emotion, were easily angered, and were capable of capricious acts of violence toward human beings. For instance, later in Genesis J tells us that Yahweh, disgusted with the direction his creation had taken, destroyed most earthly creatures in a massive genocidal and specicidal flood.[21]

An anthropomorphic likeness is probably the first thing that most people envision when they think about God. The "old man in the sky" is the picture that Michelangelo used on the ceiling of the Sistine Chapel. Whether it is an angry old man or a kindly grandfather, this is the image of God from our childhood, and for many, it carries into adulthood as well. When Jesus taught his followers to pray to "our Father," this solidified the visual image for most Christians.

---

20. Genesis 2:4—3:24
21. Genesis, chapters 7 and 8.

deconstructing god 67

Around 600 BCE, two hundred years after J wrote his creation narrative, another writer—known to scholars as *P* or the Priestly writer—described a deity who dwells apart from the world, a transcendent God. In P's poem of creation, found in the first chapter of Genesis, we meet a God who operates on a cosmic scale and creates the universe with the spoken word.[22] P is a writer in the Elohist tradition of the northern tribes who wrote during the exile of the Judean elites in Babylon (607–537 BCE). Instead of the name Yahweh, P uses the Canaanite term *Elohim*. This image of an almighty God goes hand-in-hand with an equally ancient worldview of a three-tiered universe—heaven above, the earth in the middle, and the dwelling place of the dead below. In this creation story, however, God begins with a two-tiered world: the heavens in a domed layer above and the earth in a flat layer below.

P tells us that God created heaven and earth, not out of nothing, but from a pre-existent primordial watery chaos:

> *And Elohim said, "Let there be a dome* [some texts read "firmament"] *in the midst of the waters, and let it separate the waters from the waters. So Elohim made the dome and separated the waters which were under the dome from the waters which were above the dome. And it was so. Elohim called the dome sky* [some texts read "heaven"].
> *And Elohim said, "Let the waters under the sky be gathered into one place, and let the dry land appear." And it was so. Elohim called the dry land earth and the waters that were gathered together he called seas.*[23]

A few verses later, Elohim creates a variety of lights which he places in the heavenly dome—a greater light to rule the day and a lesser one to rule the night. Finally, Elohim scatters a multitude of stars on the surface of the dome to twinkle at night.

Ancient civilizations believed that there were two primary bodies of water, one in the sky and one on the earth, and that something structural—a dome or firmament—was necessary to keep the water of the heavens (which fell as rain) separated from the waters of the earth (rivers, lakes and seas). Further, this dome was the structural support required for the movement of the sun, moon and stars above the earth. In early Mesopotamian thought, the earth was portrayed as a flat disk floating in a vast ocean. This is the same image portrayed in Genesis.

In addition to this primitive understanding of the nature of the universe, the two-tiered model was gradually identified with two aspects of

---

22. Genesis 1:1–25
23. Genesis 1:6–10

reality, the natural below and the supernatural above. Parallel structures of power were seen to exist above and below the firmament. Just as an earthly king had a royal court filled with nobles, generals, priests, and servants, God was envisioned on a resplendent throne in the clouds surrounded by the supernatural creatures of a divine court—angels and archangels, seraphim (six-winged beings according to Isaiah) and cherubim (four-faced winged creatures according to Ezekiel). When kings and their armies went to war, their national gods were imagined to battle each other in the sky with heavenly "hosts" or armies. The Hebrew Bible frequently refers to God as "the Lord of hosts" which means "Yahweh of the armies." For the ancients, the nation with the more powerful god determined the outcome of earthly affairs.

Yahweh meets Plato

With the rise of Christianity in the centuries after the death of Jesus, the intertwined Gods of the Hebrew Bible were further transformed by the ideas of Greek philosophy. Just as we saw in the merger of Canaanite and Hebrew religious traditions, now a new syncretism or blending took place. In many ways, as Christianity developed in the Hellenistic world, we find more of a substitution than a blend, replacing the passionate interventionist God of Hebrew tradition with the God of cool detachment imagined by the Greeks. Beginning with the Apostle Paul's missionary journeys around the Mediterranean, the center of the religion about Jesus the Christ shifted from the traditional Hebrew culture of Galilee and Judea to the larger Greco-Roman world. It soon became a religion of Gentiles—Hellenistic pagans who were more familiar with Greek ideas about God than Hebrew ideas. And the natures of God in these two traditions could not be farther apart.

Two aspects differentiated Greek pagan religion from Hebrew religion. On the one hand was the tradition of the twelve Olympians, the major gods of the Greek pantheon—from *pan*, meaning "all," and *theos* (*theh'-os*) meaning "god"—a term that referred to a temple dedicated to all the gods. Headed by Zeus and Hera, the contentious family of Greek gods dwelt on Mount Olympus. They represented various aspects of the natural world and human culture. Their Roman counterparts were headed by Jupiter and Juno. These gods grew out of ancient Greek mythology that like every culture sought to explain the mysteries of the world and the seeming randomness of human life. Like Yahweh, these anthropomorphic gods were human beings writ large. They were violent, passionate, and devious, and required continuous sacrifice to gain their assistance and avoid their anger. In the

Roman Empire, beginning with Augustus (63 BCE—14 CE), sacrifices were also offered to the emperor, who was seen as an earthly manifestation of (a) god or the son of (a) god.

In the Hellenistic world, tolerance regarding other religions was the norm. Other gods and cults were accepted as long as one did not ignore the worship due the emperor and the civic gods of one's community. However, unlike Judaism, Greek and Roman religion did not have an ethical dimension. There were no moral codes to obey. Religion was all about the correct performance of the rites and rituals in temples dedicated to the gods. Ethics fell under philosophy, and in Greece, that had a long tradition. It was Greek philosophy that influenced ideas about God in Christianity for centuries to come.

The dominant philosophical traditions of the Greco-Roman world at the time were Stoicism, Platonism, and Epicureanism. Of the three, Platonism was the dominant philosophy that influenced Christian ethics and theology. The Platonic understanding of God—referred to as *Theos (theh'-os)*—was a transcendent, eternal "unmoved mover" who is all-powerful, all-knowing, and unchanging. But Greek philosophies differed in their conceptions of God. For instance, the Stoic philosophers believed that God was *immanent*, equating God with the totality of the universe. This did not fit well with the Hebrew concept of Yahweh and Elohim who were seen as creators who each stood apart from the universe. Platonist philosophers agreed with the Hebrew view. They believed that an immanent God who was somehow present in all of creation was not possible. They reasoned that a creator cannot be part of their creation. They viewed Theos as *transcendent*, beyond the universe. When they referred to Theos as *eternal*, they meant that God also exists entirely outside the realm or dimension of time. The terms "eternal" and "eternity," in the strictest sense, do not mean "lasting through all time." The term for that is "everlasting," not eternal. Being all-powerful, God could make any material object last through all time, but it would not be eternal in the way God was thought to be eternal: not governed or bound by time and space. As an unmoved mover, Theos was thought to be without emotion and utterly passionless—a far cry from the character of Yahweh. Change would make a perfect God less than perfect, so Theos became unchanging or immutable. Platonic philosophers saw Theos as pure mind. Thus God could no longer be described in anthropomorphic terms. As an all-knowing being, Theos would know everything—past, present, and future. And because God knows the future, there must be some manner in which the future is already set. All of these concepts shaped orthodox Christian theology over many centuries and brought about a jumble of conflicting ideas about the nature of God.

In a sense, the movement to Greek philosophical concepts of God consigned Yahweh, Elohim, and the many diverse images of God from the Hebrew Bible, to the dustbin of Christian history. The Hellenistic church turned its back on its Jewish origins. Christianity had essentially tossed out the God that Jesus proclaimed. The unemotional, passionless, removed, and unmoved mover of the universe could not possibly be described with Jesus' metaphor of a loving and compassionate father.

Greek philosophy also introduced the concept of *logos* (*log'-os*), familiarized to Christian thought by John's gospel. Although usually translated by Christians as "word," logos is more accurately translated as "thought" or "reason." Three centuries before Jesus, Stoic philosophers proposed that the logos described the divine reason or creative intelligence that is implied in the order of the universe, giving it form and meaning. For them, humans possess a small portion of the divine logos that sets us apart from lower forms of life. For the Hellenistic Jewish philosopher Philo of Alexandria (25 BCE–50 CE)—a contemporary of Jesus and Paul—the logos was seen as the approachable aspect of an inapproachable and incomprehensible God. Philo believed that one cannot communicate directly with God, but can come to know and understand God through the logos, a kind of intermediary being or spirit that provides insight into the mind of God and reveals God's governing plan for the world.

John's gospel picks up this ancient concept, equating the spiritual figure of the Christ with the logos of God, the intermediary. For John, Jesus had become God's knowable mind and creative intelligence. During his life, Jesus was known as a teacher of great wisdom. After his death, the mystical and cosmic Christ now became seen as the spiritual aspect of God that could be known, the mind of God that could be more clearly understood. For Paul, the logos of God replaced the Torah of God as the benchmark of religious understanding.

When the prologue to John's gospel refers to Jesus as the logos, the author is declaring that the same wisdom and intelligence that is evident in all creation can be found in the peasant teacher Jesus. John believed that the creative intelligence that shaped the universe was incarnate in Jesus, and the wisdom expressed by Jesus gives us a glimpse of the inapproachable transcendent mind of God. The creative, imaginative approach to living taught by Jesus brought about a different quality of life, a deeply authentic life incarnating love and compassion to such a remarkable degree that much of the world simply cannot grasp it.

> *In the beginning was the logos, and the logos was with Theos, and Theos was the logos. He was with Theos in the beginning. All*

> *things came into being through him, and without him not one thing came into being. What has come into being in him was life, and the life was the light of all people. The light shines in the darkness, and the darkness did not grasp it.*[24]

For John, Jesus as the logos expresses a message of love—the "word of life"—that brings about a new kind of life, a new quality of life, just as God's words at creation brought all of life into being.

creator and comforter

The human belief in God is essentially predicated on two fundamental human needs. First, we need to understand the universe—how it came about, how it works, what it all means. This is primarily an intellectual need. When faced with the mystery of the cosmos and with things we simply cannot explain, God is often the human answer. Second, we need to feel that someone greater than us cares for us and looks out for our welfare. This is a psychological need. When faced with pain and suffering, with emptiness and despair, with tragedy and death, the nearness and compassion of God is frequently our answer. Many humans believe that God will walk beside them, protect them from harm, and comfort them, like a loving parent with a child.

A theme runs through the Hebrew Bible that hints at this kind of dual nature to God—both the remoteness of God and the intimate nearness of God. The aspect of presence, closeness, and nearness is sometimes portrayed as the intimate *spirit* of God to contrast the transcendent separation of God the creator. This is captured beautifully in Psalm 139 where Yahweh is found both far and near—both cosmically incomprehensible and personally present.

> *Yahweh, you have searched me and known me.*
> *You know when I sit down and when I rise up;*
> *you discern my thoughts from far away.*
> *You search out my path and my lying down,*
> *and are acquainted with all my ways.*
> *Even before a word is on my tongue,*
> *Yahweh, you know it completely.*
> *You hem me in, behind and before,*

---

24. John 1:1–5

> *and lay your hand upon me.*
> *Such knowledge is too wonderful for me;*
> *it is so high that I cannot attain it.*
>
> *Where can I go from your spirit?*
> *Or where can I flee from your presence?*
> *If I ascend to heaven, you are there;*
> *if I make my bed in Sheol, you are there.*
> *If I take the wings of the morning*
> *and settle at the farthest limits of the sea,*
> *even there your hand shall lead me,*
> *and your right hand shall hold me fast.*[25]

The prophet Isaiah agrees with the psalmist regarding the protective nature of God as a metaphorical father.

> *For I, Yahweh your God, hold your right hand; it is I who say to you, "Do not fear, I will help you."*[26]

So, we find two dimensions of God to be important. God is simultaneously both cosmic and personal. God plays the distinctly different roles of creator and comforter. Another way of saying this is that God is both transcendent (wholly separate from and beyond the material universe) and omnipresent (a presence that permeates the material world no matter where we go). For some theologians, it is difficult to comprehend a God who is both cosmically transcendent and intimately personal, but that is the nature of supernatural theism.

Accordingly, I will explore the nature of God in two parts. First, I will look at human ideas about God's general role in the larger universe; then I will examine ideas about the God's relationship to humanity in particular.

---

25. Psalm 139:1–10
26. Isaiah 41:13

CHAPTER 4

the God of the cosmos

In the beginning Elohim created the heavens and the earth. And the earth was a formless void and darkness covered the face of the deep, while the spirit of Elohim swept over the face of the waters. Then Elohim said, "Let there be light"; and there was light. [1]

—THE FIRST CREATION ACCOUNT OF GENESIS BY "P" (C. 800 BCE)

In the day that Yahweh elohim made the earth and the heavens, when no plant of the field was in the earth and no plant of the field had grown . . . Yahweh elohim formed the man from the dust of the ground, and breathed the breath of life into his nostrils; and the man became a living being. [2]

—THE SECOND CREATION ACCOUNT OF GENESIS BY "J" (C. 600 BCE)

In the beginning was the logos, and the logos was with Theos, and Theos was the logos . . . All things came into being through him, and without him not one thing came into being. What has come into being in him was life, and the life was the light of all people. [3]

—THE GOSPEL OF JOHN (C. 90–100 CE)

As we saw earlier, the creation stories in Genesis imagine a two-tiered universe—the heavens in a domed layer above and the earth

1. Genesis 1:1–3
2. Genesis 2:4–7
3. John 1:1–3

in a flat layer below. In later Jewish thought, a third tier was added below the earth. In Hebrew, it was called *She'ol* (*sheh-ole'*) or *Sheol*—a place beneath the soil where both the bad and the good would go upon death. This dwelling place of the dead is an obvious human conclusion since human bodies have been buried beneath the soil since Paleolithic times. Sheol is sometimes compared to Hades, the gloomy twilight afterlife of Greek mythology where people continued their existence as "shadows."

In the Hebrew Bible, we find several instances of travel between the two realms of heaven above and the earth below. In a wilderness dream, the ancient patriarch Jacob envisioned a ladder connecting heaven and earth with angels climbing up and down.[4] The story of Moses recounts that he climbed a tall mountain to approach God who had descended from the heavenly dwelling place in a cloud.[5] And we are told the prophet Elijah ascended bodily into the skies above while still alive.[6]

But in New Testament mythology, the travel between the three tiers of creation increases dramatically, especially in regard to Jesus. In the gospel of John, Jesus is said to declare that he and his message came down from heaven, as did manna in the desert to the early Hebrews.

> *For the bread of God is that which [or he who] comes down from heaven and gives life to the world.*[7]

It was intended as a metaphor, not a description of an actual event. But this concept of Jesus' descent from heaven was embodied in the fourth-century Nicene Creed. According to the Apostles' Creed, after his execution on Friday, Jesus descended into Hades/Hell based on an obscure passage in the New Testament's First Letter of Peter.[8] Although the four gospel accounts

---

4. Genesis 28:11–19

5. Exodus 19:1–25

6. In 2 Kings, chapter 2, the prophet Elijah is taken up into the heavens in a whirlwind accompanied by a flaming chariot and horses made of fire.

7. In John 6:31–51, Jesus calls himself the "bread of life," comparing himself to the manna eaten by the Hebrews in the desert wilderness of the Sinai Peninsula after their escape from Egypt. Exodus chapter 16 portrays manna—an excretion of desert insects—as arriving on the ground in the morning with the dew. (The Hebrew *Manna* is related to the Aramaic question "*man hu?*" for "What is it?") In Psalm 78:24–25, manna is described as falling like rain from the sky or heaven. John's gospel used the metaphor "bread of life" to show that the way of Jesus gives life to the world.

8. This is based on a passage in 1 Peter 3:18–19. These two verses contend that after his death, Jesus preached to those in "prison," a reference to those who dwelt in Hades. Based solely on this single passage the church later proclaimed in its creeds that Jesus descended "into Hell" or, in more recent versions, "to the dead."

the god of the cosmos 75

do not literally say anything about his descent from heaven at his birth or his descent into hell after his death, they do report that God "raised" Jesus from his burial tomb on Sunday—which theoretically can be viewed as ascending from Sheol/Hades (the place of the dead) to earth. Later, we are told that the resurrected Jesus ascended into the heavens.[9] At some point in the future, the church claims that Jesus will return by once again descending from the heavens to earth. As Jesus comes down to the earth, the saints (believers, who are both living and dead) will rise into the air to greet him before they all return to earth together to dwell in an apocalyptic kingdom.[10] Up and down, up and down, like an Otis elevator with three floors.

For a millennium and a half after the death of Jesus, Christians continued to believe in the literal reality of a three-tiered universe and a God "up there" who is separate from us and our existence. Much of our theological language, including that of the fourth century creeds commonly used in churches today, still reflects this outmoded three-tiered flat-earth worldview.

a God who lives "out there"

In 1963, John Arthur Thomas Robinson (1919–1983), the Anglican bishop of Woolrich, a suburb south of London, published a small but controversial book titled *Honest to God*. In it, Robinson described a major theological shift which had occurred from a God "up there" to a God "out there" over the previous 500 years. [11]

After the Copernican revolution in the sixteenth century, the biblical three-tiered image of the universe was gradually shattered. In 1514, Nicolaus Copernicus (1473–1543), the medieval Polish astronomer, formulated the first explicitly heliocentric or sun-centered model of the solar system. "'Up" and "down" no longer worked very effectively in relation to this new concept of the heavens and the earth.

Still, the advance of science has not stopped the church from continuing to use the ancient cosmology of a three-tiered universe. For many

---

9. Acts 1:6–12

10. 1 Thessalonians 4:15–17. In Paul's letter to the church at Thessalonica, he was dealing with the fact that some members of that church had died before the anticipated return or "second coming" of Christ to earth. Paul suggested that when Jesus descends from heaven, the dead will rise first to greet him, followed by the living faithful. Together, they would greet Jesus in the sky and then accompany him back down to witness the general resurrection of the dead on the earth. The belief in the "Rapture" is based on an erroneous reading of this text.

11. Robinson, *Honest to God*, 11–18.

Christians, the language of the fourth-century creeds is no longer a literal reality but is instead accepted (or tolerated) as a poetic metaphor. But this language restricts our thinking about God and makes it difficult for the church to progress beyond a pre-modern worldview in this increasingly postmodern world.

As John Robinson pointed out fifty years ago, the language of a three-tiered universe no longer works for many, even metaphorically. For instance, the idea of a Hell "down there" has gradually diminished from the modern mind, because in the Copernican scheme we can no longer place it anywhere in the universe as we understand it. Hell has no counterpart dimension for a heaven, which is now located somewhere "out there," perhaps beyond space in another dimension. Thus the ancient language of a literal Hell has begun to completely fall apart for most Christians.

Many Christians now imagine a God who exists somewhere beyond the universe, beyond observable space and time. Some people place God and heaven in another dimension of reality in order to make the concept of God still continue to work somehow with modern astrophysics. Whether God resides "out there" physically or metaphysically (meaning without material form or substance) is unclear and varies from person to person. But in the revised supernatural theistic image, God is still imagined as a being that is separate from our human existence and distinctly different from creation: watching, judging, and intervening in human history.

Yet for centuries, theologians have debated the nature of God. Is God a person-like being similar to the God of the Hebrew Bible or is God an abstract concept like the God of the Greek philosophers? In the Middle Ages, these polarities were discussed by the theologians Anselm of Canterbury (1033–1109) and Thomas Aquinas (1225–1274). Anselm, a Dominican monk, priest, and philosopher who became the archbishop of Canterbury, defined God as that "being than which no greater can be conceived"—the greatest, most perfect being imaginable. Almost 200 years later, the Italian Aquinas, another Dominican monk, priest, and philosopher, wrote "by 'God,' however, we mean some infinite good"—one of humanity's highest ideals and objectives. Somehow, in Christian theology, God became a superior being for some and an abstract concept for others.

a panentheistic God

In many respects, speculation about the nature of God has been fairly stable until recent times. One continuing characteristic of God from the fourth-century Council of Nicaea to the rise of modernity in the eighteenth century has been God's separateness from humanity—God's complete transcendence from all of creation. However, in the twentieth and twenty-first centuries, new ideas have arisen. Some theologians and philosophers now speak about a *panentheistic* God. This is not a God who is a person-like being separate from us, but a God who is present in all things—in nature and in humanity. This means that God is not out there somewhere, but is right here, part of the fabric of the universe and of our lives. Panentheism is a term devised over 150 years ago by German philosopher Karl Christian Friedrich Krause (1781–1832), referring to the concept of God as being present in everything, and everything being present in God. He argued that the world itself and humanity, its highest component, constitute a living organism integrated with and surrounded by a divine essence.

Panentheism is different from *pantheism*, which means that everything (*pan*) is God (*theos*). Pantheists believe that God and creation are the same. In contrast, panentheism (from *pan en theos*) means that everything is *in* God—God encompasses and embodies all of creation, but is ultimately greater than creation. Panentheists often use the metaphor of a fish in a tank. The water in the tank is like God—it surrounds the fish and flows through the body of the fish. The fish is in the water, but the water is more than the fish.

Marcus Borg offers another analogy in his book *The God We Never Knew*:

> I sometimes seek to explain the difference between panentheism and supernatural theism by inviting my students to imagine how one might diagram God in relation to the universe. I suggest representing the universe with an oval. Where is God in relation to the universe?
>
> Supernatural theism thinks of God as being outside of the oval; God and the universe are spatially separate. Panentheism would represent God as a larger oval that includes the oval of the universe; God encompasses the universe and the universe is in God. [12]

Within this framework, we can begin to think of ultimate reality not as a separate being, somewhere out there, but as a creative force or a cosmic essence that is present in everything, yet is still greater than everything. The term panentheism may be fairly recent, but the concept is ancient, reflected in Paul's words to the people of Athens as he paraphrases the Greek

---

12. Borg, *The God We Never Knew*, 51. This quote is found in footnote number 2 at the end of the chapter called "Thinking About God: Why Panentheism?"

philosopher Epimenides: "For in him [*Theos*] we live and move and have our being."[13]

There are some similarities between panentheism and the "Force" of the Star Wars mythology. As Obi-Wan Kenobi said "The Force is what gives a Jedi his power. It's an energy field created by all living things. It surrounds us and penetrates us. It binds the galaxy together."[14]

So at this point, we have two fundamentally different understandings of the nature of God: 1) supernatural theism, which holds that God is greater than and separate from creation, and 2) panentheism in which God is greater than but intricately woven throughout creation. Both are human constructs that attempt to make sense of how things came to be and what role, if any, God has in the creation and operation of the universe. These theologies come to different conclusions based on different observations, revelations, and the creativity of the human mind.

a God of continuing process

Process theology is a model that incorporates the essential ideas of panentheism but speculates at a deeper level about the fundamental nature of the universe. In the early decades of the twentieth century, English mathematician and philosopher Alfred North Whitehead (1861–1947) argued that creation is not static; it is in continual process, constantly evolving. His "process philosophy" challenged the ideas of Plato and Aristotle who understood reality to be made up of inert substances that endure through time. Classical philosophy held that change is merely accidental and not essential to reality. In contrast, process philosophy contends that change is the essential nature of reality. Reality does not consist of changeless things but of new and ever-changing experiential events. Momentary events at the atomic and sub-atomic level are the ultimate things that make up the cosmos. The events of the past continuously synthesize into uniquely new events, which Whitehead called "occasions of experience," that provide the ground for the changes that become future events. The idea that the present incorporates the changes of the past suggests that there is a consciousness in the universe that reacts, learns, and transforms at every level of reality.

---

13. Acts 17:28. Paul is quoting the 6th century BCE Greek philosopher-poet Epimenides. In his work *Creta*, Epimenides addresses God, the "holy and high one" with the words "For in you we live and move and have our being."

14. George Lucas, writer and director, *Star Wars Episode IV: A New Hope* (Lucas Films, 1977).

Process theology proposes that God is this ongoing underlying consciousness of the changing universe.

Whitehead's philosophy developed in reaction to scientific advances of the twentieth century—including Einstein's theory of relativity and quantum mechanics—that radically changed all the basic assumptions of science and mathematics. He attempted to incorporate these new understandings, but in contrast to secular scientific view of a solely material universe, Whitehead wanted to believe that a divine moral center to the universe still existed, so he devised a philosophical framework that would continue to accommodate God as an actor, although not an omnipotent one.

In one way, process philosophy states the obvious: the universe today is different from the universe yesterday. The great 13.7-billion-year story of the universe is a story of evolution, of continual change toward ever greater complexity, diversity, and consciousness. Process theologians propose that a panentheistic God is part of that changing reality, encompassing all the experiential events of the universe, but also surpassing them. If God is interwoven with creation, they reason, God is also in process, evolving along with the rest of creation. In Whitehead's view, God is learning and changing. God is still becoming.

But, in process theology, God has both a changing aspect and an unchanging character. The actions that take place in the universe over the course of time can affect and change God. But, the eternal essence of God—such as God's goodness and wisdom—remain constant.

Process theologians suggest that if God is an all-powerful being as supernatural theism claims, there is no observable evidence of that in the ongoing processes of the universe. Things are simply allowed to happen. In process philosophy, free will and self-determination characterizes everything in the universe, not just within human activity, but at the particle level as well. Process theologians contend that God cannot control any series of events in the universe, in human history, or in any individual's destiny, but instead God influences the exercise of universal free will by offering possibilities. They argue that God's power is one of persuasion rather than coercion. One writer suggested that God is the blueprint or recipe of the world, providing direction to a constantly changing universe. God entices or tempts things toward a certain direction, toward a divine will or intention. To say it another way, God has a will in everything that happens, but not everything that occurs is God's will. Though not omnipotent, God is still central to the operation of the universe—more like a coach than a commander, more of a mentor than a monarch.

Process theologians and philosophers suggest that the best description of ultimate reality is found in the act of *creativity*, which is at the basis of all that exists. Whitehead characterized creativity as the principle of "novelty," the process that turns something into something else. God thus is seen as the essence of the creative evolutionary process of the universe.

Process theology contends that God and the universe are mutually creative. God is the creator of the world in the sense that an orchestra conductor is a creator—organizing and directing elements into a harmonious direction. But instead of the universe following a detailed symphonic score, it is playing improvisational jazz. The universe and God learn together from experience and invent new melodies. The world creates God in the sense that these improvisations are part of God's being and God must adapt and change, while guiding things toward an intended direction.

Process theology is a creative solution that attempts to reconcile an evolving universe with a cosmic God. But it is simply another in a long line of attempts to redefine our understanding of God as human knowledge expands and older concepts no longer capture the human imagination.

the sacred story of creativity

Creation myths are part of every culture's history. The creation narratives of the Hebrew Bible provided one way of describing both the how and the why of creation, putting the world, nature, and human life in the context of God's goodness. Today, some scholars and scientists are looking for a new mythology to guide us, because they believe that humans still must have a powerful mythical story of how the world was created and how humanity became part of it, even as the old mythologies begin to fade. What's more, there is a sense that a new sacred story would replace the many varied mythologies of the world's religions with a new story based on common human observation, not on divine revelation. Revelation has resulted in contrasting stories that divide us. Some believe that observation can result in a sacred story that unites us. A new interdisciplinary field is now describing the great story of the cosmos as a sacred narrative of an evolving universe. It draws on the latest findings from many disciplines, such as astronomy, cosmology, geology, biology, natural history, and anthropology.

Sometimes called the "epic of evolution," or "big history," or the "great story," it offers a meaningful way of telling the evolving history of all that is. It puts the human story in the context of the larger story of the universe, helping us realize that we are not the center of creation, but the beneficiaries of it. It looks at the developing history of the cosmos in three chapters of successively smaller time scales: the creation of the universe (beginning 13.7 billion years ago), the formation of our solar system (4.6 billion years ago), and the development of life on earth (3.6 billion years ago). Humans enter the picture with the evolution of the great apes (18 million years ago), the rise of the Homo genus (2.3 million years ago), and the development of modern humanity (200,000 years ago). This epic takes us on a vast sweep of history from the formation of stardust to the growth of human consciousness. Big history describes a gradual evolutionary process in which something changes into a different and usually more complex form—the continual emergence of something new.

Loyal Rue (b. 1944), a professor of philosophy at Luther College describes it this way:

> *In the course of these epic events, matter was distilled out of radiant energy, segregated into galaxies, collapsed into stars, fused into atoms, swirled into planets, spliced into molecules, captured into cells, mutated into species, compromised into ecosystems, provoked into thought, and cajoled into cultures. All of this (and much more) is what matter has done as systems upon systems of organization have emerged over thirteen billion years of creative natural history.*[15]

Told as a sacred myth, this story locates humanity's place and purpose within the ongoing process that is the universe. It tells the tale of the cosmos in a methodical way that addresses complexity, directionality, purpose, and the survival of the most cooperative and compassionate beings. It tells us we are part of something greater than ourselves. Today, we urgently need a story that connects us to the earth—that links our destiny with the life of the planet. Although belief in God is not a necessary component of this sweeping narrative, there are both theistic and non-theistic versions of it.

God as serendipitous creativity

Harvard theologian Gordon Kaufman (1925–2011) saw the epic process of evolution as a "serendipitous creativity." In his writing, Kaufman substitutes *creativity* for the traditional idea of God as creator, because that term calls forth the old supernatural image of a cosmic person standing outside the world. He believes that God as a personification of the process of *creativity* better aligns with what modern science has revealed—"the enormous expansion and complexification of the physical universe from the Big Bang

---

15. Rue, *Everybody's Story*, xii.

onward, as well as the evolution of life here on Earth, and the gradual emergence of human historical existence."[16]

Why creativity exists, or has led us to this point, is in Kaufman's mind an inexplicable mystery.

> We do not know why or how creativity comes about; it is a profound mystery. The mark that identifies the occurrence of creativity is its consequence; something strikingly new, something transformative has come into being and has become a significant feature of the ongoing world.[17]

God as the ground of being

Christians who have embraced modernity have largely rejected the literal interpretation of the creation accounts in Genesis. Yet even those who deny God's role at the beginning of creation still wonder how everything began. If there is no other role left for God in a secular world, there is still the question about the Big Bang and whether there was a pre-existent creative force we can call "God." German-American theologian Paul Tillich (1886–1965) tried to address the idea of a pre-existent creative essence with the term "the ground of being." By this, he means that God is the basis for the existence of all things, that force or power that holds everything else up.

In 1948, Tillich published a collection of his sermons under the title *The Shaking of the Foundations*. In one sermon, "The Depth of Existence," Tillich claimed that God is not found at the distant heights of creation, but at the most profound depths of our lives.[18] Tillich was reacting to the theology of his contemporary Karl Barth who contended that God is "wholly other," meaning that God is fully separate from God's creation, including humanity. But for Tillich, God is not a separate being, but is the ground of all being, the essence underlying everything that exists, the very essence behind life itself. He interchangeably used terms for God like "ground of being," "power of being," "essence of being," "essence of life," "source of existence," and "ultimate reality."

The God that Paul Tillich describes is not the God of supernatural theism who is a being above all other beings. According to Tillich, a "being" can only exist in space and time. Therefore, since beings are finite, the creator of all beings must be an infinite reality beyond time and space. In other

---

16. Kaufman, *In the Beginning*, 43.
17. Kaufman, *Jesus and Creativity*, xiv.
18. Tillich, *The Shaking of the Foundations*, 52–63.

words, God cannot be a being. Tillich argued that God is a symbolic image we use to refer to the ground or foundation of all being, the essence of being itself, the basis upon which all things exist and from which all things derive. Another way of saying this is that God is an infinite essence that permeates the finite existence of our lives.

I must admit that as much as I try to comprehend Tillich's ground of being, it is a hard concept for me to digest. I keep looking for a beginner's guide—*Paul Tillich for Dummies*—to help me grasp what he is getting at. Author Glenn Chesnut (b. 1939) puts the ground of being in the context of the Big Bang in order to make it more intelligible, at least for me.

> *Modern physicists tell us that the world of nature in which we live had a beginning in time, around 13.7 billion years ago. It burst into existence in what they call the Big Bang, where all the matter and energy in the physical universe—along with time and space itself—came exploding simultaneously into being. But what was there before the Big Bang? That was the ground of being, that infinite Mystery which has always existed, continues to exist as that which keeps our present physical universe in existence, and will always exist, for it exists by necessity . . . And in addition, the ground of being is by necessity something even more extraordinary yet. Space and time were not created until the Big Bang occurred, which means that the ground of being lies outside of the box of space and time . . . This ground of being is the infinite itself, the boundless, what the pre-Socratic philosopher Anaximander called the apeirôn (ah-peh-ee'-rohn), that primary existent out of which everything else in the universe came into being and was formed . . .*
>
> *The ground of being is immaterial and incorporeal [not composed of matter], because it is not composed of the electrons and protons and neutrons and other types of matter which form our physical universe. It is omnipotent because it is not subject to the law of entropy, and can never run down or decay. It is also ineffable, which means that we cannot talk about it in ordinary human words, because even the greatest scientists cannot fit it into their mathematical equations and precise definitions.*[19]

So, according to Tillich, God is not a being that exists in any conceivable way but is instead the ineffable, infinite, immaterial essence of all being in the universe. In the end, this is simply another human construct, a sophisticated way to place God before the Big Bang.

---

19. Chesnut, "The Ground of Being: God and the Big Bang," 2–5.

God as mystery

Again and again, the word *mystery* comes up when discussing God. The mystery of the universe, the profound mystery of creativity, the great mystery of life—all of these contemporary constructs of God eventually point to mystery. What came before the Big Bang? It's a mystery. Why does anything exist at all? It's a mystery. How does cosmic creativity work? It's a mystery. Why do we have conscious minds? It's a mystery. So, is that where one finally finds God—only in mystery?

Some propose that all one can really say about God is that God is a mystery—that God is beyond all knowing or defining, beyond all human understanding. A transcendent God is beyond our limited intellectual capacity to comprehend. And, if one says that God is beyond all knowing, then one must admit to being an agnostic (meaning "one who has no knowledge")—not in the sense of not knowing about the *existence* of God, but not knowing about the nature, substance, quality, and purpose of God. In other words, if we declare God to be a mystery, we are saying that there must be a God, but we don't have the faintest clue as to God's character or how God operates in the world. But, if that is our theological position, how does that image of God help to shape our lives?

Now, there may be a significant difference between declaring that God *is* a mystery and believing in God *as* mystery—God not as an unknowable being or an indefinable creative power, but as mystery *itself*. When we say that God is *a* mystery, we imply that God is incomprehensible and utterly inexplicable. But declaring God *as* mystery suggests that God is the personification of all those things about the universe that we don't or can't understand. It is not that God is unknowable, but that God *represents* the unknowable. In this sense, "God" is a language symbol for everything that exceeds our knowledge and comprehension. As we try to take in the awesome nature of the incredibly vast and wild universe, at some point we come face to face with mystery, the limits of our understanding, and the boundaries of the human intellect.

God in the gaps

This brings us to a theological argument known as "God in the gaps." This perspective proposes that our gaps in scientific knowledge must be taken as evidence or proof of God's existence. When we come to the end of our capacity to understand how the universe operates or how specific parts of nature came to be, then we resort to God as the only possible explanation.

This is the argument employed not only by conservative Christian "creationists"—who reject the idea of the evolution of the universe and the human species—but is also embraced by evolutionary panentheists and process theologians. For in both of these widely divergent viewpoints there is a common thread that unifies their seemingly opposed positions. Both are clinging to some remaining role for God in the creation and operation of the universe. It usually follows this logic: If there is a gap in understanding of some aspect of the natural world, then the cause must be supernatural, the cause must be God.

To counter this argument, Lutheran theologian and pastor Dietrich Bonhoeffer (1906–1945) wrote from prison the year he died,

> How wrong it is to use God as a stop-gap for the incompleteness of our knowledge. If in fact the frontiers of knowledge are being pushed further and further back (and that is bound to be the case), then God is being pushed back with them, and is therefore continually in retreat. We are to find God in what we know, not in what we don't know.[20]

As Bonhoeffer suggests, the position of the creationists will inevitably be pushed back further and further as science explains more aspects of the natural world. Mystery is a connecting point between the religious and scientific communities. When confronted with the awesome mystery of the universe, many religious people view creation and the Creator as simply beyond human understanding. Scientists have another viewpoint. When confronted with the mystery of the universe, they find renewed impetus to discover a better understanding. In the scientific worldview, a mystery is something to be solved, not accepted.

Still for those who proclaim ultimate reality to be a mystery, we should be clear that an unknowable, unsearchable, unfathomable God was not the God of Jesus. Quite the opposite. Jesus found God in what he knew. Jesus found God in the human experience. The various concepts of God as an anthropomorphic creator or God as creativity itself are a discussion of divinity at a cosmic scope—life at its most macro and micro levels. As far as we know, Jesus never speculated on any of that. He was more concerned about how we treat one another.

If we are to discover a conception of God that makes sense in a postmodern world, I think we need to abandon speculation about a cosmic God—a creator God—and move to the human experience with the presence of God throughout history. Understanding what God may represent at the level of human history and individual life is a very different discussion.

20. Bonhoeffer, *Letters and Papers*, 311.

CHAPTER 5

the God who intervenes

I read the book of Job last night. I don't think God comes out well in it.[1]
—VIRGINIA WOOLF (1882–1941)

We stated earlier that our belief in God is predicated on two human psychological needs—the intellectual need to understand the universe and the emotional need to feel that someone greater than us cares for our welfare. Whether God is defined as a symbol for the ground of all being, or the creative intelligence of the universe, or the personification of creativity itself, many people believe that God is also intensely personal—an intimate reality in their daily lives. Theological thinkers have explored that concept for thousands of years. Therefore, we need to explore the possibility of God's relation to human life in order to arrive at any conclusions about the meaning of God and God's power in a postmodern world.

Someone has said that most humans believe in a God of some kind, so the principle question facing us today is not 'Does God exist?' but rather 'How do I relate to God?' How does one relate to ultimate reality if it is simply an impersonal essence of reality, or the personification of a creative process, or the embodiment of a cosmic life force?

---

1. Woolf, *The Letters of Virginia Woolf*.

the presence of God

In *Honest to God*, Bishop John Robinson (1919-1983) said that:

> *God is, by definition, ultimate reality. One cannot argue whether ultimate reality exists. One can only ask what ultimate reality is like—whether, for instance, in the last analysis what lies at the heart of things and governs their working is to be described in personal or impersonal categories.*[2]

Many of the images of a panentheistic God are very impersonal in nature. In *The Heart of Christianity*, Marcus Borg, who supported a panentheistic image of God, addressed this point:

> *In the Christian tradition, as in most religions, God is often spoken of as "personal"—as a personlike being with personal characteristics. But is God personal? Supernatural theism unambiguously affirms this, whereas Panentheism seems to some people to be disappointingly impersonal. So, is God personal? If so, in what sense?*[3]

Borg then offered some rationale to allow panentheists to use personal language in reference to God:

> *Whatever God is ultimately like, our relationship to God is personal. This relationship engages us as persons at our deepest and most passionate level. I am persuaded that God has more the quality of a "presence" than a nonpersonal "energy" or "force." To use language Martin Buber used, I am persuaded that God has more the quality of a "you" than an "it," more the quality of a person than of an impersonal "source."*
>
> *Moreover, I think God "speaks" to us. I don't mean an oral or aural revelation or divine dictation. But I think God "speaks" to us—sometimes dramatically in visions, less dramatically in some of our dreams, in internal "proddings" or "leadings," through people, and through devotional practices and scriptures of our tradition. We sometimes have a sense—I sometimes have a sense—of being addressed.*[4]

So even if God is not a person-like being, Borg proposes we can still conceive of God in personal ways and use human relational language in reference to God.

2. Robinson, *Honest to God*, 29.
3. Borg, *The Heart of Christianity*, 70–71.
4. Ibid, 72–73.

Is God a presence? Writer, poet, and social activist Thomas Merton (1915–1968) believed that God's presence in the world was obvious. But he also claimed that most people rarely see it. Marcus Borg quoted Merton's description of God's revelation in all things at all times:

> Life is this simple. We are living in a world that is absolutely transparent, and God is shining through it all the time. This is not just a fable or a nice story. It is true. If we abandon ourselves to God and forget ourselves, we see it sometimes, and we see it maybe frequently. God shows Himself everywhere, in everything—in people and things and in nature and events. It becomes very obvious that God is everywhere and in everything and we cannot be without him. It's impossible. The only thing is that we don't see it.[5]

the power of God

At the center of our myriad conceptions of God is always a discussion of God's power. As God's power in the universe diminishes in the human mind due to increasing scientific understanding of its operation, God's relationship with humanity may become the final arena in which the question of God's power continues to engage us as an ongoing debate. The power of God is the central question about the reality of God in a postmodern world. Is God all-powerful as many supernatural theists believe? If so, does God sometimes choose to withhold divine power? Or does God possess only limited power—guiding and persuading humanity toward a desired goal? Has God stepped back from human involvement as the Deists claim and largely left us on our own? Or, has God relinquished cosmic control and joined with humanity in a partnership of limited power in earthly affairs? Finally, is it possible there has never been a transcendent force for good among us, but only humanity's weakness at work in the world all along? And if we eventually discover there is no divine power at the center of our lives, is the universe ultimately without intrinsic meaning and purpose?

the four Gods of America

In 2005, the Baylor University Institute for Studies of Religion conducted a major study of the religious beliefs of the American population.[6] For

---

5. Ibid, 155. Also, Borg, *The God We Never Knew*, 47. Borg took the quote from an audiotape of Merton made in 1965.

6. Baylor Institute, *American Piety in the 21st Century*.

over fifty years, the Gallup Poll has consistently shown that 95 percent of Americans say they believe in God. Baylor researchers wanted to know just what *kind* of God people actually believed in. Previous research had never probed very deeply into the question. So the Baylor Religion Survey began to ask questions to determine how people would describe their image of God.

After sifting the data, the Baylor researchers defined four fundamentally different Gods based on two variables:

- God's engagement with the world—the extent to which individuals believe that God is directly involved in personal and worldly affairs
- God's anger with the world—the extent to which individuals believe that God is angered by human sins and tends toward punishing, severe and wrathful characteristics

The four different characters of God they uncovered are described in simple A, B, C, D terms:

- an **Authoritarian** God—engaged with the world and angry with humanity
- a **Benevolent** God—engaged but not angry
- a **Critical** God—not engaged with the world but still angry with humanity
- a **Distant** God—not engaged and not angry

In each case, the God described by Americans is a variation on the God imagined by supernatural theism.

The Baylor researchers found that nearly a third of all Americans believe in an *Authoritarian God*. This group generally thinks that God is highly involved in their daily lives and world affairs. They tend to believe that God helps them in their individual decision-making and is ultimately responsible for global events such as economic upturns or disastrous tsunamis. They also tend to feel that God is quite angry over human sin and is ready and willing to mete out punishment to those who are unfaithful or ungodly. The defining characteristic of the Authoritarian God is holiness, which means that God cannot tolerate any kind of sin. In this view, when human beings violate God's holiness, God must punish them. This is the view of God in most atonement theories.

Like believers in the Authoritarian God, the quarter of the population who believe in a *Benevolent God* also tend to think that God is very active in our daily lives. But these individuals are less likely to believe that God is angry and acts in wrathful ways. Instead, the Benevolent God is mainly a force of positive influence in the world and is less willing to condemn or punish individuals. These believers are more likely to see God's hand only in the miracles of life, not in the disasters. The defining characteristic of the Benevolent God is compassion. A compassionate God is gracious, loving, and forgiving.

Believers in a *Critical God* represent another quarter of Americans. They feel that God is largely absent from direct influence in daily life and does not interact on the world stage. Nevertheless, this God still observes the world and views the current state of humanity unfavorably. This group believes that although divine justice is not consistently meted out on earth, God's displeasure will surely be felt in another life.

Just ten percent of believers believe in a *Distant God*. They believe that God is not active in the world and is not especially angry either. These individuals tend to think about God as a cosmic creative force who set the laws of nature in motion and then stepped back. As such, God does not intervene in the world and does not judge our individual actions or world events.

the American religious landscape

The authors of the Baylor study believe that these four personalities of God are probably better descriptors of the American religious landscape than labels like conservative and liberal or Protestant and Catholic.

The region of the country one lives in seems somewhat related to the four images of God. Southerners tend towards an authoritarian and holy God active in all earthly affairs. Midwesterners tend towards a benevolent and compassionate God whose influence is seen in the good things of life. Easterners disproportionately tend towards belief in a critical God who does not interfere with humanity and West Coasters tend towards belief in a distant God removed from daily life. So, in the South and Midwest, God is seen as interventionist, while on the East and West coasts, God is largely uninvolved. And in the East and South, God is viewed as very angry, while in the Midwest and West, God is much nicer.

In addition, about five percent of Americans believe there is no God. Atheists are certain that God does not exist. Some religious people maintain that atheism leads to personal immorality or amorality, because they reason that only a God promising an eternal reward or threatening an eternal punishment will get people to act in moral ways. Nevertheless, atheists often hold very strong perspectives concerning the morality of human behavior and ideals of social order. They just have no place for the supernatural in their worldview.

Interestingly, atheists, agnostics, and supernatural theists largely share the same image of God—a wholly other being who exists somewhere "out there." Supernatural theists believe in this image, atheists reject it, and agnostics say they simply don't have enough information to be sure one way or another, or possibly they don't want to commit one way or the other. Someone once quipped that an agnostic is simply an atheist without conviction.

a deist God

The image of the distant or absent God, held by one out of ten people, has its roots in the Enlightenment of the seventeenth and eighteenth centuries. At the time, science was demonstrating that the laws of nature could explain many natural events such as the weather. For the first time in history, God was no longer necessary to direct the daily operation of the world. As a result, many intellectuals, who were still unwilling to deny the existence of God, began to reason that God was simply absent and removed from the world's affairs, perhaps resting after the magnificent act of creation. They saw God as the "grand architect" but not the building supervisor.

A philosophy called Deism arose among many famous thinkers and writers, including American statesmen like Thomas Paine, George Washington, and Thomas Jefferson. They believed in an impersonal God, a kind of remote watchmaker. They imagined that God had wound the world up like a pocket watch and let it go on ticking without any further intervention. In their view, God has very little interest in the ongoing development of the universe and has generally left it alone. The deist God does not usually interfere in human events and is certainly not active in individual lives. These Enlightenment Deists also believed that Jesus was a great moral teacher but was not a divine or semi-divine being. Therefore classical deism is not considered Christian in the most orthodox sense.[7]

an interventionist God

In contrast to the deist view, which never attracted a majority of Christians, just over half of the American people today see God as an omnipotent

---

7. An interesting argument against those who claim that America was founded as a Christian nation.

interventionist. This is the predominant view among those who hold a traditional and conservative theology. They believe that an all-powerful God not only intervenes, but takes sides. Many American Christians believe that God favors the United States of America in a divinely appointed role among nations, as God once favored the Hebrews over the people of other nations according to the stories of the Hebrew Bible.

The biblical narrative is certainly on the side of an interventionist God who chose a particular nation in history. The Hebrew Bible is filled with images of Yahweh and Elohim acting to shape, destroy, punish, rescue, and discipline the ancient Israelites. These ancient stories tell us that God heard the cries of the oppressed Hebrew slaves and rescued them from bondage in Egypt. God guided the Hebrew people through the wilderness with pillars of fire and smoke to lead them to the land of Canaan. There, God directed them to slaughter the previous inhabitants—every man, woman and child. Still later, God acted with harsh judgment by sending the invading armies of Assyria and Babylonia to destroy the farms and homes of the Hebrew people and carry them away into captivity and exile. God then rescued a remnant of the Hebrew people by using the king of Persia as God's agent (a divinely-appointed messiah) to release them from captivity. Thus in these narratives, the Bible paints a picture of a God who is active in history, who favors one particular people, and who shapes national and international events. The great American myth that shapes its own civil religion is that God has now chosen the United States to be that people.

an arbitrary and unjust God

Many proponents of the interventionist God also believe that God has a master plan for life on earth, and within that, a detailed plan for each of us to play. I have never found any biblical support for this idea, but it is quite pervasive in conservative Christian culture and belief. However, if God is exercising a master plan for human existence, then God must be held responsible and accountable for everything that happens on earth, either causing it (by intervening) or permitting it (by choosing not to intervene).

Following the logic of a "cosmic plan," an interventionist God would be responsible for everything from natural disasters to terrorist acts—as conservatives Jerry Falwell (1933–2007) and Pat Robertson (b. 1930) have been quick to tell us. Carrying the logic further, the omnipotent interventionist God must also be at work when babies die in their cribs or when people contract cancer. If there is a detailed plan involving individuals, then the people who are mugged in our city streets or abused in their homes are unfortunate victims of that plan. Accordingly, God's "will" is revealed in car crashes, cross burnings, and concentration camps. An interventionist God acting in history causes wars to occur and leads certain nations to victory over others. In other words, if one believes in a cosmic plan by an omnipotent interventionist God, then God must be held accountable for all the evil and suffering we experience. But many religious people are unwilling to accept that logic.

As we have seen, those who believe in a benevolent God are more likely to see God's hand only in the miracles of life and not in the disasters. This is a way to give an interventionist God the benefit of the doubt, maintaining a balance between the idea that God is all-powerful and the belief that God is essentially good. (The word *God* derives from the Old English word for "good.") But, to believe in a God who is both omnipotent *and* compassionate requires both a blind faith and a blind eye to reality.

We are often told by conservative Christians that God performs daily miracles, intervening in human lives to heal and save individuals from disaster and disease. But more frequently we observe that God does not intervene for many of our loved ones, our friends, and our neighbors who experience sickness, suffering, and death.

The problem with an omnipotent interventionist God (even a benevolent one) is that human experience reveals this kind of God to be arbitrary and unjust. Some people *do* experience miraculous cures from disease, but most others do not. Some are spared in traffic accidents, many others die. Some lives are uneventful, others are beset by tragedy. Our fundamental belief that God rewards good and punishes evil is challenged by the reality around us. The faithful do not get any special treatment in this world. Pain, loss, and death are common denominators for us all.

Logically, if God is truly omnipotent, then the world is exactly the way God wants it to be. And, following the logic of God's omnipotence, we must assume that human misery and injustice are part of God's cosmic plan. As human beings, we are simply incapable of understanding why this could be so. The omnipotent God may be great, but simple observation tells us that the interventionist God is surely not good or fair.

is God good?

If, as the interventionists claim, God is truly in charge and is directing all aspects of life on earth, we then have a theological problem. God's interaction leads to the theological question of *theodicy*, which tries to reconcile evil and suffering in the world with the concept of a God who is benevolent, just, and all-powerful. The term theodicy essentially means "the justice of God," derived from the Greek words *theos*, meaning God, and *dikē* (dee'-kay), meaning justice.

If God causes or allows pain and suffering to happen, one must begin to wonder why. This leads some people to believe that when bad things happen, God is either testing us or punishing us. Given that mindset, we look within ourselves for fault. We review our lives for some sin or transgression that has angered God. And most of us do not have to look very far.

Some Christians propose that unmerited suffering is necessary to our spiritual growth—that a testing of our belief in the goodness of God leads to a stronger faith in the end. Yet for many others, rather than strengthening their faith, inexplicable suffering leads to no faith at all.

The real faith crisis comes when bad things happen to good people, particularly innocent children. We then become very confused. Why would God do that? The glib answer we often receive is that "God acts in mysterious ways." Some people propose that there must be a good reason for this cruelty, but understanding it is well beyond our capabilities. They tell us that it is all part of a plan that will one day be revealed. In the midst of our misery and sorrow, Paul's letter to the Romans is sometimes quoted—"And we know that in all things God works for the good of those who love him."[8] Yet, when we stand at the grave of a loved one, it is hard to swallow that smarmy line. Our grief cannot accept any possible goodness or good outcome in the death of someone we love.

the affliction of Job

In his book *When Bad Things Happen to Good People*, Rabbi Harold Kushner (b. 1935) claims that our understanding of God has to change if we are to make any sense out of pain and suffering. Kushner examined the story of Job in the Hebrew Bible.

In the prologue to the biblical story—perhaps written in the sixth or fifth century BCE—Satan (a character whose name means "the adversary" and who is a part of Yahweh's heavenly court) obtains Yahweh's permission to test the unsuspecting Job, whom Yahweh regards as "a perfect and an upright man." Satan wants to know if Job will continue to trust in Yahweh's goodness if Job loses all those worldly things which he attributes to Yahweh's generosity—his health, wealth, family, and well-being. Yahweh agrees to a cosmic contest at Job's expense. Nearly everything that Job has—his

---

8. Romans 8:28

children, his flocks and herds, and his wealth—are taken from him, and he is physically afflicted with a painful disease. The main part of the book consists of lengthy speeches by Job and three friends who come to "comfort" him.

Kushner proposes that there are three fundamental concepts at work in this story. First, that God is all-powerful and causes, or allows, everything to happen in the world. Second, that God is fair and just—rewarding good or faithful people and punishing the wicked. Third, that Job (insert your name or any other person's name here) is a good or faithful person.

As long as Job is healthy and wealthy, we can believe all three of these statements at the same time with no difficulty. When Job experiences suffering—when his children are killed, his possessions are lost, and his health is destroyed—we then have a problem. We can no longer make sense of all three propositions together. We can now affirm any two only by denying the third.

If God is all-powerful and just, then Job must be a sinner and deserves what is happening to him. If, however, Job is good ("a perfect and an upright man" according to the text) and God causes him to suffer, then God is not being fair and just. If Job was not deserving of punishment and a just God did not cause this suffering to happen, then God is not all-powerful, or at least God withholds divine power in the face of human suffering.

The story conveniently uses the character of Satan to get God off the hook when it comes to the suffering experienced by Job. In the narrative, Yahweh does not directly cause Job's suffering; Satan does. The implication of the book of Job is that all human suffering is part of a cosmic game and each of us will at one time or another be tagged, "You're it!"

Job's so-called friends side with Yahweh's power and holiness, proposing that Job is a sinner and deserves what he got. Job, on the other hand, believes that Yahweh is unfair and unjust. Rabbi Kushner suggests that we should choose the third option. He proposes that we must give up the idea that God is all-powerful. We must admit that God is not in charge of life's events if we want to hang on to God's essential goodness.

In the play *J.B.* by Archibald MacLeish (1892–1982), which is based on this story, the character of Nickles, who takes on the role of Satan in a contemporary dramatization of the story of Job, sings this refrain:

> *If God is God, He is not good,*
> *If God is good, He is not God.*[9]

---

9. MacLeish, *J.B., A Play in Verse*, 11.

However, to propose that God is not all-powerful pits us against a deep and pervasive image of God. The idea of an omnipotent God is at the heart of Christianity today. A powerful God who can give us what we want is at the foundation of most people's intercessory prayer life. Popular Christianity repeatedly claims, "God answers prayer." When God does not deliver a positive response, we experience another crisis of faith. The proponents of the omnipotent God then give us the standard caveats: sometimes they say God's answer is "No," while at other times they tell us we need to realize that God works in a different time frame than humanity—"God's time." For me, neither answer is very satisfying. The concept of an all-powerful, interventionist, *and* loving God is incomprehensible based on my own life experience.

an incomprehensible God

Of course, many would say that God is necessarily incomprehensible. To be God, God *must* be inexplicable and unintelligible to humans. God *must* be an inexpressible mystery. Not just as the great mystery behind the creation of the universe, but the mystery behind human suffering as well. We are told that is what makes God, God. Incomprehensibility is God's defining characteristic according to many. In addition to the simple anthropomorphic images of Yahweh in Genesis, there are other fantastic accounts of God's strangeness found in biblical revelations.[10] God, who is seen as eternal, is deemed to be of an entirely different order from any finite human being.

Many biblical writers have declared that we can never truly know or understand God. Paul wrote to the people of the house churches in Rome, "How unsearchable are his judgments and how inscrutable his ways."[11] In saying this about God, Paul was recalling the words of the prophet Isaiah, "Have you not known? Have you not heard? Yahweh is the everlasting God, the Creator of the ends of the earth. He does not faint or grow weary; his understanding is unsearchable."[12] Isaiah expands on the difference between human and divine understanding this way, "For my thoughts are not your thoughts, nor are your ways my ways, declares Yahweh. For as the heavens are higher than the earth, so are my ways higher than your ways and my thoughts than your thoughts."[13]

---

10. See the heavenly visions in Isaiah 6:1–8, Ezekiel 1:26–28, Daniel 7:9–10, and Revelation 4:1–11.

11. Romans 11:33

12. Isaiah 40:28

13. Isaiah 55:8–9

In the story of Job, one of his friends counsels him not to question the ways of Yahweh (substituting the term *El*) because, "Surely El is great, and we do not know him; the number of his years is unsearchable."[14] And later the friend says, "El thunders wondrously with his voice; he does great things that we cannot comprehend."[15] Finally, he urges, "Hear this, O Job; stop and consider the wondrous works of El." At this point in the story, Yahweh steps into the dialog and personally addresses Job, speaking from a whirlwind. Yahweh challenges Job with this question, "Where were you when I laid the foundations of the earth?"[16] Then, for the next three chapters, Yahweh goes on to list his accomplishments in the creation of the natural world, especially in regards to wild creatures of which Yahweh seems particularly proud. The intent of the rambling lecture is to humble Job into abject submission to Yahweh's magnificence and effectively put an end to any further questions Job may have about Yahweh's ethical behavior and fairness in the world.

a God of freedom

Some theologians tell us that God is always active in the world but has a profound respect for human freedom. That explains why God does not act when we are in distress. If God were to always intervene for our good, this theology suggests, we would exist as part of a coercive universe with no freedom to act on our own, no personal choices to make. This is known as the doctrine of "free will." According to this philosophy, God gives humans the freedom to live as they choose. Proponents of free will see a God who is omnipotent but who chooses to limit divine power and lets us murder, dominate, and plunder one another as we please.

But, if free will accounts for all human acts of evil such as slavery, rape, war, and genocide, and if natural causes account for hurricanes and tsunamis, and if lifestyle choices, germs, carcinogens, and heredity account for most illness, and if there is at least *some* element of chance in the world, then when does an omnipotent God act at all? Is there any observable evidence for God acting in the world for good, or for that matter, acting in *any* way?

---

14. Job 36:26
15. Job 37:5
16. Job 38:4

a God of predetermined outcomes

In contrast to human free will, other Christians believe that everything has been decided in advance. This is the doctrine of "predestination." The reformer John Calvin (1509-1564) was a proponent of this concept. Human beings only have the illusion of free will. God not only knows exactly what we are going to do, God has pre-determined our behavior according a mysterious plan. In essence, the story has already been written, the end is already known, and we are unwitting actors in the drama following a script not of our own device. According to the doctrine of predestination, only a select few—the so-called elect—are destined for salvation. Other than these 144,000 (according to some interpretations of the Book of Revelation)[17] extremely lucky (and some would claim, deserving) people, God condemns everyone else to Hell. Proponents of this theology suggest that one can tell those who are part of the chosen elect by their material success. Calvinists believe that God blesses and rewards the virtuous and punishes the wicked in this life as well as the afterlife.

I have never observed any evidence to support this belief. In fact, we often witness the contrary—bad things happen to good people, and good things happen to bad people. The wicked often prosper while the righteous suffer. Are we to believe that the super-rich one percent of the population are the predestined elect of God? Can we accept a theology in which the wealthy have been chosen to experience God's favor while the suffering poor are ignored?

the death of the omnipotent God

In *A History of God*, Karen Armstrong (b. 1944), relates the impact of the Holocaust on the concept of an omnipotent interventionist God, especially among many contemporary Jews. Armstrong describes the horrors witnessed by Nobel Prize winner Elie Wiesel (1928-2016) at the Auschwitz and Buchenwald death camps:

> *One day the Gestapo hanged a child. Even the SS were disturbed by hanging a young boy in front of thousands of spectators. The child who, Wiesel recalled, had the face of a "sad-eyed angel," was silent, lividly pale and almost calm as he ascended the gallows. Behind Wiesel, one of the other prisoners asked: "Where is God? Where is He?" It took the child a half an hour to die, while the prisoners were forced to look him in the face. The same man asked*

---

17. Revelation 7:1-7

the god who intervenes

again: "Where is God now?" And Wiesel heard a voice within him make this answer: "Where is He? Here he is—He is hanging here on this gallows." [18]

Karen Armstrong comments:

> Dostoevsky had said that the death of a single child could make God unacceptable, but even he, no stranger to inhumanity, had not imagined the death of a child in such circumstances. The horror of Auschwitz is a stark challenge to many of the more conventional ideas of God... Many Jews can no longer subscribe to the biblical idea of a God who manifests himself in history, who, they say with Wiesel, died in Auschwitz. The idea of a personal God, like one of us writ large, is fraught with difficulty. If this God is omnipotent, he could have prevented the Holocaust. If he was unable to stop it, he is impotent and useless; if he could have stopped it and chose not to, he is a monster. Jews are not the only people who believe that the Holocaust put an end to conventional theology.[19]

For some people, if the idea of God is to continue to exist, a new image of God is necessary. The God of a majority of Americans—omnipotent, interventionist, and supernatural—no longer works for many other people who observe the real world of pain, suffering, and evil.

an absent and silent God

For many Christians, God is a daily reality in their lives, but for many others, God is simply not there. God cannot be found or experienced anywhere. They long to feel God's presence and God's love, but instead they experience emptiness and isolation. They worship God in church, but find that God is not present in the sanctuary. They pray fervently to God, but realize that their prayers often go unanswered. In the end, there is only silence. The biblical character of Job cried out to God in despair, "I cry to you God, but you do not answer. I stand before you, and you don't even bother to look."[20]

Barbara Brown Taylor (b. 1951) describes this emptiness in her book *Leaving Church: a Memoir of Faith*, in which she relates her experiences at a small Episcopal church in rural Georgia.

---

18. Armstrong, *A History of God*, 375. She briefly summarizes the story told by Wiesel in *Night*, 76–77.

19. Ibid, 375–376.

20. Job 30:20

> *On my worst nights I lay in bed feeling like a single parent, unable to sleep because I knew I did not have enough love in me to go around. God was the boundless lover, but for many people God was the parent who had left. They still read about him in the Bible and sang about him in hymns. They still believed in his reality, which made it even harder to accept his apparent lack of interest in them. They waited for messages from him that did not arrive. They prepared their hearts for meetings that never happened. They listened to other Christians speak as if God showed up every night for supper, leaving them to wonder what they had done wrong to make God go off and start another family.*[21]

Mother Teresa (1910–1997), who ministered to the needs of the poor, sick, orphaned, and dying in India for over 50 years, felt a similar absence and silence in her life. It began soon after she set up her Missionaries of Charity in Calcutta in the late 1940s and continued until her death in 1997. She interpreted it as a loss of faith.

> *If there be a God—please forgive me. When I try to raise my thoughts to heaven, there is such convicting emptiness that those very thoughts return like sharp knives and hurt my very soul. I am told God loves me—and yet the reality of darkness and coldness and emptiness is so great that nothing touches my soul.*[22]

Even Jesus on the cross experienced the absence of God.

> *And about three o'clock Jesus cried with a loud voice, "Eli, Eli, lema sabachthani (ay-lee', ay-lee', la'-ma, sa-bakh-tha'-nee)?" that is, "My God, my God, why have you forsaken me?"*[23]

Theologian Peter Rollins (b. 1973) comments on the crucifixion experience of Jesus in his book *Insurrection*:

> *On the Cross, Christ is rejected by his friends, betrayed by the religious authorities, and crucified by the political leaders. We witness here, in the starkest of terms, the loss of all those structures that ground us and give us the comfort that life makes sense. More than this, Christ experiences the loss of that which grounds each of these realms—God.*[24]

---

21. Taylor, *Leaving Church*, 74–75.

22. Kolodiejchuk, *Mother Teresa: Come Be My Light*, 187.

23. Matthew 27:46. Because the author of Matthew's gospel first quotes the Aramaic words before offering a Greek translation, this passage lends validity to the authenticity of these words as coming from the lips of Jesus.

24. Rollins, *Insurrection*, 23.

He continues:

> *Radical doubt, suffering, and the sense of divine forsakenness are central aspects of Christ's experience and thus a central part of what it means to participate in Christ's death.*[25]

So the sense of God's absence, the sense that God has abandoned and forsaken us, is not a unique experience of people who simply lack enough faith. For Rollins, it is the central experience and meaning of the cross in history. Jesus experienced not just abandonment by his friends, he ultimately felt abandoned by God as he suffered an agonizing death. There was no divine rescue. Instead, Jesus like the rest of us was allowed to suffer and die alone.

So, is God present with those who suffer, or has God abandoned us in our time of need? Was God truly hanging on a gallows with a child who slowly strangled at Auschwitz? Was God nailed to the cross with Jesus as he died from asphyxiation? Or were they, and countless other victims of evil, simply abandoned by an uncaring omnipotent God, and left to agonize alone? The key existential question asked by many Christians is "Where is God in our time of need?" Are we now on our own as we muddle through life? I keep thinking of the catch-phrase "Elvis has left the building." Is that often true of God when God's presence is most needed?

Perhaps a different understanding of God is needed—no longer a transcendent God of creation and supernatural intervention, but a God of weakness and suffering, dwelling in our midst.

---

25. Ibid, 29.

CHAPTER 6

the apocalyptic Christ

And on the way Jesus asked them, "Who do people say I am?"
And they answered him, "John the Baptist; and others, Elijah; and still others, one of the prophets."
Jesus asked them, "But who do you say I am?"
Peter answered and said, "You are the Logos, existing in the Father as His rationality and then, by an act of His will, being generated, in consideration of the various functions by which God is related to his creation, but only on the fact that Scripture speaks of a Father, and a Son, and a Holy Spirit, each member of the Trinity being co-equal with every other member, and each acting inseparably with and interpenetrating every other member, with only an economic subordination within God, but causing no division which would make the substance no longer simple."
And Jesus said, "What?"[1]

The study of the nature of Jesus is called *Christology* (*kris-tohl'-oh-jee*). There are two approaches to this study: "Christology from above" and "Christology from below." The former emphasizes the divine nature of Jesus that starts with the historic confessions and dogma shaped by the first seven ecumenical councils (between 325 and 787 CE), while the latter highlights the human nature of Jesus and traces the process by which the church eventually elevated him to the godhead over a period of centuries. Two recent book titles illustrate the difference. When New Testament scholar Bart Ehrman (b. 1955) published

---

1. A commonly-used joke for Trinity Sunday, source unknown. I have been unable to trace this particular trinitarian formula.

How Jesus Became God in early 2014, a group of five evangelical scholars quickly responded with *How God Became Jesus*. The first book is a Christology from below, while the second is Christology from above. Where you start makes all the difference as to where you end up.

In ancient Israel, the leaders of church and state—kings and high priests—were anointed with olive oil as a ceremonial sign of their new office. The oil was an outward and visible sign of a new status—a consecration for an important task. The practice was common throughout the Near East. Egyptian paintings show the pharaoh being anointed with oil. The biblical stories state that when both Saul and David were anointed, the spirit of Yahweh came upon them powerfully.[2] Of all the individuals who were anointed for their offices, the king was in a special sense *Yahweh's anointed one*.[3] In Hebrew, the word for anointed is *mashiach (mah-shee'-akh)*. The Greek translation is *christos (kris-tos')*. From these we get our English words *Messiah* and *Christ*.

Kings and high priests were anointed, but so were other key figures throughout the history of the Hebrew people. Prophets—those social critics who called upon the nation and its leaders to change their political and economic direction—were also sometimes anointed and would therefore be considered messiahs. The messianic role in Israel could thus be that of prophet, priest, or king. If Jesus is to be considered the messiah in any sense, it would have to be as a prophet. He was never chosen and appointed as a priest of the temple or as a head of state, nor did he seek these grandiose roles. Instead, he was a critic of both institutions—a force for social and religious transformation and change. Still, we have no biblical record that Jesus was ever anointed with oil for his prophetic task nor did he seek the title of messiah.[4] But that did not stop his followers from thrusting that title on him.

Early on, some followers of Jesus began to believe that he was the Jewish messiah—a long-awaited military conqueror and king who would bring their nation to victory and glory after centuries of subjugation. Perhaps that

---

2. 1 Samuel 10:9–11, 1 Samuel 16:13. This image is repeated when Jesus is baptized at the Jordan by John the Baptizer.

3. Psalm 20:6. "Yahweh will help [save, deliver, rescue, give victory to] his anointed."

4. All four gospels present an anointing story in which Jesus was a guest for a meal when a woman entered the room and anointed him with an expensive perfume. In two accounts, he is anointed on his head and in two accounts on his feet. The details, including the location and the identity of the woman vary from account to account. See Mark 14:3–9, Matthew 26:6–13, Luke 7:36–50, and John 12:1–8. In Mark's and Matthew's accounts, the anointing on his head is to prepare Jesus for his burial, not for his messianic task.

idea took shape even before his death. Certainly that is the image that presents itself in the gospel of Mark, written about four decades after the crucifixion. According to Mark, as Jesus walked toward the newly-constructed Hellenistic city of Caesarea Philippi that lies north of the Sea of Galilee, he asked his disciples, "Who do people say that I am?" Some of the disciples replied, "John the Baptist." Others said "Elijah" or "One of the prophets"—all references to contemporary and ancient prophets, not regal or military figures. Jesus persisted: "But who do you say that I am?" Only Simon Peter answered him: "You are the messiah." In both Mark's and Luke's gospels, Jesus declines to confirm or deny Peter's declaration.[5] He simply orders his disciples not to discuss the conversation with anyone.[6] Matthew, however, expands the episode—first having Jesus praise Peter and then claim that this confession would become the basis of his future church. Jesus sternly orders the disciples to tell no one of this discussion. Why keep this idea a secret? Because it was a dangerously seditious claim. The messiah was not a spiritual or religious figure, but a decidedly political one, and thus a threat to the powers that be.

It was only at the synagogue in Nazareth as portrayed in Luke's gospel that Jesus alluded to himself as a messiah, and then did so specifically by quoting the language that the prophet Isaiah had used to refer to himself—as a messianic prophet, not a messianic king. Other than that one instance reported in a single gospel, Jesus never spoke of himself as the messiah. But as indicated in all the synoptic gospels, Peter believed Jesus fulfilled the traditional messianic role of a conquering king. In the end, Jesus was executed because powerful figures in Jewish society were frightened that a messianic figure—whether self-proclaimed or acclaimed by others—could lead to civil strife if he incited a popular messianic movement aimed at violent rebellion and revolution. For the Apostle Paul, Jesus was also seen as the messiah. His writings predated the gospels and greatly influenced their theology. Writing in Greek, Paul called Jesus by the Greek equivalent of *mashiach*—*ho christos* (*ho kris-tos'*) or "the Christ"—sometimes using his name and title so tightly linked ("Jesus Christ" and "Christ Jesus") that the Christ was no longer simply a title or role, but part of Jesus' resurrected identity.

---

5. Interestingly, the majority opinion was that Jesus was a prophet, not the messiah. Not just any prophet, but a great miraculous prophet from Israel's past—Elijah—or a renowned contemporary—John the Baptizer.

6. Mark 8:27–33. See parallels in Luke 9:18–22 and Matthew 16:13–23. This story is not found in John's gospel. In Matthew's version, Jesus commends Peter and declares that he will build his church on Peter's confession. This is one of only two references "the church" in the gospels. It is surely a later addition.

The word *mashiach* or *messiah* appears only 39 times in the Hebrew Bible and in most cases it refers to the current ruler of Judah or Israel, although there are a few other variations. In Leviticus, the term is applied to the high priest.[7] In Psalm 105, the entire Hebrew people are called "God's anointed."[8] And when the Persian king Cyrus the Great (c.600–530 BCE) released the Hebrew people from captivity in Babylon soon after 538 BCE, the prophet Isaiah called him a messiah, in the sense that he was acting as God's agent to liberate the people from captivity and oppression.[9]

But it was King David (c. 1040–970 BCE) who became the Hebrew prototype for all potential messiahs. He held a special place in the hearts and minds of the people of Israel. In the biblical narrative, David—an acclaimed warrior—defeated the Philistines, and was crowned king over the united kingdom of Judah and Israel, establishing Jerusalem as his capital. He ruled the nation for four decades as their first great king, and before his death, he laid out the plans for the first temple in Jerusalem, built by his son Solomon. Yahweh promised David that his offspring would rule the nation forever.

As a result, David became the messianic model for later generations. As his royal line stretched out over the next four centuries, with varying results, the term *messiah* began to refer not just to the present anointed king, but to an ideal king. When the Davidic line ended during the Babylonian captivity (607–537 BCE), messiah became a code word for a new king from the "root of Jesse," a reference to David's father. For the next six centuries, the messiah was seen as a future political and military leader who would reclaim the throne of David, save the people from foreign oppressors, and restore the nation to its former glory.

a failed messiah

When the title *messiah* or *christ* was applied to Jesus by his Jewish and Hellenistic followers, some confusion is sure to ensue if one examines the historical job description of the ideal king and conquering hero. Although he met the definition of a messianic *prophet*—challenging the injustice of his society and speaking truth to power—his prophetic ministry began not with anointment, but with a baptism in the Jordan River. In any event, Jesus repeatedly rejected the roles of both priest and king, even though the gospel writers tried to suggest the kingly role for Jesus at his trial and execution and

7. Leviticus 4:3
8. Psalm 105:12–15
9. Isaiah 45:1

the writer of the New Testament letter known as Hebrews later cast Jesus in the role of great high priest.[10]

John's gospel has the disciple Nathanael declare to Jesus, "Rabbi, you are the Son of God! You are the King of Israel!"[11] This passage links the title "son of God" with the role of the messiah as the "king of Israel," indicating that both are political terms. But Jesus never became the king of Israel or of Judea or of anywhere, even though he was executed with the derisive sign "King of the Jews" above his head. On one occasion, he reportedly fled from a crowd because he believed they were about to force him into that role. This happened after the story of feeding five thousand people in the wilderness:

> *When the people saw the sign that he had done, they began to say, "This is indeed the prophet who is to come into the world." When Jesus realized that they were about to come and take him by force to make him king, he withdrew again to the mountain by himself.*[12]

The people see a prophet and want to elevate him to the role of king as a challenge to Rome. Any charismatic person could conceivably fill the bill as long as people would willingly follow him to battle. Rather than overthrowing the present kingdom and establishing a new one, Jesus announced that God's kingdom was already present—spread out upon the land—yet hidden. And Jesus saw God as the ruler, never himself. Like David and Judas Maccabeus, Jesus was a peasant, but unlike them, he did not become a military leader. He modeled servanthood, not domination, and he taught the way of peace and forgiveness. But most importantly, he was executed by Roman authorities. This could not be the fate of someone who was expected to overthrow the enemies and oppressors of the Jewish people and establish a great kingdom with authority over other nations. Rome and their Judean collaborators squashed Jesus like a bug, He clearly failed the test of the long-awaited victorious messiah.

And yet, some of Jesus' followers declared him to be the anointed one. That could only be true if the term messiah was completely redefined in prophetic terms, or if his royal messianic role was somehow to be played out supernaturally after his death.

---

10. Hebrews 4:14
11. John 1:49
12. John 6:14–15

a second-chance messiah

As the early church tried to put the life and death of Jesus into the context of Jewish history, the role of messiah somehow needed to be redefined if Jesus was to fill the role. Certainly, prophets had been anointed in the past, and although that technically made them messiahs, the role of *the* messiah was still expected to be a military leader and king, not a social critic. The people were looking for a liberator. They weren't looking for someone to free them from iniquity or sin; they wanted freedom from Rome. Moreover, the peasants were looking for freedom from debt and the oppressive economics of the wealthy aristocracy. The pre-resurrection Jesus did not fulfill these expectations of the messiah, but a post-resurrection Jesus had the opportunity to fulfill the hopes and dreams of the people in a spectacular fashion. As Paul and other New Testament writers looked back at Jesus, they were convinced that his resurrection gave him a second chance. He didn't fit the role of messiah in his lifetime, so the role was projected into gloriously imagined future events. And for Paul, it was an impending future. The transition from the human Jesus to the cosmic Christ was dependent on this shift in perspective.

Imperial power and glory are very seductive forces—certainly more impressive than the apparent weakness (at least in many culturally-bound male eyes) of compassion, forgiveness, and nonviolence. I imagine there were some in the early Jesus movement, and many today, who could not comprehend God's presence in any form of perceived human weakness. The life of Jesus ended in a humiliating defeat on a rebel's cross, and though Paul saw the resurrection as a vindication by God, for many Hellenistic Christians in a world dominated by Roman reverence for Augustus Caesar, this was apparently not enough.

These followers believed that Jesus had ascended to heaven and hoped that he would soon return to earth to get the job done properly. Therefore Jesus was confessed as the messiah, not on evidence from his past life, but on belief in a future role. What these followers anticipated and what they fervently desired was the quick return of Jesus in power, majesty, and glory administering the violence of God upon all evildoers and oppressors of the Jewish people.

The developing mythology of the victorious Christ soon became a militaristic image of Jesus descending from the clouds in splendor and might to defeat the powers of the present age and to put all nations under his control.

The myth proclaimed that Christ's kingdom would become the greatest empire in history and would last for a thousand years. A messianic age of peace would be ushered in, but it would be a peace achieved by cosmic violence. The humble and nonviolent kingdom of God is replaced with the image of a glorious kingdom ruled by the conquering Christ.

This mythology became a central motif in Christianity over the centuries. But the whole concept of the second coming of Christ makes a mockery of everything Jesus stood for. It attempts to remake the image of Jesus the peasant prophet into the image of Augustus Caesar, the glorious imperial ruler.

the son of God

The Apostle Paul believed that Jesus was appointed to the role of the *son of God* after his resurrection from the dead.[13] For Paul, this newly elevated status reflected a vindication by God of Jesus' humiliating death and seeming defeat on the cross. Paul did not intend this metaphor as a literal claim about the biological parenthood of Jesus. Paul certainly never believed that Jesus had the genetic matter of Yahweh in his being, or as was stated in a creed over three centuries later that Jesus was "one substance with the Father." It would have been absurd and abhorrent to a first-century Jew to believe that a finite human could also be the infinite God of the cosmos, or conversely that a transcendent God dwelling apart from creation would take on an earthly human form—although this was commonly accepted in Greek and Roman religions, and eventually, centuries later, in Christianity as well. Instead, Paul's metaphor was a statement about the intimate relationship that Jesus had with God.

Two different Greek words are translated as *son* in English. The first, *teknon* (*tek'-non*), refers to a child of either sex by physical descent—a biological son or daughter. The second, *huios* (*hwee-os'*), is a legal descriptor for an heir, often by adoption. When the New Testament writers speak of Jesus as the son of God, they employ the Greek phrase *huios theou* (*hwee-os' theh'-oo*)—*theou* meaning God. Thus, Jesus is the *adopted* son of God. Similarly, Paul uses the plural version—*huioi theou* (*hwee-oh'-ee theh'-oo*)—for the followers of Jesus who are called the adopted *sons of God* (or *children of God*, if you prefer). Singular or plural, it has the same meaning about the relationship to God. Divine paternity is purely a metaphoric relationship, not

---

13. Romans 1:4

biological. Paul stated that anyone who is led by the compassionate spirit of God becomes God's adopted child.[14]

In most ancient temple-states—like those of Sumer, Akkadia, Egypt, Babylonia, Assyria, and Israel—the ruler was considered an earthly representative of the national god, often regarded as the appointed or adopted son of the god. In some cases, the ruler was seen as a living manifestation of the god, but this was not the case in Israel. Throughout the ancient world, the expression *son of God* was not a term of divinity—it was a label for a political leader. In ancient Hebrew culture, the term *son of God*, referred primarily to the anointed king of Israel.[15] For instance, Psalm 2 was written for the coronation of a king at Mount Zion, the prominent hill located at the center of ancient Jerusalem. This was a song written for an adoption ceremony. In this poem, the psalmist has Yahweh declare:

> *I have anointed my king on Zion, my holy mountain. I will proclaim the decree of Yahweh: You are my son; today I have become your father. Ask of me, and I will make the nations your inheritance, the ends of the earth your possession. You will rule them with an iron scepter; you will dash them to pieces like pottery.*[16]

The son of God in this poem is envisioned as a mighty warrior who is destined to become an iron-fisted ruler of the surrounding nations. In a temple-state, consummate military and political power was seen as a necessary prerequisite for divine sonship.

The image of Jesus as a warrior king is forcefully portrayed in the last book of the New Testament, the apocalyptic book of Revelation, which was written somewhere around 90 CE. Within sixty years after his death, Jesus had been transformed into an agent of God's vengeance. The author of Revelation pictures Jesus—metaphorically referred to as the Word of God, and dripping in blood—leading the armies of heaven in a consummate bloodbath on the earth. Obviously, the language is symbolic, but the essence of retribution is clear.

---

14. Romans 8:14

15. Although this was the primary understanding of the phrase, the term was not used exclusively to refer to the king. Elsewhere in the Hebrew Bible, the term "sons of God" refers to angels or members of the heavenly court (Genesis 6:1–4), and the phrase "son of God" was used to describe all the entire people of Israel (Exodus 4:22–23). It was also used to describe an individual who practices justice toward the poor (Wisdom of Solomon 2:18, which is not included in the Protestant Bible).

16. Psalm 2:6–8. This psalm has often been associated with King David (c. 1040–970 BCE), but may also date from a later period in Israel's history after the Babylonian exile (607–537 BCE). In any event, the association of the term "son of God" with the anointed king of Israel is an early and well-known Hebrew tradition.

> From his mouth comes a sharp sword with which to strike down the nations, and he will rule them with a rod of iron; he will tread the wine press of the fury of the wrath of God the Almighty. On his robe and on his thigh he has a name inscribed, "King of kings and Lord of lords."
>
> Then I saw an angel standing in the sun, and with a loud voice he called to all the birds that fly in mid-heaven, "Come, gather for the great supper of God, to eat the flesh of kings, the flesh of captains, the flesh of the mighty, the flesh of horses and their riders—flesh of all, both free and slave, both small and great" ... and all the birds were gorged with their flesh.[17]

This is one of the most disturbing images in the bloody battle in Revelation—the call for birds to "gather for the great supper of God" where the flesh of kings, military leaders, and the mighty will be consumed along with their followers—the great and the small. Carrion will feast on the flesh of God's enemies! If that's not an image of unbridled revenge, I don't know what is. The great supper of God! What a dramatic and horrifying contrast to the celebratory wedding banquet images found in the parables of Jesus.

Because, the term *son of God* was generally used to refer to a king or an emperor, it carried a powerful political significance. In Paul's hands, calling Jesus the son of God was a clear political critique of the Roman Empire and of its current leader, whether it was Augustus, Tiberius, Caligula, Claudius, or Nero, all of whom ruled during Paul's lifetime.

In 42 BCE, two years after the death of Julius Caesar (100–44 BCE), the Roman Senate declared the assassinated Roman dictator to be *Divus Ilulius* (dee'-voos ee-loo'-li-oos) or the "deified Julius," elevating him to the status of a god. Later, his adopted son Octavian (63 BCE–14 CE) was deemed by the Senate to be *Divi Filius* (dee'-vee fee'-li-oos), or "son of the divine one." When Octavian became the first Roman emperor, known by the title Augustus Caesar, he ushered in an era of peace and stability—the *Pax Romana* or Roman Peace—which allowed the devastated lands and economy of Rome to flourish once again. As a military leader, Octavian had ended a disastrous civil war by defeating his political rivals through a decisive military victory. In response, the Senate of Rome awarded him the title *Augustus* (ow-goos'-toos) a religious description meaning "the illustrious one" or "the revered one." Due to his immense military and political power, and in recognition of the benefits that he had restored to the social fabric, Augustus soon became the central character in a new Roman imperial religion. He was worshipped and revered throughout the Roman Empire as the "son of god," the "king

---

17. Revelation 19:11–21

the apocalyptic christ 111

of kings," the "lord of lords," the "prince of peace," and the "savior of all humanity." As we know, these terms were later applied to Jesus, beginning with the writings of the Apostle Paul and amplified in the book of Revelation.[18]

When Paul called Jesus the *son of God*, he was making a decidedly anti-imperial statement that contrasted the servanthood and nonviolence of this peasant prophet to the militaristic power and iron-fisted rule of the emperor of Rome.[19] In contrast to the Pax Romana, Jesus offered humanity a different kind of peace—one found in a lifestyle of love, generosity, and forgiveness. It was a peace achieved through nonviolence and compassion, not through warfare and domination. It was a peace which could be found in a close-knit and inclusive community that demonstrated a special concern for the weakest and most vulnerable members in their midst. Jesus called his followers to a different kind of life, a qualitatively richer and deeper life, a more profoundly authentic human existence. In Paul's mind, if anyone was to be called the son of God, it should be Jesus, because Jesus reflected and revealed the true character of a compassionate God, while the emperor of Rome did not.

Paul expressed his belief that Jesus became the adopted son of God at his resurrection in writings from the mid-50s CE. If we follow the development of this idea through the subsequent writings in the New Testament, we see the divine sonship of Jesus moving back earlier and earlier in his life as the metaphor took root and grew. Fifteen to twenty years later, Mark's gospel (written c. 70) moves Jesus' adoption as a son of God back to his baptism in the Jordan River.

> *In those days Jesus came from Nazareth of Galilee and was baptized by John in the Jordan. And just as he was coming up out of the water, he saw the heavens torn apart and the spirit descending like a dove on him. And a voice came from heaven, 'You are my son, the beloved; with you I am well pleased.'*[20]

---

18. Revelation 17:14: "the Lamb will conquer them, for he is Lord of lords and King of kings." The title "prince of peace" comes from Isaiah 9:6: "For a child has been born for us, a son given to us; authority rests upon his shoulders; and he is named Wonderful Counsellor, Mighty God, Everlasting Father, Prince of Peace." First Timothy 4:10 parallels the "savior of humanity" assertion: "For to this end we toil and struggle, because we have our hope set on the living God, who is the Savior of all people, especially of those who believe."

19. Paul's letter to the Romans 1:1–5 reports that Jesus is "declared to be Son of God with power according to the spirit of holiness by resurrection from the dead." Additional Pauline references to Jesus as the "son of God" are found elsewhere in Romans, 2 Corinthians, Galatians, Ephesians, and Colossians.

20. Mark 1:9–11

Another fifteen years later, Matthew and Luke (c. 85) place it at his birth, and in fifteen more years, the gospel of John (c. 100) elevates Jesus to a divine role in the creation of the universe.[21]

> In the beginning was the logos, and the logos was with Theos, and the logos was Theos.[22]

This represents a remarkable transformation of the status of Jesus as the son of God in less than five decades.

born of a virgin

The general reader of the New Testament assumes that the four gospel portraits of Jesus are historically accurate accounts of Jesus' life and ministry. Most Christians have been taught that the scriptures are divinely inspired and thus unquestionably accurate. Therefore, if there are differences between the gospels, they cannot possibly be significant, and the four accounts can be easily blended or harmonized with one another. For instance, the two different birth stories in the gospels of Matthew and Luke have been blended for so long that the average Christian is not aware that they are entirely different and inconsistent accounts. Nor is the average Christian aware that the gospel of Mark—the earliest written gospel—not only says nothing about Jesus' birth, but it also says nothing about Jesus' bodily resurrection and ascension into the sky.[23] It merely ends with an empty tomb.

A close reading of the gospels creates a problem for the reader. They simply do not agree. The virgin birth of Jesus is a good example of the unreliability of the Biblical texts.

Jesus died around 30 CE. As we said earlier, the earliest writings of the New Testament are the letters of Paul written in the 50s, about 20 years after the crucifixion. Paul's writings predate the earliest gospel—that of Mark—by about 20 years. Paul says nothing about Jesus having a miraculous conception and birth. He only says that Jesus was born of a woman.[24]

Mark's gospel, written about 70 CE, likewise has nothing to say about the birth or early life of Jesus. These two facts together indicate that for the

---

21. Matthew 1:18-23, Luke 1:26-35, John 1:1-5

22. John 1:1. Logos can be understood as the "word" or the "creative intelligence" of God.

23. Any reputable translation of Mark's gospel will note that the last twelve verses of the final chapter (Mark 16:9-20) are not part of the earliest copies of this gospel, and are therefore a later addition.

24. Galatians 4:4

first half century after the death of Jesus, the birth of Jesus was a non-issue. There was certainly nothing miraculous to crow about. In addition, two additional early sayings gospels—Q and Thomas—also are silent about a supernatural birth.

Then, around 80 or 85, the gospels of Matthew and Luke were written. They both knew one key fact—that Jesus was from Nazareth. But both writers also wanted to convince their readers that Jesus was the messiah, and that meant integrating two so-called "prophecies" into the story, one about a birth in Bethlehem and the other about being born of a virgin.

By the first century, Jewish scholars had compiled various lists of verses from their scriptures that they believed referred to a coming messiah. Many of these texts were seen as prophecies or future predictions. However, most were simply intended for the time and place in which they were written, and had no long-term future implications. One of these so-called prophecies was that the messiah would be born of a virgin—a young woman who had conceived a child miraculously without sexual intercourse.

This is an important doctrine for many Christians because they believe that the virgin birth is a sign of Jesus' divinity. However, modern readers need to understand that in first century Judaism the virgin birth of the messiah, while unprecedented in Jewish thought, would never have been a sign of his divinity (an idea that would have been abhorrent to the Jews), it was simply a sign in ancient cultures of a remarkable person who was destined for an extraordinary human role.

This so-called prophecy, however, was the result of a simple mistranslation of a verse in the book of Isaiah. When the Hebrew Bible was first translated from Hebrew to Greek several centuries before the birth of Jesus, the translators used the Greek word *parthenos* (*par-then'-os*), which means "virgin," instead of the correct term *kore* (*kor-eh'*) to translate the original Hebrew word *almah* (*al-maw'*), which means "a maiden" or "a young woman of marriageable age." There is a specific Hebrew word for virgin: *bethulah* (*beth-you-lah'*). Isaiah did not use it—nor did he mean or imply it.

The mistranslation of this text from Isaiah led directly to the church doctrine about the virginity of Mary. This in turn led to even more farfetched ideas about Mary in the Roman Catholic Church—for instance, that Mary herself was herself immaculately conceived so that she was born without original sin, and that her other children were really Jesus' adopted cousins—allowing Mary to remain a sinless virgin until her death and bodily "assumption" into heaven.[25]

---

25. From the Latin word *assumptio* (*ah-sump'-tee-oh*), meaning "a taking."

If one carefully reads the Isaiah text in its original context, one wonders how it ever became a prophecy about a future messiah. About seven centuries before the birth of Jesus, the prophet Isaiah (active c. 740–701 BCE) had advised King Ahaz of Judah (c. 755–715 BCE) that he was playing with fire by allying himself with the powerful King Tiglath-Pileser III of Assyria (d. 727 BCE) and turning his back on the neighboring nations of Israel and Aram (modern Syria) that were under assault by the Assyrians. Isaiah pointed to a young pregnant woman in the court of King Ahaz, and predicted that her child would be a son named *Immanuel* (*im-maw-noo-ale'*), meaning "God [is] with us." He also predicted that before the child reached the age of three (eating solid foods and knowing the difference between good and evil), the armies of Assyria would bring untold destruction to the region.

Isaiah said to the king and his court:

> *Hear then, O house of David! Is it too little for you to weary mortals, that you weary my God also? Therefore Yahweh himself will give you a sign. Look, the young woman is with child and shall bear a son, and shall name him Immanuel. He shall eat curds and honey by the time he knows how to refuse the evil and choose the good. For before the child knows how to refuse the evil and choose the good, the land before whose two kings you are in dread will be deserted. Yahweh will bring on you and on your people and on your ancestral house such days as have not come since the day that Ephraim departed from Judah—the king of Assyria.*[26]

This was clearly a short-term prophecy about a geo-political situation facing the kingdoms of Judah, Israel, and Aram. It required no prophetic foreknowledge into the future, just a savvy take on the current international situation. Centuries later, however, two sentences in this text were taken completely out of context and treated as a prophecy about a future Jewish messiah.

> *Therefore Yahweh himself will give you a sign. Look, the young woman is with child and shall bear a son, and shall name him Immanuel.*[27]

In the Greek mistranslation of the Hebrew text, a *young woman* became a *virgin* and for those who looked for a future messiah, a miraculous virgin birth was now a requirement. Here is how the words of Isaiah were used in Matthew's gospel:

---

26. Isaiah 7:13–17
27. Isaiah 7:14

> Now the birth of Jesus the Messiah took place in this way. When his mother Mary had been engaged to Joseph, but before they lived together, she was found to be with child from the Holy Spirit. Her husband Joseph, being a righteous man and unwilling to expose her to public disgrace, planned to dismiss her quietly. But just when he had resolved to do this, an angel of the Lord appeared to him in a dream and said, "Joseph, son of David, do not be afraid to take Mary as your wife, for the child conceived in her is from the Holy Spirit. She will bear a son, and you are to name him Jesus, for he will save his people from their sins." All this took place to fulfill what had been spoken by the Lord through the prophet: "Look, the virgin shall conceive and bear a son, and they shall name him Emmanuel," which means, "God is with us." When Joseph awoke from sleep, he did as the angel of the Lord commanded him; he took her as his wife, but had no marital relations with her until she had borne a son; and he named him Jesus.[28]

Note that the angel tells Joseph to name the child Jesus, not Emmanuel as the "prophecy" foretells. That provides a nice way to tie the prophecy to Jesus without requiring a name change. The story also implies that after the birth of Jesus, Joseph *did* have marital (sexual) relations with Mary.

In addition to Matthew's gospel, Luke's gospel also recounts the birth of Jesus and his miraculous conception, but he does not quote Isaiah. Luke too incorporates a dream—this time to Mary.

> In the sixth month the angel Gabriel was sent by God to a town in Galilee called Nazareth, to a virgin engaged to a man whose name was Joseph, of the house of David. The virgin's name was Mary. And he came to her and said, "Greetings, favored one! The Lord is with you." But she was much perplexed by his words and pondered what sort of greeting this might be. The angel said to her, "Do not be afraid, Mary, for you have found favor with God. And now, you will conceive in your womb and bear a son, and you will name him Jesus. He will be great, and will be called the Son of the Most High, and the Lord God will give to him the throne of his ancestor David. He will reign over the house of Jacob forever, and of his kingdom there will be no end." Mary said to the angel, "How can this be, since I am a virgin?" The angel said to her, "The Holy Spirit will come upon you, and the power of the Most High will overshadow you; therefore the child to be born will be holy; he will be called Son of God."[29]

28. Matthew 1:18–25
29. Luke 1:26–35

Matthew and Luke created two very different narratives to describe the circumstances around the birth of Jesus. They both knew that the messiah was expected to be born in the city of King David's birth—Bethlehem—based on another "prophecy" from the book of Micah.[30] Because Jesus was widely known to be from Nazareth, each author found it necessary to craft a different tale to integrate Jesus' birth in Bethlehem. In Luke's gospel, Mary and Joseph live in Nazareth and travel to Bethlehem for an imperial census. In Matthew's gospel, Mary and Joseph live in Bethlehem (no census and no travel is mentioned). They later escape to Egypt after the birth (to fulfill another "prophecy"), and then out of fear, they eventually move to the town of Nazareth. These two gospel stories are widely different, and yet every Christmas they are mashed together in a seamless whole so that few know that the narratives do not agree on their so-called "facts."

About fifteen years after the gospels of Matthew and Luke, the gospel of John was written. There is absolutely nothing in John's gospel about a virginal conception. So prior to the gospels of Matthew and Luke, the record is silent about a miraculous birth, and after Matthew and Luke were written, John's gospel says nothing about a unique pregnancy. What does all this have to say about the literal factuality and internal consistency of the New Testament? In the opinion of many biblical scholars, it calls it all into question.

In ancient times, it was often claimed that important religious figures had miraculous births. Horus, an Egyptian god, was believed to have been born of the virgin Isis. Images of Isis holding the infant Horus on her lap have been said to influence later paintings of the Madonna and child. Krishna, a central figure of Hindu belief, was claimed to have been born without a sexual union by "mental transmission" from the mind of the divine Vasudeva into the womb of the virgin Devaki. The Babylonians believed that their god Adonis was born of the virgin Ishtar, commonly called the *Queen of heaven*. The Persian Zoroastrians believed that the prophet and philosopher Zarathustra (or Zoroaster) was conceived when the god Ahura Mazda, the creator of the universe, descended from heaven to visit the virgin Dughdova. Prince Siddhārtha Gautama, who became the Buddha, was reportedly divinely conceived in a dream in which his mother Māyā was touched on her side by Samantabhadra, an enlightened being, who was mounted on a white elephant.

In Greek mythology, many fabled heroes were reputably born of a mortal woman and a god. Perseus, the legendary founder of Mycenae and of the Perseid dynasty, was said to be the son of the god Zeus and the mortal

---

30. Micah 5:2

Danaë. Minos, a mythological king of Crete, was a son of Zeus and Europa, a noble Phoenician woman. Asclepius, the Greek god of medicine and healing, was believed to be the son of the god Apollo and Coronis, the daughter of a king.

Great historic figures were also considered divinely conceived. Plato (c. 424–347 BCE) was said to have been born by the union of the god Apollo with his mother Perictione. Likewise, Alexander the Great (356–323 BCE) was said to have been conceived when a thunderbolt fell from heaven and made his mother Olympias pregnant before her marriage to Philip of Macedon. And most importantly for the early church, the Roman Emperor Augustus (63 BCE–14 CE) was reportedly conceived when his mother Atia was worshipping in the temple of Apollo. She fell asleep and was impregnated by the god in the form of a snake.

All of these myths of divine conception—a well-established ancient tradition—preceded the birth of Jesus and clearly influenced the first-century audience of pagans who were attracted to the emerging Jesus movement. Today, when confronted by these pagan stories of divine conception, many Christians will of course assume that they are simply fanciful myths, having no basis in reality. But as for the virginal conception of Jesus, the fourth-century creeds of the church and 1,600 years of Christian dogma insist that this story is unquestionably true.

There is one more point on the topic of the virginal conception of Jesus that is sometimes raised: if Mary knew that Jesus had been conceived miraculously and was somehow divine, why did she and Jesus' brothers think he had gone completely out of his mind when he began to heal people and gather a band of disciples at the outset of his ministry? According to Mark's gospel, Jesus' family, including his mother, wanted to take him back home and restrain him.[31] So much for a divinely-conceived Jesus.

the son of man

Jesus did not speak of himself as either the messiah (the Christ) or the son of God—which we have seen are both references to a military conqueror and ruler. These were titles attributed to him by others. According to the gospels, the only self-referential title he used was the *son of man*. No one else calls Jesus by this term. It was an image he apparently claimed for himself, but which the church has generally dropped in favor of son of God. However, where the phrase *son of man* is used in the gospel accounts, modern English translators often capitalize it as *Son of Man* to ensure that we will

31. Mark 3:21

understand the use of the term in a very specific context—as a reference to a supernatural figure found in the book of Daniel and as a divine title. In Daniel's dream, this figure comes before God on the clouds of heaven and is given dominion over a never-ending empire on earth. Daniel's Son of Man fits nicely with the exalted image of Jesus in that other apocalyptic New Testament book—Revelation. But the phrase *son of man* has other less-exalted connotations in the Hebrew Bible.

For a better understanding of the term, it is helpful to look at Walter Wink's groundbreaking book, *The Human Being: Jesus and the Enigma of the Son of the Man*. Wink explains that in much of the Hebrew Bible the term *son of man* or *ben 'adam* (*bane aw-dawm'*) was used to describe a specific human being or humanity in general. The Hebrew word *adam* (*aw-dawm'*) can be translated as either the generic term "man" or the specific name "Adam" depending on the context. The phrase *son of man* simply means a human being. Many scholars insist that when Jesus used the term, he meant that he was just one of the boys, a regular fellow, a typical human. Of course, the phrase comes across as very male-oriented, and it is. Wink suggests that if we prefer, we can translate it more broadly as "child of the human," "humanity's child," or "the human one." When rendering *ben 'adam* in English, translators sometimes use "human being," "mere man," or "O mortal" as substitutions when referring to people other than Jesus. We see this usage in translations of the book of Ezekiel in the Hebrew Bible, where Yahweh employs the term to refer to Ezekiel, to whom Yahweh had appeared in a bizarre vision. There are 107 occurrences of *ben 'adam* in the Hebrew Bible, 93 of which are found in the book of Ezekiel. And they all mean "human being."

The apocalyptic book of Daniel was written four hundred years later than Ezekiel, sometime around 167 BCE in Judea. Their latest foreign ruler, Antiochus Epiphanes IV (*an-tee'-uk-us ep-if-an-ace'*) of the Seleucid (*sih'-loo-sid*) Empire, had outlawed Hebrew religious rites and traditions and ordered the worship of Zeus as the supreme god in the Jewish temple. The Jewish people were being forced at the point of a sword to convert to paganism. It was a time of severe social and religious crisis that led to widespread martyrdom and the Maccabean revolt.

The author of the book of Daniel recounted a series of dreams in which he sees "one like a son of man" coming on clouds of heaven before the throne of God—"the Ancient One"—to receive universal and everlasting dominion on earth.

> *As I watched in the night visions,*
> *I saw one like a son of man*

coming with the clouds of heaven.
And he came to the Ancient One
and was presented before him.
To him was given dominion
and glory and kingship,
that all peoples, nations, and languages
should serve him.
His dominion is an everlasting dominion
that shall not pass away,
and his kingship is one
that shall never be destroyed.[32]

Although some biblical scholars and theologians suggest this points to the second coming of Jesus, the verses that follow explain that the *son of man* in Daniel is not a supernatural or divine individual, but rather a metaphor for the entire people of Israel.

The kingship and dominion
and the greatness of the kingdoms under the whole heaven
shall be given to the people of the holy ones of the Most High;
their kingdom shall be an everlasting kingdom,
and all dominions shall serve and obey them.[33]

the *son of man* in the gospels

There are 81 *son of man* sayings in the four gospels, although many of these are parallel repetitions. Walter Wink contends—as Marcus Borg has suggested—that some sayings of Jesus in the gospels are pre-Easter and others are post-Easter, meaning that some derive from the historic Jesus and others derive from the later apocalyptic Hellenistic church. Jesus spoke in Aramaic. He would have used the Aramaic phrase *bar enash* (*bar en-awsh'*) to refer to himself as a son of man. The Greek New Testament texts use the phrase *ho huios tou anthropou* (*ho hwee-os' too anth'-roh-poh-oo*), literally *the son of the man*, with the second definitive article included.

In the gospels, the son of man sayings fall into three distinct categories. The first are proverbs about the role and authority of the son of man in Jesus' Galilean context. These could refer to both Jesus and his followers.

32. Daniel 7:13–14
33. Daniel 7:27

The second group describes the passion of the son of man (Jesus)—his suffering and death in Jerusalem. The third collection points to a future return of the son of man on the clouds of heaven. The first group may have been actually uttered by the historical Jesus, while the second and third groups most likely stem from writers of the early church looking back at the passion of Jesus in retrospect and looking forward to an imminent return of Jesus as an apocalyptic judge and ruler over Israel. To sort all of the son of man sayings into these three categories would take more space than allowed in this book, but a discerning reader can see the differences.

The enigma is why Jesus might have used this third-person reference to himself, if he did. He was certainly capable of referring to himself as "I" as is evident in these three gospel parallels.[34]

> *Who do people say that I am?* (Mark)
> *Who do the crowds say that I am?* (Luke)
> *Who do the people say that the son of man is?* (Matthew)

This indicates that sometimes the usage is dependent, not so much on Jesus, but rather on the gospel writer. But the interpretation of the term depends on whether one has a Christology from above or a Christology from below.

Jesus and God

I do not believe that the historical Jesus was God. Yet, Jesus had a relationship with God that was extraordinary. Jesus went beyond a simple belief in God to pursue a radical life centered in a powerful trust in God's love and compassion. Contrary to common sense, Jesus trusted that God's abiding concern for the poor and God's passion for the least among us would someday triumph over the injustice of the world. Ignoring conventional wisdom, Jesus trusted that human kindness and generosity would eventually transform the status quo of selfishness, greed and apathy. Against all reasonable odds, Jesus trusted that the power of love and non-violent resistance would ultimately overcome entrenched evil and brutality. This kind of radical trust seems truly mad given the realities of a world beset by evil and suffering. It invites one to be an open target for the contempt and dismissal of intimidating political, economic, and religious powers. And it inevitably calls one to become a willing martyr in the ongoing struggle to overturn the unjust systems of the world.

---

34. Mark 8:27, Luke 9:18, Matthew 16:13

Jesus trusted that the radical change of the reign of God would not come about easily. It would require dedication, risk, and suffering. Jesus never promised that the transformation of the social, political, and economic systems of domination would occur overnight. He never proclaimed that a sudden cosmic event would magically change the world in the twinkling of an eye. Neither did he promise that he or his followers would live to see the change he envisioned. Instead, Jesus trusted that a life of compassion and service in a suffering world would make a progressively small difference, one person at a time, one act at a time, just like the action of a tiny mustard seed in a well-tended garden, or a bit of yeast in a large batch of dough. In everything he did and said, Jesus trusted that God would provide the courage and strength to help his followers muddle through the overwhelming odds stacked against the lives of humble people, trapped in poverty and condemned as social outcasts. Jesus trusted that the spirit of God would empower and encourage a powerless people to prevail over oppressive social systems that were created to serve the narrow interests of a privileged few. Jesus calls us to that task. He calls us to that journey. He calls us to that life.

CHAPTER 7

sin and atonement

To err is human—but it feels divine.

—MAE WEST (1893–1980)

Do nothing from selfish ambition or conceit, but in humility regard others as better than yourselves. Let each of you look not to your own interests, but to the interests of others.[1]

—PAUL, THE APOSTLE (C. 5–67 CE)

Traditionally, Christian theology and practice has concentrated on issues of sin and salvation. Personal redemption from God's righteous wrath has become more important than the transformation of human behavior or the struggle for justice in human society. In orthodox theology, we are passive recipients of God's grace, not hands-on actors in the transformation of the world.

The third chapter of Genesis introduces us to a mythological origin of human sin—the story of temptation and disobedience in paradise.

> *Now the serpent was more subtle and crafty than any other wild animal that Yahweh Elohim had made. He said to the woman, "Did Elohim really say, 'You shall not eat from any tree in the garden'?" The woman said to the serpent, "We may eat of the fruit of the trees in the garden; but Elohim said, 'You shall not eat of the fruit of the tree that is in the middle of the garden, nor shall*

---

1. Philippians 2:3–4

you touch it, or you shall die.'" But the serpent said to the woman, "You will not die; for Elohim knows that when you eat of it your eyes will be opened, and you will be like gods, knowing good and evil." So when the woman saw that the tree was good for food, and that it was a delight to the eyes, and that the tree was to be desired to make one wise, she took of its fruit and ate; and she also gave some to her husband, who was with her, and he ate. Then the eyes of both were opened.[2]

Clearly the story in Genesis is about humans becoming like the gods, creating their own morality—defining right from wrong, good from evil. But in the Apostle Paul's theology, this is a strategic story about how sin entered the world through the disobedience of one man (Adam, not Eve) and how it required the sacrifice of one man (Jesus) to overcome its legacy among us.

Therefore, just as one man's trespass led to condemnation for all, so one man's act of righteousness leads to justification [absolution, exoneration] *and life for all. For just as by the one man's disobedience the many were made sinners, so by the one man's obedience the many will be made righteous.*[3]

For fundamentalists, the story of Adam and Eve is not a metaphorical tale of origins. They believe the story of our descent from one man and one woman must be literally true if Paul's theology is to be taken at its word. Therefore the theory of human evolution from earlier primates is seen as a theological threat. If sin did not enter the world through the first divinely-created human, the Pauline salvation story falls apart, at least in the conservative mind.

As the early church merged ancient Greek philosophy with their own theological thoughts about God, sin, and redemption, they encountered a dilemma. Because God was seen as perfect and good, God's creation must also be good and perfect. And that is what the Priestly writer declared around 800 BCE: "Elohim saw everything that he had made, and indeed, it was very good."[4] Centuries later, Plato (c. 424–347 BCE) disagreed. For him only spiritual realities were good. The entire material world—including human beings—was an imperfect and evil creation. Platonists reasoned that a good and omnipotent God would make nothing bad. Some argued that there must have been two creators. A second creator—a *demiurge* (*dem'-ee-urj*), from the Greek *démiourgos* (*day-me-oor-gos'*), meaning an artisan

---

2. Genesis 3:1–7. The fruit of the tree would make one "wise." Interestingly, the term *Homo sapiens* means *wise man*.

3. Romans 5:18–19

4. Genesis 1:31

or builder—must have created our imperfect sinful reality, while the first creator was responsible solely for the non-material world. That was a neat and tidy theory, allowing Theos to remain a perfect and good being. However, apart from some Gnostic theologians, most Christian thinkers could not accept the possibility of dual creators.

Saint Augustine (354–430 CE), a Bishop of the city of Hippo in North Africa, who was the first major and perhaps the most influential Christian philosopher, solved this dilemma by making a distinction between the period from the moment of creation to the introduction of sin in the Garden of Eden and the time that has followed since. Up until the disobedience in the garden, everything had been perfect and good. (Perhaps for a week or two?) It was reasoned that Adam and Eve had been endowed by God with free will—the choice to sin or not to sin. Therefore, it was humanity—not God—that introduced sin into the world by eating the forbidden fruit of the Tree of Knowledge of Good and Evil. But Augustine believed that since the fall from grace in the Garden, humanity is no longer truly capable of free will; we are now all condemned to sin because of a biological inheritance. Augustine believed that our sinful nature is passed from generation to generation by our "concupiscence," our debased sexual longings and libidinous appetites. In other words, we are condemned to sin by virtue of our natural sexual drives. The "original sin" committed by Adam and Eve thus infects and contaminates each of us who are conceived sexually and who accordingly deserve God's wrath and punishment as sinful beings. This is why the virgin birth of Jesus becomes so important in Christian theology. Jesus is professed to have been conceived without sexual intercourse; therefore he was born without sin—the only sinless human being since Adam and Eve. (Unless you are Roman Catholic, and then Mary is the first.)

The doctrine of original sin as developed by Augustine is a case of autobiography becoming theology. Augustine's first insight into the nature of sin occurred when, as a child, he and a number of friends stole a few pears they did not really want or need from a neighborhood garden—an act of sin parallel to that of Adam and Eve. Augustine believed that by nature he had a propensity for sin and crime. In his youth, he lived a hedonistic lifestyle, associating with young men who boasted of their bi-sexual conquests. He later observed that his youthful sex drive led him to confuse the search for love and friendship with the satisfaction of his sexual desires. As he said, "The bubbling impulses of puberty befogged and obscured my heart so that it could not see the difference between love's serenity and lust's darkness." Augustine believed that his lust was so strong that it had overcome his ability to choose the good.

> *I was bound not by an iron imposed by anyone else but by the iron of my own choice. The enemy had a grip on my will and so made a chain for me to hold me a prisoner. The consequence of a distorted will is passion. By servitude to passion, habit is formed, and habit to which there is no resistance becomes a compulsion. By these links, as it were, connected one to another (hence my term a chain), a harsh bondage held me under restraint.[5]*

At about the age of 19, Augustine began a lengthy affair with a young woman of a lower social class, angering his mother. The woman remained his unmarried lover for over thirteen years and gave birth to his son Adeodatus. Later, Augustine abandoned his mistress and child in order to prepare himself to marry a young heiress in a match arranged by his mother. Because he had to wait two years until his eleven-year-old fiancée came of age, he quickly took another mistress. Augustine eventually broke off his engagement with the young girl and abandoned his second mistress. He later saw his sexual appetites as evidence of his inherently sinful nature. Augustine's sense of guilt about the sins of his early life and a belief in his own innate sinfulness impacted Christian theology for the next sixteen hundred years leading to a Christian obsession with sexual behavior.

But, according to social gospel theologian and pastor Walter Rauschenbusch (1861–1916), until first Paul and later Augustine developed the doctrine of sin and salvation, the temptation and fall of humanity in the Garden of Eden was not of theological importance in the Hebrew Bible. The idea of original sin and our need for redemption is simply not there.

> *There are scarcely any allusions to the story in the Old Testament. The prophets were deeply conscious of the sins of men, but they did not base their teachings on the doctrine of the fall . . . In the synoptic sayings of Jesus there is not even a reference to the fall of Adam . . . Not until we come to Paul do we find any full and serious use of the story of the fall in the Bible.[6]*

In Hebrew tradition, sin is a specific act of commission or omission. People can atone for their sins and a gracious God will forgive them. Yom Kippur, a day to atone for the sins of the past year, is the most significant holy day of the Jewish year. It is a day of prayer and fasting to demonstrate repentance and make amends. In order to atone for a sin against another, one must seek out the injured person and work toward reconciliation before Yom Kippur. For Paul and Augustine, however, sin is an inherited human

---

5. Augustine, *Confessions*. Book 8, Chapter 5.
6. Rauschenbusch, *Social Gospel*, 40.

condition. It requires a cosmic sacrifice by the Christ to atone for the sinful nature of humanity. These two approaches demonstrate the difference between sins and sinfulness, actions versus an existential state of being.

Although the church has built its entire doctrine of human redemption on the story of the fall, Jesus and the earlier Hebrew prophets paid little attention to it. Once again, we see the difference between the gospel *of* Jesus and the gospel *about* Jesus, which is immersed almost entirely in personal salvation from the inherited guilt of original sin—something Jesus said nothing about. Absolutely nothing.

As Rauschenbusch points out, in the gospel *about* Jesus:

> *The traditional doctrine of the fall has taught us to regard evil as a kind of unvarying racial endowment, which is active in every new life and which can be overcome only by the grace offered in the Gospel and ministered by the Church.*[7]

But, Rauschenbusch says, in the social gospel *of* Jesus, evil becomes "a variable factor in the life of humanity, which it is our duty to diminish for every young life and for every generation."

The theology of original sin needs to be put to rest. It is one of the chief ideas that distorts our understanding of Jesus as a teacher of love and a prophetic critic of the domination system into an apocalyptic Christ whose sacrificial death was more significant than his life.

the nature of sin

Sin is anything but original. According to some theologians, sins are actions that violate God's will, intentionally or unintentionally. Sins are sometimes viewed as any action that disrupts the ideal relationship between that individual and God, and to a lesser extent between that individual and other human beings. The Roman Catholic Church divides sinful behavior into two categories: venial and mortal. The least corrupt are *venial* sins (meaning forgivable sins) which are minor infractions. *Mortal* sins—major crimes—result in a complete separation from God and eternal damnation in hell. Of course, these categories are completely human constructions—based on a human classification of good and evil behavior, which according to the story we read in Genesis is the actual original sin.

In the New Testament, the English word *sin* is most commonly translated from the Greek *hamartia (ham-ar-tee'-ah)* that signifies missing the mark. It is a failure, a fault, or an error—human behavior that does not

---

7. Ibid, 43.

measure up to an ideal standard. Some have compared it to an archery contest, or perhaps a handgun shooting range, where the target is widely missed. And when we miss, according to some theologians, it is our own damn fault, or in the case of original sin, the damn fault of our entire species. The traditional confession of sins in the Latin mass intoned, "*mea culpa, mea culpa, mea máxima culpa*" (translated as "my fault, my fault, my greatest fault"), while the penitent's right fist beats on the chest three times. The Lutheran confession of sins for Ash Wednesday puts it this way: "We have sinned by our fault, by our own fault, by our own most grievous fault in thought, word, and deed, by what we have done and by what we have left undone."

Today, another group of theologians has begun to see sin not as missing a target of ideal human behavior, or violating any number of select divine commandments, or even being born in a state of rebellion against God or an existential separation from God, but rather as the fundamental state of ego-centrism that consumes our lives. This understanding of sin is consistent with the gospel *of* Jesus. At its core, sin in both the individual and the social context is rooted in human self-centeredness, self-obsession, and selfishness. It is found in the condition of living for oneself alone and a callous disregard for the needs of others. My desk dictionary lists 142 compound words that begin with the word *self*, including self-absorption, self-concern, self-centeredness, self-importance, self-indulgence, self-interest, self-righteousness, self-serving, and selfishness. This is the underlying nature of human sin—an overwhelmingly dominant focus on myself, my needs, and my desires. This finds expression in the ancient domination system where selfishness is the core value of the economic system created by elites and where selfishness and suspicion of others is cultivated among the working classes to keep them at odds from one another in order to preserve the status quo that primarily benefits those at the top.

sin as selfishness

If one wants to think about children being born in a condition that leads to sin, human selfishness is it. Humans are profoundly selfish beings. We are all born that way. It is the natural state of every infant. A baby is only aware of his or her own needs and insists that those be met immediately. As we mature, we learn to balance our needs with those of others—family, friends, spouse, and children. Yet, we still feel a powerful pull to put our own needs first. This may be more culturally true for men than for women, but selfishness affects us all. Selfish egocentrism results in a preoccupation with one's own internal world. Egocentrics regard themselves and their own opinions or interests as being the most important or valid.

As humans, our hearts are filled with worry, insecurity, and self-concern. We are anxious about the future. Whether we admit it or not, we perceive the world as a cruel place, and realize that in a largely selfish world, others will surely be indifferent to our needs and welfare. We thus believe we must care for ourselves first and provide for our own future security at the expense of anyone else. The self thus pursues goals that attempt to insulate and protect it from a seemingly random and harmful universe. We search for a sense of security through wealth, possessions, pleasure, prestige, power, exclusive solidarity, and self-centered religion. In the process, our hearts become concentrated in our materialistic culture and the things that conventional wisdom deems to be of importance.

This focus on the self often leads to alienation, isolation, and separation from others. A life lived for one's self results in a hard and cold heart. It drives out compassion and concern for the needs of others. It often spawns a desire to dominate and control others in service to the self. Selfishness is at the root of the ancient domination system in which a few control the economic life of the many, extracting their productivity to maintain luxurious lifestyles.

Individuals will always sin. They will continually make bad choices and they will inevitably screw things up in their personal lives. But contrary to what some conservative preachers may claim, most humans are not totally depraved. Aside from some sociopaths, the majority of us may be frequently dishonest, sometimes immoral, occasionally unscrupulous, and now and then wicked, but few are totally and hopelessly evil. Says Rauschenbusch:

> *We are equipped with powerful appetites. We are often placed in difficult situations, which constitute overwhelming temptations. We are all relatively ignorant, and while we experiment with life, we go astray. On the other hand, we are gifted with high ideals, with a wonderful range of possibilities, with aspirations and longing, and also weighted with inertia and moral incapacity to achieve. We are keenly alive to the call of the senses and the pleasures of the moment, and only dimly and occasionally conscious of our own higher destiny, of the mystic value of personality in others, and of God.*[8]

Following Jesus involves a movement away from self-obsession and toward the needs of other people. We begin the journey of transformative discipleship by denying ourselves and emptying our hearts of self-centered devotion.

8. Ibid, 45.

> *Then he said to them all, "If any want to become my followers, let them deny themselves and take up their cross daily and follow me."*[9]

The call to deny oneself often sounds like a Lenten discipline. It conjures up images of people renouncing chocolate, Cheetos, or cheeseburgers. But Jesus is talking about something more fundamental. It is a call to give our lives to love and compassion. And it is a call to put the needs of other people first. Jesus is our model. Dietrich Bonhoeffer called him "the man for others."[10]

Although most New Testament translations use the phrase "let them deny themselves" in this quote from Luke, a few others offer variations like "let them forget themselves" or "let them give up the things they want." The New Living Translation says, "You must turn from your selfish ways." Jesus calls us out from the lordship of selfishness to a new mode of life. He calls us to risk everything for that new mode of thinking and living.

Jesus was not crucified as a sacrifice for the sins of humanity; he was executed because his message threatened the wealthy and powerful forces of his day. He was willing to pay the price of martyrdom for his friends—the poor, the hungry, the sick, the weeping, the outcast. The religious and state authorities wanted him out of the way. They wanted to shut him up and put an end to his movement.

Theology professor Sharon Baker Putt (b. 1960) wrote one of the most compelling arguments against the traditional Christian theology that the death of Jesus was required blood atonement for the sins of humanity in order to satisfy the offended holiness of a judgmental God. She contrasts this traditional atonement theology to the teachings of Jesus by rewriting the parable of the prodigal son.

> *A man had two sons. The younger son demanded his inheritance from his father, left home, squandered it, and returned home, admitting to his father that he had sinned and begging for forgiveness.*
>
> *The father responded, "I cannot simply forgive you for what you have done. You have insulted my honor by your wild living. Simply to forgive would be to trivialize your sin. Justice, forgiveness, and reconciliation cannot occur unless the penalty for your sin is paid. Either you must be punished or you must pay back the honor you stole from me.*
>
> *The older brother spoke up, telling his father he would pay the debt of his younger brother. The brother worked day and night to pay the debt until he died of exhaustion. The father's wrath was*

---

9. Luke 9:23
10. Bonhoeffer, *Letters and Papers*, 382.

> *finally placated against the younger brother, and they lived happily until the end of their days.*[11]

Baker argues that if the parable had read like this, then traditional atonement theologies would make more sense. Instead, Jesus portrayed a compassionate, loving father who saw his son from afar and ran to him, embraced him, and celebrated his return without regard to the son's past behavior. No confession of sin was required to receive complete and total forgiveness. No blood atonement was necessary to resolve the debt. The parable is about pure, unconditional love. End of story.

---

11. Baker, *Executing God*. This excerpt was printed in a book review by Deanna Thompson in "The Christian Century," April 30, 2014. Online: http://www.christiancentury.org/reviews/2014-04/executing-god-sharon-l-baker

CHAPTER 8

heaven and hell

In the sweet by and by, we shall meet on that beautiful shore.[1]
—SANFORD FILLMORE BENNETT (1836–1898)

You will eat, bye and bye, in that glorious land above the sky.
Work and pray, live on hay, you'll get pie in the sky when you die.[2]
—JOE HILL (1879–1915)

In popular Christianity, the afterlife is what it is all about. As Marcus Borg has said, if he had been told at the age of twelve that heaven did not exist, he would have most certainly wondered why anyone should be a Christian at all.[3] After all, getting to heaven is the sole purpose and point to being a Christian, isn't it? For many people, it clearly is.

The belief in heaven is so pervasive that it manifests itself in an enduring folk religion that has become thoroughly enmeshed with our culture. I frequently hear people talk about a departed friend or family member smiling down from heaven. Dad is said to be organizing the angels into a golf league and Mom is busy planning heavenly parties. In the popular imagination, life on earth is simply continued in heaven. Cartoons show those who have died standing among the clouds replete with white robes, halos, harps, and wings. Jokes about St. Peter at the Pearly Gates complete this broad caricature of heaven in the popular imagination.

1. Bennett, Sanford F. and Joseph P. Webster, "In the Sweet Bye and Bye," 1868.
2. Joe Hill (Joel Emmanuel Hägglund), "The Preacher and the Slave," 1911.
3. Borg, *The Heart of Christianity*, 10.

Beliefs about a heavenly afterlife are many and varied. If you put ten Christians together in a room (not to mention people of other faiths) and ask them about life after death, you will get ten very different answers. But the widespread belief in heaven is more an expression of human wish-fulfillment than it is a clearly-defined biblical concept. For instance, four out of ten Americans believe that animals—at least their cherished pets—also go to heaven.[4] The desire to be reunited with animal companions in heaven is a clear indication that wish-fulfillment drives most of our beliefs about life after death.[5] When it comes to heaven, it's not what is true that is important. It's what we *want* to be true that forms our most cherished beliefs.

I've frequently heard from many very sincere people that they believe there must be a heavenly afterlife because so many people are suffering here on earth from abject poverty, hunger, and disease. Heaven thus becomes a compensation for earthy misery. It's what Joe Hill sang about in his parody of the hymn "The Sweet By and By." His lyric reads "Work and pray, live on hay, you'll get pie in the sky when you die." Based on this reasoning, the goal of traditional Christianity has been to convert as many people as possible to faith in Jesus so that they can go to heaven after their short, brutal lives and avoid the eternal life of suffering in hell that a just God demands of those who may not hold the proper beliefs or lifestyle. Pastor and author Rob Bell has a different answer in his book *Love Wins*: a loving God would not condemn any of God's children to hell and thus everyone is taken into heaven after death. Even if one rejects the idea of hell, heaven always seems to survive in the religious imagination.

The idea of "universal salvation" holds that people of every faith and no faith at all are saved (usually meaning that they are welcomed into heaven in the presence of God). But if that is true, it is not necessary to convert anyone to a certain set of religious beliefs. Whether the program is mass conversion of two-thirds of humanity or not, neither one of these approaches—a limited "special salvation" or an unlimited "universal salvation"—says that the real effort should be put into mitigating suffering on this side of the grave. If one is really concerned about those who suffer from deprivation, then elimination of hell on earth is the real issue, not pie in the sky when you die. Folks who feel sorry for those who suffer in this world should act

---

4. Sussman, "See Spot Go to Heaven?"

5. In his novel *Animal Farm*, George Orwell described an animal's view of heaven. The animals were told by their leaders that after their miserable lives were over they would go to a place in which 'it was Sunday seven days a week, clover was in season all the year round, and lump sugar and linseed cake grew on the hedges." This is surely a farm animal's wish fulfillment. Pet owners expect an even better future for their animal friends—especially for dogs, with their unconditional love; cats, I'm not so sure of.

to end their suffering in "the here and now," not compensate them in "the there and then."

an ancient belief

The concept of heaven is rooted in the ancient human belief that the gods—like Yahweh, Zeus, and Odin—lived somewhere above the clouds. Jesus, who was enculturated in that ancient worldview, reportedly spoke of God dwelling in the heavens: "Our father in the sky" was the beginning of the prayer he taught his followers, at least according to Matthew's version.[6]

Below the earth lay the place of the dead which the Hebrews called *Sheol* (*sheh-ole'*). It is sometimes compared to the Greek's *Hades* (*hah'-dace*), where the dead continue their existence as "shadows."[7] In fact, the word "Hades" was substituted for Sheol when the Hebrew Bible was translated into Greek and it continued to be used in the New Testament to refer to the abode of the dead. In Hebrew lore and Greek mythology, Sheol and Hades were resting places for *all* the dead, not just a place reserved for wicked people. The term "Sheol" was sometimes simply used as a reference to "the grave" or more harshly to "the pit." Isaiah uses that metaphor for Sheol. In a mocking tone, he commented on the death of the king of Assyria and Babylon:

> *You said in your heart . . .*
> *"I will ascend to the tops of the clouds,*
> *   I will make myself like the Most High."*
> *But you are brought down to Sheol,*
> *   to the depths of the Pit.*[8]

In the ancient Hebrew tradition, everyone—even the greatest and noblest—ends up buried in a pit in the ground.

the rich man and Lazarus

Sheol plays a role in one of the stories told by Jesus in the gospel of Luke—the parable of the rich man and Lazarus.

---

6. Matthew 6:9. Luke's gospel simply says "Father" (Luke 11:2)
7. The more typical English pronunciation is *hay'-dees*.
8. Isaiah 14:12, 14–15

> There was a rich man who was dressed in purple and fine linen and who feasted sumptuously every day. And at his gate lay a poor man named Lazarus, covered with sores, who longed to satisfy his hunger with what fell from the rich man's table; even the dogs would come and lick his sores. The poor man died and was carried away by the angels to be with Abraham. The rich man also died and was buried. In Hades [Sheol], where he was being tormented, he looked up and saw Abraham far away with Lazarus by his side. He called out, "Father Abraham, have mercy on me, and send Lazarus to dip the tip of his finger in water and cool my tongue; for I am in agony in these flames." But Abraham said, "Child, remember that during your lifetime you received your good things, and Lazarus in like manner evil things; but now he is comforted here, and you are in agony. Besides all this, between you and us a great chasm has been fixed, so that those who might want to pass from here to you cannot do so, and no one can cross from there to us."[9]

Some people believe this short story suggests the existence of heaven and hell after death, although heaven and hell are never mentioned in the tale. The story describes a poor man being carried away by angels after his death to some unspecified location where he resides with the Jewish patriarch Abraham. In Hebrew lore, resting in the "bosom of Abraham" was a metaphor for a place of comfort, similar to a child being tenderly held in a father's lap or at a mother's breast. The implication in modern minds, however, is that this is a description of heaven. Likewise, the story tells of a rich man who was tormented in Hades after his death. Presumably, this describes hell.

But Jesus' listeners recognized this story simply as a description of their understanding of Sheol, not of an afterlife in heaven and hell—of which they had no conceptual framework. Semitic folklore imagined Sheol as a great cavern beneath the ground. In the gospel story, we are told that there are two levels to Sheol, separated by a wide chasm—one, a place of torment below, and the other, a place of comfort above. Some would claim this is merely a subtle difference from our modern understanding of heaven and hell, but it is a difference nonetheless and should not be glossed over.

In Greek mythology, the realm of Hades is the misty and gloomy abode of the dead where the disembodied souls of all humans go. There were many variations of the Hades premise recounted in different Greek myths over time, with descriptions of separate sections of Hades reserved for people whose lives merited different rewards or punishments. The *Elysian Fields* was a place of enjoyment reserved for heroes and other people favored by

---

9. Luke 16:19–31

the gods. In some myths, the souls of these heroes were reunited with their physical bodies, but this was rare. The *Asphodel Meadows* was a less perfect version of existence for those whose lives were balanced between good and evil deeds. For those judged worthy of punishment, *Tartarus* was a deep gloomy place of torment and suffering. These ancient ideas probably helped shape the story of the rich man and Lazarus. Imagine the poor man in the Elysian Fields with the patriarch Abraham, while the rich man discovers himself in Tartarus.

Some scholars doubt that Jesus actually told this story—that it was included by Luke and put on the lips of Jesus because it fit one of the writer's themes about the dangers of wealth. At the time, there were many folk tales about a reversal of situations after death—the comfortable rich being afflicted and the suffering poor being comforted. In this story, the rich man is not being tormented for doing evil deeds, or for worshipping false gods, or for not accepting Jesus as his Lord and savior, or even for simply being rich; his punishment comes from the fact that he was indifferent to the obvious suffering of the destitute Lazarus who lay at the gate of his palatial estate. Obviously, Jesus was concerned about the plight of the poor and the dangers of wealth. But did Jesus really declare that his listeners would experience eternal punishment if they did not get with his program of compassion, generosity, charity, and justice?

weeping and gnashing of teeth

Jesus said very little to suggest there would be an everlasting punishment (or an everlasting reward, for that matter) after death. There are only eight references to what we might call "hell" in the gospels. In addition to the story of the rich man and Lazarus in Luke's gospel, there are six sets of sayings found in the gospel of Matthew and one saying in Mark's account. In contrast to most Christian theology, these sayings about God's judgment and punishment are based on the fruitfulness of one's life and not on the orthodoxy of one's religious beliefs. According to Matthew, the judgment of God will result in a reward or punishment based on how one treats one's brothers and sisters in direst need.[10] Matthew declares that people whose lives do not produce the good fruit of compassion and generosity will be "thrown into the furnace of fire" or "cast into the outer darkness" where there will be "weeping and gnashing of teeth." These phrases are unique to Matthew, and many scholars agree that these are ideas and words of Matthew alone and not of Jesus.

10. Matthew 25:31–46

The first example is found in Matthew's story about the healing of a Roman centurion's servant. In this story, Jesus says:

> *I tell you, many will come from east and west and will eat with Abraham and Isaac and Jacob in the kingdom of heaven, while the heirs of the kingdom will be thrown into the outer darkness, where there will be weeping and gnashing of teeth.*[11]

There are many concepts to be unpacked in this passage, including Matthew's misleading terminology "kingdom of heaven" as a substitute for the "kingdom of God"—but the outer darkness, the weeping, and the toothgnashing are our current focus.

In addition, Matthew's gospel cites four examples of judgment and punishment in parables told by Jesus, beginning with the parable of the weeds gathered at harvest time that adds the image of a fiery furnace.

> *Just as the weeds are collected and burned up with fire, so will it be at the end of the age. The son of man will send his angels, and they will collect out of his kingdom all causes of sin and all evildoers, and they will throw them into the furnace of fire, where there will be weeping and gnashing of teeth.*[12]

Next, is the parable of the fisherman's net:

> *Again, the kingdom of heaven is like a net which was thrown into the sea and gathered fish of every kind; when it was full, men drew it ashore and sat down and sorted the good into vessels but threw away the bad. So it will be at the close of the age. The angels will come out and separate the evil from the righteous, and throw them into the furnace of fire; there men will weep and gnash their teeth.*[13]

The parable of the wedding banquet follows:

> *Then the king said to the attendants, "Bind him hand and foot, and throw him into the outer darkness, where there will be weeping and gnashing of teeth."*[14]

The series concludes with the parable of the talents:

---

11. Matthew 8:11–12
12. Matthew 13:40–42
13. Matthew 13:47–50
14. Matthew 22:13

> *As for this worthless slave, throw him into the outer darkness, where there will be weeping and gnashing of teeth.*[15]

Matthew's reference to a "gnashing of teeth" may have been influenced by Psalm 112 that speaks of the earthly fates of the just and the unjust. To the righteous who act with compassion and justice, the psalmist observes:

> *They have distributed freely, they have given to the poor;*
> *their righteousness endures forever;*
> *their horn is exalted in honor.*
> *The wicked see it and are angry;*
> *they gnash their teeth and melt away;*
> *the desire of the wicked comes to nothing.*[16]

In addition, there is one more Matthean example of punishment in the famous account of a final judgment by God. Jesus describes the fate of those who do not feed the hungry, clothe the naked, welcome the stranger, or visit the sick and imprisoned:

> *Then he* [the Son of Man] *will answer them, "Truly I tell you, just as you did not do it to one of the least of these, you did not do it to me." And these will go away into eternal punishment, but the righteous into eternal life.*[17]

What these stories and sayings from the early Jesus movement suggest is that the determining factor between eternal reward and eternal punishment (whether actual or metaphorical) is not an issue of orthodox belief but of compassionate practice.

These six sayings of punishment are found exclusively in Matthew's gospel and are seen nowhere else in accounts of Jesus' teachings. Therefore, scholars conclude that this tradition does not derive from Jesus, but comes from the writer of Matthew's gospel.

Finally, there is a saying in Mark's gospel, which predates Matthew's gospel by about fifteen years. It refers to "hell" as a place where "the worm never dies and the fire is never quenched."

> *If any of you put a stumbling block before one of these little ones who believe in me, it would be better for you if a great millstone were hung around your neck and you were thrown into the sea. If*

---

15. Matthew 25:30
16. Psalm 112:9–10
17. Matthew 25:31–46. Matthew does not attribute this last phrase to Jesus, but instead inserts it as his own comment.

> *your hand causes you to stumble, cut it off; it is better for you to enter life maimed than to have two hands and to go to hell, to the unquenchable fire. And if your foot causes you to stumble, cut it off; it is better for you to enter life lame than to have two feet and to be thrown into hell. And if your eye causes you to stumble, tear it out; it is better for you to enter the kingdom of God with one eye than to have two eyes and to be thrown into hell, where their worm never dies, and the fire is never quenched.*[18]

The English word "hell" with its undying worm and unquenchable fire has been misleadingly substituted in some Bible translations for the Greek word *Gehenna* (*gheh'-en-nah*), a term that referred to the Valley of Hinnom—in Hebrew *Ge Hinnom* (*gay-hin-nome'*)—one of the two principal valleys surrounding the Old City in Jerusalem. Historians believe this valley had been a site where Canaanite followers of prosperity gods like *Baal* (*bah'-al*) and *Moloch* (*moh'-lock*) sacrificed their first-born children by fire.[19] It is commonly thought that the valley later became the general disposal site for all the refuse of Jerusalem. It has been said that the dead bodies of criminals, the carcasses of animals, and the city's rubbish were burned there in a constantly tended fire. Gehenna thus became a symbol for punishment or destruction after death.

The undying worm (or maggots) and unquenchable fire referenced by Mark are also stock biblical images for the destruction of evil. The book of Isaiah ends with this verse:

> *And they shall go out and look at the dead bodies of the people who have rebelled against me; for their worm shall not die, their fire shall not be quenched, and they shall be an abhorrence to all flesh.*[20]

So we see a handful of references to punishment after death in the gospels, mostly from one author. The question addressed by biblical scholars is whether these sayings originated with Jesus or whether they served the purpose of the authors we call Matthew, Mark, and Luke, and therefore originated with them. The authenticity of these sayings must finally come down to the question of who Jesus was and what he was about. Jesus preached love for one's enemies, urged continual forgiveness toward those who have hurt us, and told us to pray for those who persecute us. Does this teacher of radical love and compassion then turn around and condemn people to an eternity of suffering in some form of final retribution? Does Jesus believe

---

18. Mark 9:42–48
19. 2 Kings 23:10, Jeremiah 32:35
20. Isaiah 66:24

that a God of love—a compassionate, welcoming, accepting father—will ultimately treat God's children this way? Many conservative Christians would enthusiastically say "Yes!" because the existential fear of eternal punishment is the foundation of their belief system. But I think not.

I believe that the stories Jesus may have told—like the parable of the rich man and Lazarus, or the last judgment by the Son of Man—were not about our contemporary understanding of life after death in heaven or hell; they were stories about the importance of heaven and hell in this world—paying attention to the beggars at our gates. As the reformer John Calvin (1509-1564) once said, "Hell is not a place but a condition." It is a daily human condition for far too many people. The followers of Jesus are not called to consign unbelievers to a place of suffering after death, but to deliver all people from the living hell of destitution, hunger, illness, and violence.

images of heaven

Biblical imagery is powerful and continually shapes the contour of a place called heaven in the minds of many Christians. About 2,800 years ago, in the eighth century BCE, the prophet Isaiah reported a vision of God's royal dwelling place.

> *In the year that King Uzziah died, I saw Yahweh sitting on a throne, high and lofty; and the hem of his robe filled the temple. Seraphs were in attendance above him; each had six wings: with two they covered their faces, and with two they covered their feet, and with two they flew.*[21]

It was not unusual to describe God being surrounded by exotic celestial beings. Two centuries later, the prophet Ezekiel described a much more imaginative vision of God as "something like a human being."

> *Over the heads of the living creatures there was something like a dome, shining like crystal, spread out above their heads. Under the dome their wings were stretched out straight, one toward another; and each of the creatures had two wings covering its body. When they moved, I heard the sound of their wings like the sound of mighty waters, like the thunder of Shaddai (shad-dah'-ee), a sound of tumult like the sound of an army; when they stopped, they let down their wings. And there came a voice from above the dome over their heads; when they stopped, they let down their wings.*

---

21. Isaiah 6:1-2

> *And above the dome over their heads there was something like a throne, in appearance like sapphire; and seated above the likeness of a throne was something that seemed like a human form. Upward from what appeared like the loins I saw something like gleaming amber, something that looked like fire enclosed all around; and downward from what looked like the loins I saw something that looked like fire, and there was a splendor all around. Like the bow in a cloud on a rainy day, such was the appearance of the splendor all around. This was the appearance of the likeness of the glory of Yahweh.* [22]

A lot of imaginative speculation went on about God's appearance and dwelling place, especially among apocalyptic writers like the authors of the book of Daniel in the Hebrew Bible and the book of Revelation in the New Testament. Like the writers of other apocalyptic literature, they presented a mystical divine revelation to a human recipient told in the form of visions. Using symbolic imagery, they were intended to bring comfort and hope to a community suffering to maintain the integrity of their faith.

The book of Daniel, written during the attacks against Judaism and Jerusalem by the Syrian-Greek ruler Antiochus Epiphanes IV (*an-tee'-uk-us ep-if-an-ace'*) in the second century BCE, reports a vision of God and his heavenly throne room in highly imaginative poetic language.

> *As I watched,*
> >   *thrones were set in place,*
> >   *and an Ancient One took his throne,*
> >   *his clothing was white as snow,*
> >   *and the hair of his head like pure wool;*
> >   *his throne was fiery flames,*
> >   *and its wheels were burning fire.*
> *A stream of fire issued*
> >   *and flowed out from his presence.*
> >   *A thousand thousands served him,*
> >   *and ten thousand times ten thousand stood attending him.*
> >   *The court sat in judgment,*
> >   *and the books were opened.*[23]

---

22. Ezekiel 1:22–28. Hebrew Bibles say that the one seated on the throne had a "likeness of a man (*adam*)" or a human being.

23. Daniel 7:9–10

The book of Revelation, written during a time of persecution of the early church by Emperor Domitian (ruled 81–96 CE) near the end of the first century CE, gives us a similar colorful image.

> *At once I was in the spirit, and there in heaven stood a throne, with one seated on the throne! And the one seated there looks like jasper and carnelian, and around the throne is a rainbow that looks like an emerald. Around the throne are twenty-four thrones, and seated on the thrones are twenty-four elders, dressed in white robes, with golden crowns on their heads. Coming from the throne are flashes of lightning, and rumblings and peals of thunder, and in front of the throne burn seven flaming torches, which are the seven spirits of God; and in front of the throne there is something like a sea of glass, like crystal.*[24]

John, the self-named author of Revelation, envisions those faithful people who have endured the ordeal of religious persecution as one day standing at the throne of God. The martyrs are robed in white:

> *After this I looked, and there was a great multitude that no one could count, from every nation, from all tribes and peoples and languages, standing before the throne and before the Lamb, robed in white, with palm branches in their hands.*[25]

Revelation thus presents a Christian version of the same concept introduced in the book of Maccabees—the martyrs who have died will be rewarded for their faithfulness in the face of violent persecution.

Common to all of these images is a God seated on a throne as a royal potentate and surrounded by sometimes bizarre celestial courtiers. Ezekiel and Daniel portray God as a very old man with white hair. Thunder, fire, and lightning are among the noises and sights associated with the dwelling place of this ancient God who originated as a divinity encountered in the frightening storms of nature.

Although apocalyptic literature seems to present visions of the future, the genre is really about the present. It gives hope that current persecutors will one day be defeated and that faithful martyrs will be vindicated. It is written to encourage people to hold fast under conditions of tyranny, torment, and trouble. But just because a writer has an ecstatic vision or creates a grandiose metaphor does not mean that any of this is true in any real sense. These images of God and heaven are all products of very creative imaginations.

24. Revelation 4:2–6
25. Revelation 7:9

CHAPTER 9

resurrection and eternal life

The message of Easter is that God's new world has been unveiled in Jesus Christ and that you're now invited to belong to it.[1]

—N. T. (NICHOLAS THOMAS) WRIGHT (B. 1948)

Let me begin with an obvious truth. You are going to die. I am going to die. We are all going to die. The amazing thing about human beings is the human ability to deny that truth, or to find some way around that truth. Most of us are looking for another way out of here rather than through the exit of death.

I am often struck by the peculiar line from the familiar Christmas carol "Hark! The Herald Angels Sing" which declares that Jesus was "born that man no more may die." I think there was a time in my life when I somehow believed that line. But it now seems ludicrous. Of course people will die. Jesus himself died.[2] Any sane person must agree that everyone dies. The question is "What, if anything, comes after death?" Many religions create a scenario in which life will somehow continue beyond the grave, either in a heavenly existence in some manner or in a reincarnated life on earth of some kind. Whether one's vision is linear or cyclical, everyone hopes that somehow their existence will not end.

In spite of nearly universal Christian belief about a heavenly afterlife, Jesus never proclaimed a message about life after death. It was not as if it was a foreign concept to him; the belief was widespread in the Roman Empire of

---

1. Wright, *Surprised by Hope*, 252–253.
2. The Apostle's Creed testifies that Jesus "was crucified, died and was buried."

the first century. The Egyptians believed in a shadowy existence after death, and had for thousands of years. Likewise the Greeks believed that an immortal soul continued after earthly existence ended, as did the Zoroastrians in Persia. From the south, north, and east, these ideas prevailed among the peoples surrounding Palestine. But for Jesus, otherworldliness and a future life in heaven was not a central part of his ministry or mission. His proclamation of the kingdom of God was about a transformed life on this side of the grave. It was all about how we live today, not what happens after we die.

So why is there this widespread belief—shared by most clergy—that the message of Jesus was a message about a heavenly afterlife? Perhaps uncritical acceptance of a centuries-long tradition of doctrines created by ecclesial committees and a fundamental lack of interest in serious biblical scholarship is part of the answer. But being afraid to speak the truth to laity is the major issue. Letting people believe what they want to believe is the easier path to take. After all, clergy stand by their parishioners at the graveside when a loved one dies. Comfort, not challenge, is a requirement of their job. Still, at some point it becomes necessary to tell the truth about what is really in the Bible, if in fact the Bible is to be a foundation of Christian faith. And one thing is sure—a heavenly afterlife was not central to the message of Jesus in the gospel accounts.

There are, however, three topics that Jesus talked about that most Christians—including many clergy—have often confused with the concept of a heavenly afterlife. They are (1) the kingdom of heaven, (2) the resurrection of the dead, and (3) the phrase "eternal life." These unrelated biblical concepts have been mixed together by Christian theologians and preachers in a confusing and illogical way for so long that they have resulted in a lot of misleading conclusions. So let us briefly review them for the sake of clarity and truth.

the kingdom of heaven

The first confusion about a heavenly afterlife comes from the phrase "the kingdom of heaven" as a substitute for "the kingdom of God." This terminology is found only in Matthew's gospel. In the other synoptic gospels—Mark and Luke—Jesus preaches his central message about the kingdom or reign of God on earth. Scholars believe that the anonymous author whom we call Matthew was writing to a Jewish-Christian community in which taking God's name in vain was a major concern, violating the second commandment (for some Christians) or the third commandment (for Jews). Therefore, to avoid offending God, even accidentally, Matthew substituted God's dwelling place—"heaven"—as a replacement for "God," putting a phrase on

Jesus' lips that he never uttered. In fact, if one were to translate the Greek phrase *basileia ton ouranon* (*bas-il-eh'-ah tohn oo-ran-ohn'*) into English literally, it would read as the "kingdom of the sky" or the "kingdom of the heavens," not the "kingdom of heaven." In other words, it refers to the earth's atmosphere, not a supernatural environment beyond space and time. Still, so many preachers continue to use the phrase "kingdom of heaven" both as a reference to God's dwelling place and the place of a heavenly afterlife, that widespread misunderstanding has resulted regarding the kingdom of God and its earthly connotation.

the resurrection of the dead

The second confusion about a heavenly afterlife is the concept of the resurrection of the dead. People often assume that the resurrection spoken of in the New Testament is an immediate transition from the moment of death into a glorious heavenly existence in the presence of God (or Jesus). But it's not. Biblical resurrection is the idea that the dead will someday return to a renewed life here on earth, not to a heavenly dimension. In the first century, the idea of the bodily resurrection was a fairly recent innovation in Jewish thought, espoused primarily by the Pharisees—including the Apostle Paul who claimed he was educated as a Pharisee. The Pharisees believed that those who had died as martyrs for their faith would be raised by God to experience new life in an earthly messianic kingdom and would be allowed to enjoy the fruits of their martyrdom in a renewed life as vindicated heroes. Resurrection was an issue of justice for the faithful, but was clearly a concept based on wish-fulfillment.

Throughout the Hebrew Bible there is little mention of life after death outside of the subterranean Sheol. Unlike the Greeks, the Jews did not separate the human being into two parts—the body and the soul—with an immortal soul that survived the death of the mortal body. For most of the history of the Hebrew people, they believed that when someone died, everything about that person died. Still, many believed that the dead somehow continued a shadowy existence in Sheol until their memory was forgotten.

It is only during what is sometimes called the "inter-testamental period" when the books of the Maccabees (Maccabees 1, 2, and 3) were written, that the idea of a bodily resurrection entered Jewish thought.[3] When Alexander

---

3. These books—part of a collection known as the Apocrypha—are found in Roman Catholic editions of the Bible but have largely been excluded from most Protestant Bibles. They are sometimes called inter-testamental because they were documents written after the collection Protestants call the Old Testament was assembled and before the writings of the New Testament occurred.

the Great (356–323 BCE) died, his vast empire was divided among his top generals. One of them, Seleucus (*sih'-loo-cos*) (312–280 BCE), became the ruler of an area that included Syria and the land of Israel. One of the descendants of the *Seleucid* (*sih'-loo-sid*) dynasty, Antiochus Epiphanes IV (*an-tee'-uk-us ep-if-an-ace'*) (215–163 BCE) began a concerted effort to increase the influence of Greek culture, known today as Hellenism—including the Greek pantheon of gods—among his diverse subjects, including the Jews. The Greeks were generally tolerant of other religions, and regional gods—including the Hebrew god Yahweh—were allowed to be worshipped in addition to the Greek gods. Most other religions went along with this syncretistic approach, but not the Jews. They were monotheistic, which sometimes meant that they believed in the existence of only one God, and at other times meant that they believed that their God was superior to all the other gods. When the Jewish majority refused to acknowledge the Greek gods, Antiochus stepped up his campaign of forced cultural and religious integration.

Antiochus—who took the egotistic surname "Epiphanes" (*ep-if-an-ace'*), which translates as a "manifestation [of God]"—precipitated a Jewish popular revolt in Jerusalem around the year 168 BCE by placing a statue of Zeus in the Jerusalem Temple and then sacrificing a pig at the altar. His action created a widespread uproar among the Jewish people. Antiochus then began an intense repression and persecution of resistant Jews in which many people were cruelly martyred in horrific ways. This in turn led to the successful Maccabean revolt (168–165 BCE) and the eventual independence of the Jewish people from Greek control for about a century, beginning in 164 BCE and lasting until the Roman conquest in 63 BCE.

It was during this period of insurrection and martyrdom that some Jewish thinkers began to propose that if God was just, God would raise the faithful martyrs from the dead so they could experience the new age of freedom and independence after the Greek armies of Antiochus were defeated.

The idea of the resurrection of the dead, of course, had been a part of the Zoroastrian religion in Persia for centuries. Zoroaster (or Zarathustra) was an ancient Iranian prophet, philosopher, and religious poet who may have lived somewhere between 800 and 600 BCE. The teachings espoused by his followers sound very familiar. They believed that in the beginning, all of creation was perfectly good but was subsequently corrupted by evil. The conflict between the truth and order of creation and the falsehood and chaos that threatened it involved the entire universe. Zoroastrian followers had an active role to play in the conflict through good thoughts, words, and deeds that were necessary to keep the chaos at bay. At the end of the ages, there would be a great battle between the forces of good and evil, in which good would triumph. A future savior would bring about an earthly resurrection of the dead, followed by a last judgment. Ultimately, creation would be restored to its original perfection.

Jewish thinkers began to integrate the Persian concept of an earthly resurrection into their ongoing religious theological development. Initially, the unjust suffering of the martyrs and their reward and vindication through resurrection were closely linked ideas.

By the time of Jesus, this novel theological proposition was part of an ongoing religious debate in the Jewish community. The conservative Sadducees refused to recognize the possibility of resurrection based on their orthodox reading of the Torah. It was simply not part of their traditional teachings and therefore not acceptable. The more liberal Pharisees, however, accepted, developed, and promoted the idea. The resurrection of the dead would be ushered in when a new messianic age began. The arrival of the future messiah was the key.

By this point in history, some Jewish theologians had suggested that *all* faithful people—not just the martyrs—would be resurrected to a new life when the latest oppressors—this time, the Romans—were defeated and an independent nation was again established. Still others were intrigued by the idea that evil people might also be resurrected, so that they could be judged for their past deeds and endure a physical punishment in retribution, paying them back for the suffering they had caused in others. This created a satisfying package of ideas: the martyrs and other faithful people would be ultimately rewarded, and their persecutors would receive an ultimate punishment. The tables would be turned and a final retributive justice would be meted out by God.

The apocalyptic book of Daniel, written during this period, describes the resurrection of the dead this way:

> *Many of those who sleep in the dust of the earth shall awake, some to everlasting life, and some to shame and everlasting contempt.*[4]

That is one of only two passages in the Hebrew Bible that speaks clearly about life after death, other than an existence in Sheol. The other is in the book of Isaiah, in an apocalyptic psalm.

> *Your dead shall live, their corpses shall rise.*
> *O dwellers in the dust, awake and sing for joy!*
> *For your dew is a radiant dew,*
> *and the earth will give birth to those long dead.*[5]

---

4. Daniel 12:2
5. Isaiah 26:19

The image to keep in mind from these texts is that the dead are "sleeping"—that they are unconscious and unaware of time. It is only when they awake—when their corpses rise from the dust—that they will experience renewed life.

Despite all of this inventive reasoning, the resurrection of the dead was never connected to an afterlife in heaven. According to the Jewish proponents of resurrection, when the general resurrection occurred, people would be restored to a physical life on earth. And this is the entire meaning of the resurrection in Paul's writings. Paul anticipated that the reported resurrection of Jesus signaled the beginning of a general resurrection of the dead, which he believed was imminent. The old age was ending and a new messianic age was beginning.

> *But in fact Christ has been raised from the dead, the first fruits of those who have fallen asleep.*[6]

For some first-century Jewish thinkers, it was assumed that after some period of time—perhaps after a lengthy new life on earth—the resurrected martyrs would once again perish, like Lazarus of Bethany who Jesus resurrected in John's gospel, and who as far as we know is not still walking around.[7] Even if the new existence was somehow envisioned as everlasting, it was always thought to be lived solidly on the earth—never in God's dwelling place in heaven.

Jesus on resurrection

So what did Jesus believe about the resurrection of the dead? We don't have much evidence, because as we said it was not central to his mission and message. If it had been, we'd have a lot of teachings about the life of the living dead. There is only one gospel episode we can point to in which the resurrection is discussed, and the issue was not brought up by Jesus. It is found in three parallel accounts in the synoptic gospels.[8] We are told that while he was in Jerusalem a group of Sadducees questioned Jesus about the resurrection, even though they ridiculed the idea of a bodily resurrection themselves. If the gospel stories are accurate, Jesus was quite familiar with the Pharisaic position and accepted their concept of a physical resurrection.

Several members of the Sadducean elite came to Jesus and posed a hypothetical situation based on a Jewish law in the book of Deuteronomy

6. 1 Corinthian 15:20
7. John 11:1–44
8. Matthew 22:23–33; Mark 12:18–27; Luke 20:27–39

that was intended to provide for the support of a widow and to retain her dead husband's property within her husband's family unit. The text stated:

> *When brothers live together, and one of them dies without a son, the widow of the deceased shall not marry anyone outside the family; but her husband's brother shall go to her and perform the duty of a brother-in-law by marrying her.*[9]

The Sadducees presented Jesus with this unlikely situation: a young woman marries seven brothers in turn, failing to give birth to children each time, and survives every brother until her own eventual death. The Sadducees then asked Jesus, "In the resurrection, whose wife of the seven will she be?"[10] Here is the response Jesus gave according to Mark's gospel:

> *Jesus answered them, "You are wrong, because you know neither the scriptures nor the power of God. For in the resurrection they neither marry nor are given in marriage, but are like angels in heaven. And as for the resurrection of the dead, have you not read what was said to you by God, 'I am the God of Abraham, the God of Isaac, and the God of Jacob'? He is God not of the dead, but of the living." And when the crowd heard it, they were astounded at his teaching.*[11]

Astounded? Probably bumfoozled is more like it. However, Jesus makes two points. The first seems to be that after the earthly resurrection the institution of marriage would no longer exist and everyone would be chaste and celibate. This idea would have been a great disappointment to Mark Twain (1835–1910) who believed that most folks would be extremely bored with an everlasting existence of harps and wings and stated that if heaven was to be sought after and desired, it would consist of eternal orgasm.

Eugene Peterson paraphrases the idea expressed by Jesus in Mark's gospel:

> *You're way off base, and here's why: One, you don't know your Bibles; two, you don't know how God works. After the dead are raised up, we're past the marriage business. As it is with angels now, all our ecstasies and intimacies then will be with God.*[12]

In his second point, Jesus refers to the story in Exodus where Moses encountered God in a burning bush on Mount Sinai.

---

9. Deuteronomy 25:5–10
10. Mark 12:18–27, Matthew 22:23–33, Luke 20:27–40
11. Mark 12:24–27
12. Peterson, *The Message*, 104.

> *Elohim called to him out of the bush, "Moses, Moses!" And he said, "Here I am." Then he said, "Come no closer! Remove the sandals from your feet, for the place on which you are standing is holy ground." He said further, "I am the God of your father, the God of Abraham, the God of Isaac, and the God of Jacob."*[13]

Observing that the words of God were in the present tense, Jesus tells the Sadducees that the living God is a God of the living, not of the dead. His meaning is that the great patriarchs of the past continue to live in some way—that they are still present—at least in memory.

It is difficult to know what to make out of this exchange about the end of marriage in the resurrection, about resurrected bodies being celibate or angelic in nature, and the reference to the living patriarchs. But if this is all that Jesus really had to say about the topic, I think we should move on and accept that it was not at the core of his message.

In spite of what Jesus thought or said, in the centuries after his death Christian theologians began to integrate classical Greek philosophy into Christian thinking and belief. The idea that the mortal human body is inhabited by an immortal soul was adopted by a church that was rapidly moving away from its Jewish roots. At death, some Hellenistic theologians now speculated, there is a separation between the body and the soul. In Greek thought, only the soul lived on. For Jews, however, death and resurrection were about a completely integrated body. In letters to his newly established churches, the Apostle Paul was dealing with blended communities of Jews and gentiles. Thus, he tried to blend their concepts about the afterlife—a disembodied soul lasting forever and an integrated body/soul being resurrected. He speculated that in our resurrected state we will have "spiritual" bodies, but never tries to define it or explain it.

> *So it is with the resurrection of the dead. What is sown is perishable, what is raised is imperishable. It is sown in dishonor, it is raised in glory. It is sown in weakness, it is raised in power. It is sown a physical body, it is raised a spiritual body. If there is a physical body, there is also a spiritual body.*[14]

As you read Paul's developing theology, it seems as if he was working out radically new ideas as he wrote, trying to find a balance somehow between Jewish integrated physical realities and pagan separated spiritual realities in his resurrection schema. But remember, all of this theological speculation is purely Paul, not Jesus. As someone once said, it seems as if

---

13. Exodus 3:4–6
14. 1 Corinthians 15:42–44

Paul was constantly tap-dancing, improvising a theology that would work in the empire's diverse Hellenistic context, bringing Jews and gentiles together. Paul's religious concepts ignored the historical Jesus in favor of his newly minted apocalyptic Christ.

As a result, the curious Christian ideas about the resurrection of dead bodies, the existence of a separate eternal soul, and an afterlife in a heavenly realm in the sky are a mixture of very different concepts that Paul and later Hellenistic Christian theologians managed to blend together in complete disregard to what Jesus taught. The idea of resurrected bodies being transported to a heavenly realm is simply not a sound biblical concept and was certainly never espoused by Jesus.

But once the idea of a resurrected afterlife was introduced to Christianity, the discussion of what happens to the soul at the point of death was open to even more speculation. Does the disembodied soul go immediately to heaven? When does the soul's assignment to heaven or hell occur? Is there a preliminary judgment at death and a final judgment later? Does the soul go to a waiting place, like purgatory, for a period of time? Are the body and the soul reunited when Christ returns? Are they brought together for an earthly existence or a heavenly existence? What kind of bodies will we have in the resurrection? Will they be physical or will they be spiritual? Will our resurrected bodies be perfect? Will my need for orthodontia be resolved? Will I have a perfect Body Mass Index or will I still be overweight? There is no general agreement on any of these questions about body and soul in the resurrection because there are simply no sound biblical bases to support any of this speculation other than Paul's fertile imagination and our own wish fulfillment.

In the end, our various understandings of what happens after death are simply human inventions to satisfy a natural human longing that life should not end at death. These understandings also fulfill a basic human need for justice—the need to believe that undeserved suffering on earth will be reversed in heaven, that the evil which flourishes here will be punished in an afterlife, and that faithfulness in the face of persecution will somehow be rewarded.

eternal life

The third major confusion about a heavenly afterlife comes from the phrase *eternal life* in the gospels. In several parallel accounts, Jesus was questioned by a rich young man (or a wealthy ruler) about how to obtain this kind of life. The essence of the conversation is summed up in this question and answer.

> *Then someone came to him [Jesus] and said, "Teacher, what good deed must I do to have eternal life?" ... And he [Jesus] said to him ... "If you wish to enter into life, keep the commandments."*[15]

The question about eternal life seems quite normal to modern ears conditioned by two thousand years of Christian theology. Its meaning seems obvious. We understand the question to be about life after death, a life that lasts for eternity. But for a first-century Jew, the question held a very different meaning. And the meaning becomes evident in Jesus' answer that entering into life—a real life, an authentic life, a fuller life, and a more meaningful life—can be experienced in the here and now.

Once again, English translations can lead to misunderstandings. The Greek phrase often rendered as "eternal life" is *zoen aionion* (*zoh-een' ah-hee-ohn'-ee-ohn*). The phrase is used frequently in the New Testament, especially in the gospel of John. The Greek word for "life" is *zoe* (*zoh-ee'*). The adjective *aionion* (*ah-hee-ohn'-ee-ohn*) comes from the Greek root *aiōn* (*ah-hee-ohn'*) meaning "age." It is sometimes used in Greek writing to mean everlasting—in the sense of something that goes on for ages and ages with no end—but more frequently refers to a specific age, a period of time, one of a succession of epochs in history. In this usage, it is not a reference to a never-ending life, but rather describes a type of life pertaining to a specific period or eon.

The New Testament biblical writers thought in terms of present and future eons—the "present age" and an "age to come." For centuries, Christians have viewed the age to come as the final consummation of the kingdom of God at the end of history. This is the age of the new heaven and new earth as pictured in Revelation. But the kingdom of God, according to Jesus, is experienced in the present, not the future. For Jesus, the age to come was invading, displacing, and disrupting the present age in the here and now.

Walter Wink discusses the term *aiōn* (*ah-hee-ohn'*) in his book *Engaging the Powers*. According to Wink, the New Testament writers saw the present age as the rule of the domination system—the combination of social, political, and economic structures that assure that a selfish minority will prosper at the exploitation of the vast majority. The age to come is the vision of the long-awaited in-breaking reign of God. The "age to come" is what we pray for in the Lord's Prayer when we say "may your kingdom come ... on

---

15. Matthew 19:16–17. See parallels in Matthew 19:16–22; Mark 10:17–22; Luke 18:18–23.

earth" in the midst of this colossal human mess. So, for Jesus eternal life was a reference to the life of the age to come, the life of the new age, the life of the reign of God that is breaking in here on earth.

In the teachings of Jesus, the reign of God is already present among us, but it has not fully replaced the present age of the domination system—not by a long shot. The image we need to keep in our heads is not that one age ends and then another begins, but rather that there is an overlap, with the two ages living together in tremendous tension and conflict. Hopefully, the present age is diminishing in power and the age to come is growing. But this is not assured. It all depends on us and what we do or fail to do.

For Jesus, *zoen aionion* (*zoh-een' ah-hee-ohn'-ee-ohn*) was not about life after death, but rather a quality of life experienced now—a life centered in the love of God and love of one's neighbor as represented by the two great commandments. This is the kind of life that characterizes the kingdom of God, experienced in the present. According to Jesus, we don't have to die first to experience a life immersed in the kind of love that God represents. It is available in the present through a different kind of focus, priority, concern, and action. Eternal life—the life of the age to come—reflects a very different set of concerns than we normally encounter in our acquisitive, self-centered, self-immersed culture.

By far, the largest number of references to eternal life are found in John's gospel—sixteen of them. This includes the famous verse "For God so loved the world that he gave his one and only Son, that whoever trusts in him shall not perish but have eternal life."[16] But John defines eternal life in this way:

> *And this is eternal life: that they may know you, the only true God, and Jesus Christ whom you have sent.* [17]

Marcus Borg once commented on this verse in a sermon:

> *To know God is eternal life, to know God in the present is to participate in the life of the age to come, here and now . . . At the center of John's Gospel is this affirmation that it is possible to know God in the here and now, and that knowing is the life of the age to come.*[18]

The gospel of John provides another understanding of this movement into eternal life.

16. John 3:16
17. John 17:3
18. Marcus Borg, sermon at Calvary Episcopal Church, Memphis, TN on March 16, 2001. Online: http://www.explorefaith.org/LentenHomily03.16.01.html.

resurrection and eternal life

> *I tell you the truth, whoever hears my word and trusts him who sent me has eternal life and will not be condemned; he has crossed over from death to life.*[19]

John's gospel says that eternal life is a crossing over from death to life in *this* life. It begins now. It is not a *future* state, but a *present* one. The Greek word translated as death in this passage is *thanatos* (*thahn'-ah-tos*). It has several meanings. First, it refers to the death of the body. But it can also be used metaphorically to refer to the state of one's existential condition. Metaphorical death is living in captivity to one's culture, consumed by values that separate us from the reign of God and the welfare of our neighbors, as exemplified by the current politics of selfishness in the United States. Listening and responding to the words of Jesus and trusting in the values of the reign of God enable us to cross over from this kind of death to a new kind of life. Eternal life is a compassionate response to the world of suffering.

In John's gospel, eternal life is the result of trusting in Jesus, specifically the Way of Jesus—a new way of living. This kind of life is found when we immerse our lives in the reign of God—a politics of love and compassion focused on our neighbor and the common good. Eternal life is a life engaged in the values of the coming age while we are surrounded by the powers of death that rule the present age. It is not a life after death, but a life lived in a world where we are encompassed by death. It is life lived with courage and hope in the midst of a world of death and suffering and oppression. It refers to a different *kind* of life, a different *quality* of life that is radically different from the everyday life of our culture. The great challenge of human existence is to allow our existence to be transformed into a real life, a life that is full, whole, and abundant. "I came that they may have life, and have it abundantly," said Jesus.[20]

The Scholars Version of the gospels produced by the Jesus Seminar substitutes the word "real" for "eternal" in these texts in the sense that Jesus was talking about *real* life, an authentic life, a genuine life, not the self-centered delusion that passes for life in our culture. According to John's gospel, Jesus offers us the *waters of real life* and the *food of real life*. And John quotes Peter as saying that Jesus has the *words of real life*.[21] How we obtain real life, however, is clear—by loving God and our neighbor, demonstrating that self-giving love by acts of compassion toward our brothers and sisters in need. Love, kindness, compassion, generosity, joy, and truth—these are

---

19. John 5:24
20. John 10:10
21. John 4:14, John 6:27, John 6:68

the things that are eternal. They will never perish. And these are the things that transform mere existence into life.

my Father's house

In the end, there are only about two references in the gospels that can be viewed as indications that Jesus proclaimed a heavenly reward to his followers after their deaths. (In contrast, approximately one hundred references to the earthly kingdom of God are at the center of Jesus' proclamation.)

In John's gospel, Jesus reportedly described God's dwelling place as a kind of condo complex with (depending on the translation) many abodes, homes, mansions, or resting places.

> *In my Father's house there are many dwelling places. If it were not so, would I have told you that I go to prepare a place for you? And if I go and prepare a place for you, I will come again and will take you to myself, so that where I am, there you may be also.*[22]

To begin, we must preface any words of Jesus found in the gospel of John with a caveat. John's gospel was the last of the canonical gospels to be written. It is largely composed of the author's thoughts about Jesus many decades after the crucifixion. He ponders what Jesus might say to the church of his day. And that is what he writes. So John's gospel reflects a lot of John's voice and only a little of the authentic voice of the historic Jesus. It is clearly a much more highly developed theological construct than the previous gospels and begins the centuries-long process of both glorifying Jesus and dehumanizing him.

The author of John's gospel clearly believed that Jesus came from heaven and had returned there. John's message to the followers of Jesus was that if Jesus was now in heaven, they could eventually follow him there also. The use of the phrase "my Father's house" is interesting because earlier in John's gospel, the same expression was used by Jesus to refer to the Jerusalem temple, not to heaven. Jesus used the term as he drove the money-changers and those selling sacrificial animals from the temple courts.

> *He told those who were selling the doves, "Take these things out of here! Stop making my Father's house a marketplace!"* [23]

John's gospel stands apart from the synoptic gospels of Matthew, Mark, and Luke in a much more theologically sophisticated understanding of Jesus

22. John 14:2–4
23. John 2:16

and was clearly pointing toward him as a divine being in heaven. John was a sincere follower of Jesus, but I sometimes think that reading John's gospel to understand the authentic historical Jesus is like watching Fox News to understand the realities of current politics. There is such a strong bias toward a certain point of view that getting at the historic truth is nearly impossible.

paradise

One of the most often quoted verses to support the contention that Jesus believed in an eternal life in heaven after death is found in Luke's account of the crucifixion.

> *One of the criminals who were hanged there kept deriding him and saying, "Are you not the Messiah? Save yourself and us!" But the other rebuked him, saying, "Do you not fear God, since you are under the same sentence of condemnation? And we indeed have been condemned justly, for we are getting what we deserve for our deeds, but this man has done nothing wrong." Then he said, "Jesus, remember me when you come into your kingdom." He replied, "Truly I tell you, today you will be with me in Paradise."*[24]

The word *paradise* derives from a Persian term for a walled enclosure surrounding a private park, orchard, or garden. Although the Hebrew Bible did not use this word in reference to the Garden of Eden, it became associated with that image. In later rabbinic thought there were two Paradises, one in Sheol for humanity and the other in Heaven for the heavenly court. Rabbinic literature sometimes uses "paradise" as a general expression referring to "after death."

We find only two other references to paradise in the New Testament. One is a completely bizarre passage by St. Paul:

> *I know a person in Christ who fourteen years ago was caught up to the third heaven—whether in the body or out of the body I do not know; God knows. And I know that such a person—whether in the body or out of the body I do not know; God knows—was caught up into paradise and heard things that are not to be told, that no mortal is permitted to repeat.*[25]

Finally, in Revelation, these words are directed to the church at Ephesus:

---

24. Luke 23:39–43
25. 2 Corinthians 12:3

> *Let anyone who has an ear listen to what the spirit is saying to the churches. To everyone who conquers, I will give permission to eat from the tree of life that is in the paradise of God.*[26]

The crucifixion passage in Luke's gospel is the only time Jesus mentions paradise in any of the four gospels. As the commentary on this passage in the Scholars Version says, "This saying seems out of character for Jesus." And that is the major point regarding *any* reference to a heavenly afterlife in the gospels—it is not characteristic of Jesus, his message, or his mission.

asleep in the grave

The idea that the immortal soul has an immediate entry into heaven or hell after death derives primarily from Medieval Roman Catholic theology based on the writings of Greek philosophers. The concept was later refuted by Protestant reformers in the fifteenth century, yet today it is generally accepted as a common belief by many Christians regardless of denomination.

According to centuries-old Catholic teachings, immediately after death a person undergoes a divine judgment in which the soul's eternal destiny is determined. Some disembodied souls are united with God in heaven, while others are separated from God in hell, often envisioned as a place of never-ending torment. In addition, Catholicism envisions a third state. Those souls that are not sufficiently free from the consequences of sin must first be cleansed through an intermediate state of purgatory—a process of purification—before they can be united with God. Regardless, the dead soul is immediately conscious after death and finds itself in purgatory, heaven, or hell.

Martin Luther objected to these teachings, especially the concept of purgatory. But he further refuted the idea that the soul is immediately conscious after death. And he believed that there is only one judgment—a final judgment at the end of time—that will determine the soul's fate. Luther conceived the state of the dead as a deep, dreamless sleep, removed from time and space, without consciousness and without feeling until the general resurrection at Christ's apocalyptic second coming.

> *For just as one who falls asleep and reaches morning unexpectedly when he awakes, without knowing what has happened to him, we shall suddenly rise on the last day without knowing how we have come into death and through death. We shall sleep until He comes*

---

26. Revelation 2:7

and knocks on the little grave and says, 'Doctor Martin, get up!' Then I shall rise in a moment and be with him forever.[27]

Anglican bishop N. T. (Tom) Wright (b. 1948) tries to balance these Catholic and Protestant ideas, suggesting that the sleeping soul is always conscious. He contends that the references to God's many heavenly motel rooms and the immediate access to paradise are descriptions of a temporary dwelling place, a kind of interim way station where the soul survives until the bodily resurrection on earth. He summarizes his ideas in this way:

> *In the Bible we are told that you die, and enter an intermediate state . . . We know that we will be with God and with Christ, resting and being refreshed. Paul writes that it will be conscious, but compared with being bodily alive, it will be like being asleep.*
>
> *Secondly, our physical state. The New Testament says that when Christ does return, the dead will experience a whole new life: not just our soul, but our bodies.*[28]

But Wright clarifies that after the resurrection of the dead, the body and soul will not go to heaven to be with Jesus. Jesus will instead return to the earth.

> *And finally, the location. At no point do the resurrection narratives in the four Gospels say, "Jesus has been raised, therefore we are all going to heaven." It says that Christ is coming here, to join together the heavens and the Earth in an act of new creation.*
>
> *What the New Testament really says is God wants you to be a renewed human being helping him to renew his creation, and his resurrection was the opening bell. And when he returns to fulfill the plan, you won't be going up there to him, he'll be coming down here . . . Never at any point do the Gospels or Paul say Jesus has been raised, therefore we are all going to heaven. They all say, Jesus is raised, therefore the new creation has begun, and we have a job to do.*[29]

In Tom Wright's vision of how things will happen in the resurrection, a heavenly afterlife amidst the clouds is not a part of our future. It's all about creating heaven on earth.

---

27. Kantonen, *The Christian Hope*, 37. From a sermon given by Luther on September 28, 1533.

28. David Van Biema, "Christians Wrong About Heaven, Says Bishop." *Time* (February 7, 2008). Online: http:// content.time.com/time/world/article/0,8599,1710844,00.html.

29. Ibid.

I think Wright understands the Apostle Paul correctly. This is essentially what Paul says in the letter we call First Thessalonians. It is the earliest Christian writing we have, dating from within twenty years of Jesus' death. The community at Thessalonica was concerned that some among them had died and they wanted to know what would happen to these dead friends when Jesus returned. Paul describes the dead as having fallen asleep, presumably in an unconscious state in Sheol or Hades, but does not suggest that they are dwelling in heaven with God and Jesus. Quite the opposite.

> *But we do not want you to be uninformed, brothers and sisters, about those who have fallen asleep, so that you may not grieve as others do who have no hope. For since we believe that Jesus died and rose again, even so, through Jesus, God will bring with him those who have fallen asleep. For this we declare to you by the word of the Lord, that we who are alive, who are left until the coming of the Lord, will by no means precede those who have fallen asleep. For the Lord himself, with a cry of command, with the archangel's call and with the sound of God's trumpet, will descend from heaven, and the dead in Christ will rise first. Then we who are alive, who are left, will be caught up in the clouds together with them to meet the Lord in the air; and so we will be with the Lord forever.*[30]

The process of resurrection that Paul describes works like this. With a great deal of fanfare, Jesus descends from heaven to initiate the general resurrection of the dead. As he is coming down, the dead will rise first from their graves and will join Jesus in the sky. Then, the living too will rise to greet him in the clouds. Together, they will all descend to earth to begin a new age of resurrected earthly life which will presumably last forever.

Biblical scholar John Dominic Crossan (b. 1934) once explained the schema something like this. Paul's imagery is similar to that of an imperial visit to a city or town in the empire. As the emperor draws near, heralds sound trumpets to notify the citizens of his approach. The people then come out of the city to greet the emperor on the road. As he approaches, the first thing he passes are the tombs of the dead on the outskirts of the town. Then he encounters the elated townspeople who come out to greet him. Together, they enter the town in a celebratory procession. Now imagine turning this scene from a horizontal axis to a vertical one and you have the description in Thessalonians.

That's the resurrection of the dead in a nutshell. The Apostle Paul never says that a life in heaven awaits; only a renewed life here on earth. Prior to

---

30. 1 Thessalonians 5:13–17

the resurrection, he never suggests that the dead are in heaven smiling down on us. He doesn't picture them pursuing their favorite activities in the presence of God. They are asleep—presumably unconscious—buried under the ground. That's the biblical picture. I'm sure if people really understood this creative scenario of Paul's imagination, they would be deeply disappointed. This isn't how most people imagine the afterlife. Heaven, halos, wings, and harps aren't part of the story.

But even if we understand Paul's concept correctly, it still isn't part of Jesus' teachings. Jesus was focused almost entirely on the here and now on this side of the grave. Beyond that, in terms of what happens after death, Jesus was quite vague. Vagueness, ambiguity, mystery, and unknowing are probably all we can really understand about death.

the final question

Sam Keen (b. 1931), author of the book *Hymns to an Unknown God*, reflected on the recurring questions about death from the perspective of one who has rejected pat answers and is seeking a fresh approach to life's mysteries. In a chapter entitled "Death: the Final Question" he says:

> *We might write the history of religion as the story of the variety of ways in which humans have denied death and affirmed that in some way we outlive our brief moment in time.*
>
> *Radical honesty requires us to acknowledge that we do not know what happens to us following death. We can know neither that we will survive in some new form, nor that we will be obliterated . . . Our dignity as human beings has something to do with our willingness to abide joyfully in the ignorance of our ultimate destiny.*[31]

Keen then quotes from writer Stephen Batchelor (b. 1953) who comments from a Buddhist perspective:

> *It is often felt that there are two options: one can believe in another life after death or not believe in it. But there is a third alternative: to acknowledge in all honesty that one does not know. One does not have either to assert it or to deny it; one neither has to adopt the literal versions presented by tradition nor fall into the extreme of believing that death is a final annihilation.*
>
> *To opt for a comforting, even a discomforting, explanation of what brought us here or what awaits us after death severely*

---

31. Keen, *Hymns to an Unknown God*, 249, 256.

> *limits that very sense of mystery with which religion is essentially concerned.*[32]

Keen then continues:

> *All symbols of the afterlife—heaven, reincarnation, resurrection of the body, immortality of the soul—if taken as anything more than a stuttering attempt to sing a song of hope into the silent darkness, foster illusions . . .*
>
> *In the luminous darkness through which we travel on our human journey, we are often lonely but never alone. Road-weary, overwhelmed by the magnitude of the difficulties we face during our brief days, we are tempted to despair or to settle for cheap optimism. But in the deep place of the spirit, we are moved and called forth to undertake this ongoing adventure by the yearning, restless, and creative One who—though called by many names—is still clothed in marvelous silence.*[33]

---

32. Ibid, 256. Keen is quoting from Stephen Batchelor's article "Rebirth: A Case for Buddhist Agnosticism," *Triangle: The Buddhist Review* (Fall 1992).

33. Ibid, 257, 259.

PART 3
reformation

CHAPTER 10

a God of love

I am God, says Love, for Love is God and God is Love.[1]
—MARGUERITE DE PORETE (C. 1249–1310)

Arthur Gibson (1922–1980), who taught theology at St. Michael's College at the University of Toronto, is the author of *The Silence of God: a Creative Response to the Films of Ingmar Bergman*. Bergman (1918–2007) directed 50 films and won seven Academy Awards in a career that stretched over half a century. Gibson's book is an analysis of seven films by the Swedish director. When this entire body of work is viewed as a whole, Gibson finds a shift over time from a God who is portrayed as distant and silent or who simply does not exist, to a God who is intimately present in the form of one's neighbor.

> There is the felt absence [of God] growing gradually throughout the course of the seven films into a more terribly felt presence... At the beginning, there is a silence that is held to be the proof of God's inexistence. At the end, there is a still more awful silence which reveals itself as the true silence of God. The God imagined to be nonexistent because silent, reveals his face as precisely the ultimate respecter of human freedom, whose unflinching rendezvous with man is a supremely immanent or incarnational one... The radically simplified problematic of the entire series, regarded as a solidary unit, might be stated thus. The initial questioning demands: Is God there? And the terminal answer retorts: No, now he is here![2]

1. de Porete, *The Mirror of Simple Souls*, 104.
2. Gibson, *The Silence of God*, 13–14.

In Bergman's films, we gradually become aware that people are looking for God in all the wrong places. As the characters cry out to the empty universe, God is present right beside them in the form of a friend, a family member, or even a stranger.

The Christian doctrine of the incarnation has long held that the supernatural theistic God was incarnate in Jesus Christ—God made flesh in Jesus. The terms *incarnate* and *incarnation* comes from the Latin *incarnatus* (*in-car-nah'-toos*), which means "making flesh." Think of the word *carnal*—things of the flesh—or even of *chili con carne*—chili with meat. But in Bergman's vision, God is incarnate in the neighbor, God is ultimately incarnate in everyone. It gives new meaning to the Hebrew term *Immanuel*—"God [is] with us." In addition to seeing God's presence in those around us, incarnation means we must also look for God's presence within ourselves.

a God who dwells among us

Near the end of the Bible, in the book of Revelation, we find images and metaphors intended to communicate that God would vindicate faithful martyrs and violently punish their oppressors. Although redemptive violence is a major theme, a few more positive images emerge. The author, who we know as John of Patmos, describes the image of a new city of Jerusalem descending from the heavens to the earth.

> *Then I saw a new heaven and a new earth; for the first heaven and the first earth had passed away, and the sea was no more. And I saw the holy city, the new Jerusalem, coming down out of heaven from God, prepared as a bride adorned for her husband. And I heard a loud voice from the throne saying,*
>
> *"See, the home of God is among mortals.*
>   *He will dwell with them;*
>   *they will be his peoples,*
>   *and God himself will be with them;*
> *he will wipe every tear from their eyes.*
>   *Death will be no more;*
>   *mourning and crying and pain will be no more,*
>   *for the first things have passed away."*[3]

---

3. Revelation 21:1–4

Then, in John's apocalyptic vision, an angel measures the city, which is shaped like a cube fifteen hundred miles in each dimension.[4] The cubic shape of the city reflects the configuration of the inner sanctum of the temple of Herod in Jerusalem before its destruction in 70 CE. The Holy of Holies, as it was called, had a cubic interior space of about thirty-four feet on a side. For the Hebrew people, this was the dwelling place of God on earth. In comparison, the cube-shaped city described in Revelation is almost incomprehensible in its scope.

The message at the end of the book was that humanity was now to be the dwelling place for God. The new city of Jerusalem was the author's metaphor for the church, not the institutional church which did not yet exist—but instead a symbol for the people of God in the Jesus movement. Rather than a transcendent God somewhere out there, the message was that God now dwells among us on earth.[5] God's presence among us is a source of hope and courage in the face of despair.

I like Eugene Peterson's (b. 1932) paraphrase of this passage:

> *Look! Look! God has moved into the neighborhood, making his home with men and women!* [6]

This is a different way of looking at incarnation. Rather than a transcendent God being incarnated in one special person—Jesus, God is now imagined as incarnate in everyone. God has become one with humanity. God is part of each of us, a sacred spark at the core of every human being, a divine presence hidden deep within.

For countless centuries, humans have located God outside of themselves. But, a theology of incarnation locates God within. In theological circles, this is a classic argument about the nature of God: one side views God as wholly transcendent—existing apart from us outside of creation—while a contrasting view sees God as wholly immanent—dwelling within creation, no longer external to our world. The word *immanent* comes from the Latin *in manere* (*in mah'-neh-reh*), which means "to remain within." Incarnation takes it a step further, locating God specifically within human flesh.

In *The First Coming: How the Kingdom of God Became Christianity*, Thomas Sheehan (b. 1941) proposes that Jesus' proclamation of the reign of God, and his reference to God by the intimate word *abba* (an Aramaic word that some scholars claim is equivalent to "papa" or "daddy"), was a message that God had wholly identified with God's people. And Sheehan proposes

---

4. Revelation 21:15–21
5. Revelation 21:3
6. Peterson, *The Message*, 544.

that the reign of God is the term that describes the incarnation of God in humanity.

> *Jesus proclaimed a loving Father who was already arriving among his people, bringing peace and freedom and joy. One simply had to let him in, for the kingdom of God had begun ... As Jesus preached it, the kingdom of God ... meant God's act of reigning, and this meant—here lay the revolutionary force of Jesus' message—that God, as God, had wholly identified himself with his people. The reign of God meant the incarnation of God ... The radicalness of Jesus' message consisted in its implied proclamation of the end of religion, taken as the bond between two separate and incommensurate entities called "God" and "man." That is, Jesus destroyed the notion of "God-in-himself" and put in its place the experience of "God-with-mankind." Henceforth, according to the prophet from Galilee, the Father was not to be found in a distant heaven but was entirely identified with the cause of men and women. Jesus' doctrine of the kingdom meant that God had become incarnate: He had poured himself out, had disappeared into mankind, and could be found nowhere else but there ... The doctrine of the kingdom meant that henceforth and forever God was present only in and as one's neighbor ... His proclamation marked the death of religion and religion's God and heralded the beginning of the post-religious experience: the abdication of "God" in favor of his hidden presence among human beings.*[7]

Sheehan's assertion that God is now "present only in and as one's neighbor," gives renewed emphasis to the idea that to love God and to love your neighbor are the same thing. The *only* way to love God is to love your neighbor, because the dwelling place of God is within that person.

In *God in Us*, Anthony Freeman (b. 1946), an Anglican priest, has said:

> *Organized religion has relied upon there being a gulf between heaven and earth to give it a purpose: the church's main reason for existing is to bridge this gap, to provide a means of communication between God and his world. In the one direction, it carries all official messages from God ... In the other direction it is the official channel of effective prayer to God ... Nothing is so calculated to upset this coy arrangement as the news that the gap does not exist.*[8]

---

7. Sheehan, *The First Coming*, 58–62.
8. Freeman, *God in Us*, 35.

a god of love

For Freeman, the biblical passage that illuminates the closing of the gap is the story of Pentecost in the book of Acts when God's spirit is poured out on the followers of Jesus.

> *When the day of Pentecost had come, they were all together in one place. And suddenly from heaven there came a sound like the rush of a violent wind, and it filled the entire house where they were sitting. Divided tongues, as of fire, appeared among them, and a tongue rested on each of them. All of them were filled with the Holy Spirit and began to speak in other languages, as the Spirit gave them ability.* [9]

When crowds attracted by the sound accused the followers of Jesus of being drunk on new wine, the apostle Peter replied:

> *Men of Judea and all who live in Jerusalem, let this be known to you, and listen to what I say. Indeed, these are not drunk, as you suppose, for it is only nine o'clock in the morning. No, this is what was spoken through the prophet Joel:*
>
>> *In the last days it will be, God declares,*
>> *that I will pour out my spirit upon all flesh,*
>> *and your sons and your daughters shall prophesy,*
>> *and your young men shall see visions,*
>> *and your old men shall dream dreams.*
>> *Even upon my slaves, both men and women,*
>> *in those days I will pour out my spirit;*
>> *and they shall prophesy.* [10]

According to this story, the spirit of God is now being spread out among all humanity, not just on the followers of Jesus in Jerusalem, but "upon all flesh," meaning everyone—every human being of every creed. The gospels describe the spirit of God descending on Jesus at his baptism at the Jordan River.[11] And in the book of Acts, the same thing happens to the followers of Jesus—they are filled with the spirit of God. According to Freeman, "What had seemed unique to Jesus—the bringing together of God and man—is now made completely democratic."[12]

One's interpretation of this biblical account depends on one's understanding of the meaning of God's spirit. If we accept traditional theological

---

9. Acts 2:1–4
10. Acts 2:14–18
11. Mark 1:10–11, Matthew 3:16–17, Luke 3:21–22, John 1:32–33
12. Freeman, *God in Us*, 5.

interpretations that the spirit is a person-like being apart from humanity, then the spirit of God is an external power. But if the spirit is seen as the essence of God that dwells within each of us, then it becomes possible to realize that the essence of God has been within humanity all along. Experiencing the transformative power of the spirit of God involves drawing forth that essence from within ourselves, not receiving it from an external dimension.

Walter Wink came to a similar conclusion that God dwells with and within humanity, but from a different biblical tack. In *The Human Being: Jesus and the Enigma of the Son of the Man*, Wink addresses the Genesis claim that humanity is created in the image of God.

> *To say that we humans are made in the image of God, male and female, means that we are somehow "like" God in our mundane existence. But we are not yet fully human. For now, we are only promissory notes, hints, intimations . . . If God is in some sense true humanness, then divinity inverts itself. Divinity is not a qualitatively different reality; quite the reverse, divinity is fully realized humanity. Only God is, as it were, Human. The goal of life, then, is not to become something we are not—divine—but to become what we truly are—human. We are not required to become divine: flawless, perfect, without blemish. We are invited simply to become human, which means growing through our sins and mistakes, learning by trial and error, being redeemed over and over from compulsive behavior—becoming ourselves, scars and all. It means embracing and transforming those elements in us that we find unacceptable. It means giving up pretending to be good and, instead, becoming real.*[13]

God as love

A remarkable document in the New Testament, written about 70 years after the death of Jesus, took theological thinking in the early Christian community to a significantly new level. We have no idea who wrote the treatise that we now refer to as the first epistle or first letter of John. Some authorities claim that this writer is the same author who wrote the gospel of John, but without much evidence other than tradition to back that up. Although the writing style is different, the author of "First John" seems to have some familiarity with ideas expressed in the gospel of John and may have come from the same community as the gospel writer. Whoever he was, the author

---

13. Wink, *The Human Being*, 29.

of this letter developed an extraordinary theology sometime around the end of the first century.

Here is what he wrote:

> God is love, and he who abides in love abides in God, and God abides in him.[14]

As far as I know, the New Testament has only three definitions for God: God is spirit,[15] God is light,[16] and God is love.[17] The first definition comes from the gospel of John and the second two derive from the first letter of John. So these metaphors all may derive from the same community.

Both the Hebrew *ruach* (*roo'-akh*) and the Greek *pneuma* (*nyoo'-mah*) that we translate as "spirit" mean "breath." For the ancient biblical writers, God's breath was the foundational source of life. They saw the breath of God as the animating force that gave life to the first humans and as the human essence that evaporates when we die. God as "light" probably refers to the gift of human enlightenment—innovative insights or new ways of thinking about life's purpose and meaning. But "love" is perhaps the most significant definition for God. Spirit, as breath, gives us life. It enables our very existence. Enlightenment provides some of us with the insight to see our existence in deeper, more profound ways. But love is a power that has the potential to radically transform our lives. Of all the definitions of God, love is the highest, deepest, and most powerful force in human life. It is the energy that fosters human growth and change. Love is the impulse behind empathy and concern, and is the fuel that drives compassion and justice.

The God of love that this author describes is different than the transcendent God of the universe. God as love is a description of a fully human quality as a divine power. When we reverse the phrase to its complement—love is God—we truly begin to understand the profundity of the concept. For if love *is* God, then love is recognized as the relationship and activity at the depth of human existence in which we discover a divine reality. God is thus embodied in humanity in the human relationship of love. This is what the biblical writers meant when they declared that God has now made his dwelling within humanity. Love is that incarnation. God simply becomes the name we give to that deepest quality of our human experience.

14. 1 John 4:16

15. John 4:24, "God is spirit, and those who worship him must worship in spirit and truth."

16. 1 John 1:5, "God is light and in him there is no darkness at all."

17. 1 John 4:7–8, "Beloved, let us love one another, because love is from God; everyone who loves is born of God and knows God. Whoever does not love does not know God, for God is love."

When we say that love is God, the divine is no longer a *transcendent* reality somewhere outside of the known universe (supernatural theism), nor is God an *immanent* creative reality woven through the fabric of the cosmos (pantheism and panentheism), but instead God becomes an *incarnate* reality within our hearts, within our minds, within our relationships, and in our actions. Love is a reality that animates us, empowers us, and transforms us from self-centered and selfish individuals to selfless and self-giving people.

Paul Tillich defined religious faith as "the state of being grasped by an ultimate concern, a concern which qualifies all other concerns as preliminary and which itself contains the answer to the question of the meaning of life."[18] God, then, is whatever we see as an ultimate concern, that which matters most in life, our highest value. But some of our chief values and goals may not necessarily reflect the greatest depth of human existence. Love is qualitatively different from a value like truth or beauty or loyalty or honor. Love is our deepest human experience. Perhaps because love is so powerful, it convinces us of the presence of something greater than ourselves in life. If love for another is one's ultimate concern—that which matters most in life—then love becomes one's expression of God.

> *Beloved, let us love one another, for love is of God, and he who loves is born of God and knows God. He who does not love does not know God; for God is love.*[19]

> *If we love one another, God abides in us and his love is perfected in us.*[20]

The author of John's first letter tells us three things: 1) God is love; 2) love is the incarnation or indwelling of God in humanity; and 3) we know and experience God through the experience of human love.

Scholar Don Cupitt (b. 1935) has written:

> *In the New Testament, in the First Letter of John, we are told that the words Love and God are convertible. You can't slip a knife between them. If you love your fellow human being, you know God and are in God, whereas if you don't love, you don't know God . . . The word God doesn't designate a distinct metaphysical being; it is simply Love's name.*[21]

18. Tillich, *Dynamics of Faith*, 1–29.

19. 1 John 4:7–8

20. 1 John 4:12

21. Cupitt, "All you need is love" published by the Guardian newspaper in December 1994. It can be found on the Sea of Faith web site at http://www.sofn.org.uk/press/aynil.html .

Anglican Bishop John A. T. Robinson (1919–1983) said:

> *To assert that "God is love" is to believe that in love, one comes in touch with the most fundamental reality in the universe, that Being itself ultimately has this character.*[22]

I'm not sure about love being the most fundamental reality in the universe, but it is certainly at the center of human experience.

understanding love

Love is often defined as an emotion—a strong affection, a feeling of devotion, an attraction based on sexual desire, a deep feeling of passion, or an ecstatic enjoyment. But love is far more than our emotions, which are fleeting and exist only at the surface of our being. Someone has said that "love is not a feeling; love is a verb."

Love at its deepest level is an action, an activity, a commitment. True love is a self-giving and self-denying concern for another. One working definition is that love is "a choice to do what is best for another person." Love in a family involves caring for those we love—feeding, clothing, sheltering, and educating them. It means providing them with the means of life and growth.

In *The Road Less Traveled*, M. Scott Peck (1936–2005) says that love is the "will to extend one's self for the purpose of nurturing one's own or another's spiritual growth."[23] In human experience, love is a relationship that nurtures all kinds of growth—physical, psychological, and spiritual. So, I would modify Peck's definition to say that love is giving oneself to nurture another's full humanity, concerned with his or her healing, wholeness, growth, and transformation.

If God is human love in action, then the purpose of this divine love is to nurture human life and growth, healing and wholeness, change and transformation. The presence of divine love within us calls us to become fully-human agents of love in the life of the world.

The English phrase "God is love" is written in the Greek New Testament as *theos ein* agapē (*theh'-os ayn ag-ah'-pay*). Agapē (*ag-ah'-pay*) is one of four different Greek words which we translate into English as love. *Philia* (*fil-ee'-ah*) refers to loyal friendship or a brotherly love, *eros* (*err'-os*) is used to describe passionate erotic or romantic love, and *storgē* (*stor'-gay*) is used in relation to the natural affection of family love, like the love of a parent for a child. Most usages of the word agapē in ancient Greek literature come

---

22. Robinson, *Honest to God*, 53.
23. Peck, *The Road Less Traveled*, 85.

from the writings of the New Testament where it implies a self-giving love, often an unconditional love. This is the kind of love people saw in Jesus. And for the early Christian writers, it described the love of God.

Dietrich Bonhoeffer saw Jesus as "a man for others." John A. T. Robinson, commenting on Bonhoeffer's letters from prison said:

> *Jesus is "the man for others," the one in whom Love has completely taken over, the one who is utterly open to and united with, the Ground of his being... Because Christ was utterly and completely "the man for others," because he was love, he was one with the Father, because "God is love."*[24]

Bonhoeffer believed that following the Way of Jesus is the path to correct our self-centered individualism, because it involves a transformation from being men and women focused primarily on ourselves to becoming men and women for others. He said,

> *Our relation to God is not a religious relationship to a supreme Being, absolute in power and goodness, which is a spurious conception of transcendence, but a new life for others, through participation in the Being of God.*[25]

the radical love of Jesus

All too often the human perception—and that includes the average Christian perception—of love is very shallow. I once met a woman who blithely said, "I love everybody." It's very likely that she was engaged in a game of self-deception, but also likely that she had the most superficial understanding of love—a warm feeling of friendliness, a condescending generosity, or a gentle tolerance of the shortcomings of others. Our misunderstanding and confusion about the true nature of the love expressed in the life of Jesus may come from Sunday School images of Jesus gently cradling a small curly lamb or a smiling Jesus surrounded by little children. Sometimes we hear children's sermons on Sunday mornings that portray the message of Jesus as wholesome behavior: "Be nice to one another," "Share with your brother," or "Don't hit your sister." The meek and mild Jesus of the sweetness and light gospel is sometimes expressed in Christian hymns like *Jesus Loves the Little Children*, *Jesus Loves Me, This I Know*, and *Jesus, Lover of My Soul*. Many

---

24. Robinson, *Honest to God*, 76.
25. Ibid, 76.

adults have never gone beyond this childhood understanding of Jesus and do not comprehend the excessive love he advocated.

How little we understand the extreme love of Jesus. The love expressed in his life was a dangerous love. It was a radical love of one's enemies; a call to nonviolent resistance toward evil; an unending forgiveness toward those who have harmed us; an expansive generosity with those in need; an inviting inclusiveness with marginal and despised people; and a fundamental rejection of reciprocation of any kind—both good and evil. The excessive love of Jesus is an uncompromising love that moves us toward lives of reconciliation, forgiveness, peace, and justice in a hostile world. But, the passionate love that was taught and lived by Jesus is simply too threatening to a secure and comfortable way of life. Therefore, many Christians have tamed and domesticated Jesus until he has become a pallid, flaccid promoter of saccharine sweetness for our easy consumption. In a similar way, they have domesticated the fervent love of Jesus until it has no power to remake us into transformed people. We must never confuse the radical love of Jesus with being nice. A nice person will never change the world. Only an ardent lover has a chance to bring about the kingdom of God that Jesus proclaimed.

What we need is a much more powerful understanding and experience of a love that reorients our lives and transforms us into fully-human beings, fully-human agents of the selfless love we call God. If we allow it to be unleashed, the divine love within us will not let us remain the same. The radical love we see in Jesus pulls at us; it pushes and prods us out of our insular shells. It forces us to become more than we are, more than we are comfortable with, and ultimately all we are meant to be.

If we begin to think of God as love and love as God, new insights arise. The kingdom of God now becomes the kingdom of love. We now begin to ask what life would be like if love was in charge of our social relations. What would the world be like if selfless love dominated the common life of our families, societies, and nations? What if the radical love of Jesus determined the deliberations of Congress? What if a conspiracy of love was able to reshape our laws and institutions?

love as God

Marguerite de Porete (1249–1310), a medieval French mystic, saw the possibility of divinity in humanity when she wrote the surprisingly modern statement "I am God, says Love." We know little about Marguerite's life except that she was well educated and was associated with a lay monastic movement called the Beguines. Sometime between 1296 and 1306, she wrote *The Mirror of Simple Souls* that expressed her belief that when the human spirit is truly full of love, it is united with God. As someone filled with the presence of God's love, Marguerite concluded that she was one with God. She not only saw divinity *within* herself, but saw it manifested *as* herself. She was deeply influenced by the theology of John's letters. In response, Marguerite wrote:

> I am God, says Love, for Love is God and God is Love, and this Soul is God by the condition of Love. I am God by divine nature and this Soul is God by the condition of Love.[26]

The Medieval church became alarmed by Marguerite's writings. The idea that the human self could be in union with God—even though the idea was biblical—was deemed heretical. Known as *autotheism*—from the Greek *autos* (ow-tos'), meaning self and *theos* (theh'-os), meaning God—this heresy undermined the distinction between fallen humans and their creator. As a result, the concept denied the necessity of the church and its sacraments for salvation. Followers of autotheism believed that they could communicate directly with God and did not need the Roman Catholic Church for intercession. It is a faith without the need for brokers.

Marguerite believed that when one is united with God, one cannot sin. She reasoned that as God can do no evil and cannot sin, the human soul in perfect union with God is no longer capable of evil. Conversely, if one sins, one is not acting in union with the God of love. Again, she was influenced by the First Letter of John.

> Those who have been born of God do not sin, because God's seed abides in them; they cannot sin, because they have been born of God. The children of God and the children of the devil are revealed in this way: all who do not do what is right are not from God, nor are those who do not love their brothers and sisters.[27]

John's letter clearly disagrees with the theology of Augustine, suggesting that sin is not a human condition, it is a human act. This epistle states that when the presence of self-giving love is in one's heart and mind, one will not sin, one will continually strive to choose good over evil. That may be true, but to contend that the children of God *cannot* sin is a bit of a stretch. In spite of one's best efforts, sinful acts against others will occur, intentionally or unintentionally, by what we do and by what we leave undone. Right and wrong are sometimes clear choices, but not always. Life is complex. We are doing well when we navigate through life leaving behind as little damage

26. de Porete, *The Mirror of Simple Souls*, 104.

27. 1 John 3:9–10

as possible. The journey out of natural self-centeredness and selfishness and into self-giving love is a lifelong transformation and a daily struggle. Yet, it is this continual journey that leads us to become more fully human.

In 1310, a Dominican inquisitor put Marguerite de Porete on trial in Paris for her radical views about love and sin. A commission of twenty-one (male) theologians reviewed her writings and declared them heretical. Because she refused to recant, the church condemned her to death and Paris civic officials burned her at the stake. The church incinerated Marguerite because when one affirms that God is love, mediators between God and humanity no longer become necessary. A lot of traditional Christian theology gets thrown out of the window. Orthodoxy no longer holds up under this definition of God.

God as love does not exist as a disembodied reality in the universe. Love simply does not have that character. Love is not a thing, or a being, or even the source of all being. Love is a human relationship, pure and simple. The theological proposition in the First letter of John—that God is love—teaches us that in the relationship of unselfish self-giving love, we find the presence of God. It is there—in that humble yet profound human interaction—that we find ultimate reality.

Although some may assert that a loving relationship exists between humanity and a cosmic being separate from our world, it is impossible to verify that claim apart from rare ecstatic testimonies. In reality, love must be embodied in an inter-human relationship, in actions between one human and another. In other words, we should not look for God somewhere beyond the four dimensions of space and time. God is closer to home. We find God in those whom we love and those who love us. And, as Marguerite believed, we can find God within ourselves.

deconstructing traditional theology

How we see God is the foundation of our theological framework. A radical shift in that perspective can change everything. Rather than a supernatural being somewhere "out there" or the personification of a creative process in the universe, God is now revealed as an intimate part of each of us, a spark of self-giving love at the depth of one's existence. God is not a loving being; God is love itself.

To say that God is love changes everything in relation to traditional Christian theology. It calls for a wholesale revision or elimination of ancient doctrine, dogma, and creeds. It is a paradigm change of enormous magnitude. I suspect it will not go over well. Just ask Marguerite de Porete.

Nearly everything that the church has claimed about human salvation through the death and resurrection of Jesus no longer makes sense if God is love. If we no longer accept the God of supernatural theism, then a transcendent God did not send Jesus to the earth to die for our sins. Although generations of theologians have tried to make sense out of Jesus' humiliating death on the cross by imagining it as a sacrifice to God or a ransom to Satan, his execution was not unlike that of many other martyrs, now and then. Jesus was killed as a result of the way he lived and the message he preached. He did not die to settle a cosmic score with a holy and judgmental deity over original sin. When Jesus paid the ultimate price for his convictions, his followers saw it as an example of agape love taken to the fullest extent.

> *No one has greater love than this, to lay down one's life for one's friends.*[28]

a new image of God

So, some religious thinkers—both ancient and modern—believe that God has come to dwell with humanity. Indeed, God has become one with humanity. If God is not found at the heights of creation, but at the most profound depths of our being, then a new image of God emerges. Let's assume for the sake of argument that God is a human construct, as I suggested earlier. In the proposition that God is love, "God" becomes a language symbol that represents the deepest and best part of human nature—our capacity to love, fully and deeply.

In this theological viewpoint, *God is no longer transcendent*—out there, separate from us and our world. God is now incarnate—dwelling within the hearts and minds of human beings. *God is no longer omnipotent*—an all-powerful being. Now God is as weak and powerless as we are, as weak and powerless as Jesus was on the cross. *God is no longer impassive*—unfeeling and immune to emotion. God is now present with us in our suffering and joy, and is active in our love and compassion for others. *God no longer intervenes in the world* in some magical way. God now works through us to save, to heal, to comfort, and to establish justice and peace in this life. An incarnate *God is no longer supernatural*, but is instead very natural, embodied in our loving relationships. Many atheists and agnostics could conceivably embrace this understanding of divinity, since what they have reacted to with their position of disbelief or unknowing is the image of a supernatural, interventionist, theistic God dwelling apart from creation.

28. John 15:13

Of course, like any other image of God we cannot know if this theological construct is true. But if we act like God is within us and among us as we take on the divine task of caring for the welfare of all people and all life on earth, then we make it a reality. Like any image of God, it is only necessary to believe it—and to live like we mean it—to make it real in a tangible way.

This is a conception of God that can be meaningful for modern and postmodern people. It has biblical foundations, yet it doesn't restrict God to one tribe or religion on the earth. This is a God who lives within and among *all* people. This is an image of God that transcends every religion. Perhaps this is a concept of God that does away with religion altogether—the foundation of a "religionless Christianity" and a new faith for all of humanity.

Let's be clear. This does not imply that human beings are divine beings. Divine beings are simply human constructions from ancient times. Walter Wink has suggested that divinity should be viewed as fully-realized humanity, because the spark of love's presence within each of us is there, even if the full reality of that potential love has not yet manifested itself.

To become a fully-realized human being takes time and effort. In my own understanding, that is why following Jesus is important. Through following the example and teachings of Jesus, we can begin to approach our full human potential. That is why the followers of Jesus called it the Way. It is a way to become fully human. It is a way to experience the fullness of human life. It is a way to transform human community. It is a way to change the world.

the God of Jesus

In a previous chapter I said that in order to follow Jesus, we must take his relationship with God seriously. And in any attempt to understand God in the context of a postmodern world we should determine whether a newer image of God has any relation to the one that motivated, empowered, and infused the life of Jesus.

I think the God I have discovered in this journey has both similarities and differences with the God of Jesus. As to the differences, I'm sure that Jesus would never agree with me that God is a human construct or that God is a symbol or personification. He clearly saw God in very personal terms—as a welcoming, forgiving, compassionate father. Thus, he imagined God anthropomorphically. Where I see God as love itself; Jesus saw God as an empathic self-giving lover. The God that Jesus revealed invites us to love each other to a radical degree. Jesus became a radical lover because God was the pre-eminent radical lover in his life.

As for new definitions of a cosmic deity—God as the ground of being or as serendipitous creativity—I don't think Jesus would have given any credence to those ideas, if he could have even wrapped his head around the concepts. What, if anything, came before the Big Bang was not an issue for Jesus or his generation. Although Jesus didn't know what we know about the creation of the universe, he did know about love and the lack of it on earth. Jesus fully embraced life and love, and challenged us to experience it more fully. So if you spoke to Jesus about the essence of God as love, I think he would agree. Perhaps we are aligned on the basics, the essentials, the fundamentals. The differences are just questions of theology—God talk.

As for God's power? Jesus experienced the weakness of God first hand on the cross. I don't think Jesus ever expected God to radically change the way things are. He called together a group of followers to begin that task. He challenged them to change the world in the name of love. And the work still remains.

In the end, this God of love is found in those around me, those who love me and care for me. Perhaps that is enough. And I pray that in some small way, I am able to represent the God of love and compassion to them. I also pray that love can transform me from the introverted, self-centered, and all-too-comfortable person that I am to one who is willing to enter into compassionate service to others and to effect the radical political, social, and economic change that will begin to set the world right.

When asked today if I believe in God, my response is now, "Of course I believe in God, because I believe in love." The God of ancient imagination and theological fancy is replaced by something real and tangible. I can feel love's presence and experience its power. Love soothes broken hearts, binds up wounds, and brings renewed life. Love—bound up in human flesh—is the manifestation of divinity in the world. God as love is such a simple concept. Sometimes it seems far too simple and obvious. Yet I think that it may be the most profound understanding of God that we can attain.

Jesus is enough

My own attraction to Christianity has always been Jesus, not God. Even if God did not exist at any level, Jesus has offered a path that helps meet the needs of a hurting world. The Way of Jesus provides a way forward out of the despair of poverty and violence that afflicts our world. Hopefully, the spirit of God—the spirit of love—within each of us will provide the sustenance, support, and power to follow where Jesus leads.

Here are Walter Wink's concluding thoughts in *The Human Being*:

The gist of this book is, simply, that Jesus as the son of man is enough. What a lean and pared back Christianity has to give the world is not its creeds, dogmas, doctrines, liturgies, and devotions, though some of these hold great validity for many. It offers simply—Jesus.

All Christianity has to give, and all it needs to give, is the myth of the human Jesus. It is the story of Jesus the Jew, a human being, the incarnate son of the man: imperfect but still exemplary, a victim of the Powers still victorious, crushed only to rise again, in solidarity with all who are ground to dust under the jackboots of the mighty, healer of those under the power of death, lover of all who are rejected and marginalized, forgiver, liberator, exposer of the regnant cancer called 'civilization'—that Jesus, the one the Powers killed and whom death could not vanquish. Jesus' is the simple story of a person who gambled his last drop of devotion to the reality of God and the coming of God's new world. In the process, he lived out, in his flesh and blood . . . the intimation of what that new humanity might entail. In doing so, he not only incarnated God, he changed the way people experienced God. In short, the gift of Christianity to the world, as the Hindu Gandhi saw with such lucidity, is not Christianity, but Jesus, revealer and catalyst of our true humanity.[29]

---

29. Wink, *The Human Being*, 259–260.

CHAPTER 11

a prophetic Jesus

The spirit of Yahweh is upon me, because he has anointed me to bring good news to the poor.[1]

—JESUS OF NAZARETH, QUOTING THE PROPHET ISAIAH

Jesus was born in a time of empire and rebellion. At the time of his birth, the Jews of Palestine were a conquered people. For over five hundred years, they had been the victims of empires. For the past six decades, it had been Rome.

In the years following the death of Herod the Great, a massive peasant rebellion began in all regions of Herod's territories. Three lower-class leaders arose to lead revolts in the regions of Judea, Perea, and Galilee. Each leader challenged the kingship of Herod's sons as legitimate rulers of the people. Like Saul, David, Jeroboam, and Jehu—all popular leaders of Israel's history—these revolutionaries were acclaimed by their followers as anointed or *messiah* kings.

Three Roman legions (18,000 troops) from Syria marched south through the country, methodically subduing the peasant revolutionaries. Finally, outside the walls of Jerusalem, 2,000 rebels were crucified as a warning. Crucifixion was the method of capital punishment that the Romans reserved for the lower classes—for rebellious peasants and slaves. The bodies were left on the crosses to rot and be scavenged by birds and dogs. The 2,000 crosses were a sign to the populace of the awesome power of Rome.

---

1. Luke 4:18

In Galilee, the Romans burned the capital city of Sepphoris (*sef'-uh-ris*) and took all of its inhabitants into slavery.[2]

Just four miles south of the destroyed city of Sepphoris, across a fertile valley and up in the rolling hills of the Galilee highlands, lay the small village of Nazareth. There, in the midst of this armed conflict and tension, Jesus was born to a poor peasant family. Rebellions and crucifixions were the bookends of his life.

political domination

As he grew into manhood, Jesus experienced three despotic structures of government organized for a privileged few at the expense of the common good of the majority. Galilee was a monarchy ruled by Herod Antipas, one of three sons of Herod the Great. After the removal of his brother Herod Archelaus by Rome in 6 CE, the region of Judea was ruled directly by a Roman Procurator who reported to the governor of Syria. However, the day-to-day operations were entrusted to a wealthy oligarchy (meaning *the ruling few*) of the Sadducees (*sad'-dzhoo-seez*), sometimes referred to in the gospels as "the leaders of the people," or "the chief priests and the elders." In conquered territories, it was always Rome's practice to find indigenous collaborators to rule on their behalf. And they always chose people from the wealthy class who saw it in their personal interest to support power when it advantaged them. On top of these structures was an emperor in Rome who was essentially a self-appointed dictator. So Jesus was confronted by a monarchy in Galilee, an oligarchy in Jerusalem, and a dictatorship in Rome.

People living under the oppression of a domination system generally respond to the situation in one of four ways. They may become part of the establishment; but that course is only available to a few of the most wealthy and powerful. They may simply try to cope or compromise to some degree with the ruling authorities—go along to get along—in order to survive. They may emigrate or withdraw from society in isolated communities. Or, they may take up arms and revolt. The people of first-century Palestine certainly fit this pattern of multiple responses. There were several different influential groups or parties active in the culture: Sadducees (establishment), Pharisees (compromise), Essenes (withdrawal), Zealots (revolution). Except for the Sadducees, the other three groups all hoped for a political savior to drive out Rome and set up a new rule.

---

2. Although Josephus reports this event, archeologists have not confirmed the destruction and burning.

These parties were notable factions with various political impacts, but they represented only a small minority of the population. Except for the Zealots, they were primarily composed of more-or-less literate elites who had the luxury of engaging in overt positions of political and religious cooperation or opposition. The majority of the people were subjugated and defeated peasants who were buffeted by political winds and degraded by poverty. They just tried to survive until events pushed them to the point of insurrection and rebellion. The peasants found it hard to make any significant response to oppression when they were trying to eke out an existence from the land. But as some saw their lives spiral out of control and as they lost lands, homes, and employment, violent rebellion must have been a tempting option. Jesus was born into this economic and social class.

economic exploitation

In an agricultural economy, land is the only real source of wealth. The Hebrew people considered the land of Palestine to be a gift from God. The stories of the Hebrew Bible recount the invasion and conquest of the land under the leadership of Joshua and the subsequent division of the land among the twelve tribes and their families. The land was considered a patrimony to be passed down from generation to generation. Inherited land was not to be sold, since the land belonged to God alone. However, land could be lost through indebtedness. The misfortunes of illness and drought, or the flaw of personal failings, could result in the need to borrow money against the land. Foreclosure by lenders was a tool commonly used to extend the property holdings of the wealthy. The pervasiveness of indebtedness was a major issue for first-century Jewish peasants.

By the first century, the globalization of empire was transforming the economic landscape. The Roman economy of commercialized agriculture was impoverishing the peasants of Palestine at an alarming rate. For centuries, the Hebrews had a traditional agrarian economy, raising sustenance crops on small farms. In this type of economy, the Hebrew elites who lived in the cities and who controlled the Jerusalem Temple took about 30 to 50 percent of agricultural production from the peasants in the form of religious tithes and political taxes. But when the Romans introduced commercialized agriculture, the elites took the land itself. Commercialized agriculture depends upon consolidation of farms and pastures into large estates, so that agricultural production becomes more efficient. The benefits go to a small number of wealthy landowners in greatly increased profits, resulting in a luxurious lifestyle at the expense of others.

The wealthy elites needed cash to support their lifestyles, so they looked for agricultural exports that could be traded in the economy of the wider Roman Empire. They converted small farms into extensive vineyard estates and shipped wine back to Rome. Only the rich had the means to establish large vineyards because they required tending for at least three years before they produced a usable crop.

When peasants no longer possess their own land, they cannot grow food for their own subsistence. As a result, they must work for wages to buy the food they need. But a commercialized agricultural economy does not support as many people as a traditional one. It creates a large class of expendables, people who are simply superfluous to the economic system and who must compete with one another for meager resources. Large numbers of peasants were forced to become bandits and armed revolutionaries out of desperation.

The poor fishermen and agricultural laborers to whom Jesus spoke were faced with these dehumanizing realities. They needed some good news because all the news they had was increasingly bad and getting worse.

the wilderness prophet

This was the seething social context when Jesus met the wilderness preacher known as John, the son of Zechariah—whom we know as John the Baptizer. Matthew's gospel tells us that it was John the Baptizer who introduced Jesus to the message of the kingdom of God.

> *In those days John the Baptist appeared in the wilderness of Judea, proclaiming, "Repent, for the kingdom of God is at hand."*[3]

John's prophetic message was a simple one: God was angry with the chosen people and planned to punish them, unless a dramatic change took place. The Hebrew Bible declared that God had acted previously in Jewish history using the armies of foreign empires as God's means of national punishment. God's anger was not due to individual sins, or even over a nation that had turned away from the worship of God. Instead, John declared that the issue that angered God was a lack of social justice, as prophets of earlier times had also proclaimed. John was a social prophet in a long line of social prophets who called the nation of Israel to reaffirm the just society required by their covenant with God.

3. Matthew 3:1

Peasants were losing their land. Poor people were going hungry. Children were suffering from illness and deprivation and many were without adequate clothing. In a dog-eat-dog society, people refused to help one another in the face of desperate circumstances. Those who had more simply congratulated themselves, closed their eyes, ears, and hearts, and were indifferent to the needs of those who had less. It was an oppressive and unjust society with no system of communal support for those who suffered the most. Judean society exhibited a disregard of the ancient covenant of an egalitarian society, no commitment to the common good, no obligation to being one's brother's or sister's keeper. Recurring episodes of violence were leading toward a dramatic confrontation with the most powerful military force on earth.

In John's vision, God's judgment would bring massive destruction. John pictured these events as a great forest fire before which the snakes of the forest flee, in which trees and chaff are burnt, and in which people are engulfed in a baptism of fire.[4] He also made use of the metaphors of the axe and the winnowing fan used to separate wheat from chaff. There is no reason to think that John was referring to a burning hell in the afterlife. The forest fire he described is an image of hell on earth. He foresaw not the end of the world, but the Roman destruction of Jewish life, culture, and political hopes in Palestine.

When confronted with John's dramatic words of impending doom and a call to personal conversion, the people asked, "What then shall we do?" John's response was that religious rituals could not save them. Only acts of charity and justice could avert God's anger and wrath.

> And the crowds asked him, "What then should we do?" In reply he said to them, "whoever has two coats must share with anyone who has none; and whoever has food must do likewise."[5]

These are the words of charity that John addressed to those who came to hear his message. But the call for justice was addressed to others who were far away, living in luxurious homes and palaces. In Jerusalem, it was the Sadducees, and the aristocratic families they represented, who needed to change. Closer to hand, it was Herod Antipas, the ruler of Galilee and Perea, who required a new heart. John believed that these uncaring rulers must embrace justice for the poor to forestall a simmering peasant rebellion and a massive Roman military suppression.

---

4. Matthew 3:8–11
5. Luke 3:10–11

Jesus was attracted to the message of John the Baptizer. He traveled to the Judean wilderness along the Jordan River where he was baptized by John and became one of his disciples until John was arrested and executed by Herod Antipas.

Jesus soon left the Jordan wilderness and returned to Galilee to begin his own movement. He not only carried on John's message of the kingdom of God, but it became the center of his message and mission.

> *Now after John was arrested, Jesus came to Galilee, proclaiming the good news of God, and saying, "The time is fulfilled, and the kingdom of God has come near; transform your lives, and trust in the good news."*[6]

the prophet of justice and hope

As he carried on John's work, Jesus began to form a new vision. John was right, of course. If the situation did not change drastically, many people would lose their lives in a futile struggle against the power of Rome. The suffering of many poor and oppressed peasants would only increase. Unlike John, Jesus did not feel called to save Israel by bringing everyone to a baptism of repentance in the Jordan. He decided that something else was necessary, something that had to do with the poor, the sinners, and the sick—the peasants who were the lost sheep of the house of Israel.

It appears that Jesus and John had different images of God. John saw God as a judge who was angry about human injustice. Jesus saw God as a compassionate and nurturing parent who was constantly forgiving and accepting. As a result, Jesus modified John's message of catastrophe. Jesus began to find a new way to address the coming devastation. He developed an alternative vision, a way out, a way to avert violent confrontation.

John preached actions of justice, but with his emphasis on the coming catastrophe, these actions would have been motivated by fear of judgment. Jesus no longer preached John's message of doom. Instead he preached a vision of the way things could be, the way they would be when God's rule was established on earth. Like John's message, it had to do with acts of compassion and justice. But the way of Jesus was based on hope, not fear. Jesus believed that the reign of God operates by invitation, not coercion. Unlike John's vision, which seemed to associate the kingdom of God with judgment, Jesus proclaimed that God's coming reign was "good news."

6. Mark 1:14–15

Jesus suggested that if people would begin living out the just, compassionate, and nonviolent values of God's in-breaking reign today, the inevitable destruction of violent confrontation could be avoided. It was not necessary to eliminate Roman armies to live justly. An armed rebellion would not accomplish the kingdom of God. Jesus now saw clearly the way God's ruling style could be implemented among human societies, and it began with a message of love and compassion for the least in our midst.

Jesus gathered the timeless hopes of humanity for a world of peace, justice, and equality. In words and actions, he demonstrated that the time had come for a new way of living together. The mission Jesus now embarked on was to make his vision of God's new reign clearly visible to the people of his day, and to invite them to enter as participants. John the Baptizer had relied upon a baptism of conversion and expected fruit worthy of that conversion in the lives of his followers. In a similar way, Jesus looked to the transformed lives of individuals to bear fruit in transformed homes, communities, societies, and nations.

a political vision

If we take our spiritual blinders off for a moment, we can begin to see Jesus in a new light. Imagine him in the context of a struggle for social and economic equality similar to the struggles of Gandhi and Martin Luther King, Jr. as they addressed their respective domination systems. According to Luke's gospel, Jesus began with an inaugural speech in Nazareth—his "I have a dream" speech.

> When he came to Nazareth, where he had been brought up, he went to the synagogue on the sabbath day, as was his custom. He stood up to read, and the scroll of the prophet Isaiah was given to him. He unrolled the scroll and found the place where it was written:
>
> > The spirit of Yahweh is upon me,
> > because he has anointed me
> > to bring good news to the poor.
> > He has sent me to proclaim release to the captives
> > and recovery of sight to the blind,
> > to let the oppressed go free,
> > to proclaim the year of Yahweh's favor.
>
> And he rolled up the scroll, gave it back to the attendant, and sat down. The eyes of all in the synagogue were fixed on him. Then

> he began to say to them, "Today this scripture has been fulfilled in your hearing."[7]

Jesus announced that he had come to establish the ancient Hebrew concept of the Jubilee year in which the economic debts of the poor were forgiven, debt-slaves were released, and land that had been taken in foreclosure for peasant indebtedness would be returned by rich landowners to the dispossessed. Jubilee offered an economic amnesty for the poor who had lost everything to debt. Jesus essentially announced that he saw himself as an agent for change, transformation, and liberation. Yet he never claimed the messianic role of a military liberator who effects regime change through violence, but rather established himself as a voice for radical nonviolent social and economic reformation. Jesus proclaimed himself to be a prophet, not a conquering messiah.

When Jesus announced the coming of the kingdom of God, he was announcing a social revolution. Jesus saw himself as the messenger chosen by God to deliver the good news of God's powerful new activity in the world. God's kingdom of justice was coming to replace the authority of ingrained systems of domination. The kingdom of God, as proclaimed by Jesus, was clearly political. Its very name implies the politics of God. So, at the synagogue in Nazareth, Jesus announced he was launching a political movement to bring relief to the suffering and dispossessed peasants and to re-establish God's reign of justice in Roman Palestine.

Jesus was not naïve. He knew that the call for Jubilee restoration would be rejected by the rich and powerful. It had little chance of succeeding if it required the willing participation of those at the top of society. So he addressed the domination system in a different way—a revolutionary way of living by those at the bottom of society. Jesus rejected the politics of violent revolution. He would not try to overthrow the kings and oligarchs. Instead, he and his followers would create an alternative community—a new social order in the midst of the old. And, Jesus taught, the kingdom of God was beginning immediately, starting with powerless groups at the bottom of society. The poor and the outcasts would model life in the kingdom of God for the wealthy and powerful. The least would be the most important in the new

---

7. Luke 4:16–21. The liberty that Luke takes with the Isaiah text is interesting. Of course, the anonymous author who wrote the gospel attributed to Luke was not an eye witness to the event, if it even happened. In first-century Palestine, nearly all people of the peasant class were illiterate, so it is unlikely that Jesus could read the text of Isaiah. It is estimated that perhaps only 3 percent of the population could read and write. Everyone else lived and learned in an oral culture where memory transmits the essence of a text, not a literal word for word rendition.

community, the last in this world would be given first place. The poor would welcome this dramatic change, but the wealthy would not.

a movement for change

Jesus quickly formed a political movement to create an alternative social reality. The coming of God's new social order requires a committed people with a new vision and new values. The founding of a new social reality is not a threat to the status quo when it is only a vision in the head of one person. Jesus knew that his call for Jubilee economic redistribution would threaten the rich and powerful, and would likely result in a violent reaction. He also knew that it would be relatively easy to silence a single voice. But a movement empowered by a shared vision is much more difficult to stop. When a movement galvanizes the hopes and aspirations of a larger community, authorities begin to worry. Movements can quickly get out of control.

Jesus gathered a core team of 82 disciples, with twelve in a leadership role. (Imagine King's Southern Christian Leadership Council.) Then he sent 70 of them out to the villages and towns of Galilee to prepare for his forthcoming political campaign tour to engage the peasants in a grassroots effort. In Luke's gospel we read,

> *After this the Lord appointed seventy others and sent them on ahead of him in pairs to every town and place where he himself intended to go. He said to them . . . "Whenever you enter a town and its people welcome you, eat what is set before you; cure the sick who are there, and say to them, 'The kingdom of God has come near to you.'"*[8]

Sharing food, healing the sick, and announcing the kingdom of God: these were the three assignments to the disciples as they carried the Jesus movement to the villages and towns of Galilee.

The message they shared was that God's economic justice was arriving, and it was important for every individual to get on board. How? By living out the vision of a new economic and political reality immediately! Jesus taught his followers to trust God, but more importantly to create a compassionate community to provide for each other's needs and to respond when called upon to care for and share their resources with their brothers and sisters. He taught his followers to reject selfish concerns and to pray for sufficiency—just enough for tomorrow, "our daily bread." The kingdom of God creates a social safety net for the poor, the hungry, and the homeless.

8. Luke 10:1–9

a prophetic jesus

The community of followers that gathered around Jesus left everything to follow him. They formed what is known as a "fictive family," not connected by blood ties, but by a common vision. Jesus claimed that they were now his new brothers and sisters—no longer friends, acquaintances, or neighbors, but family.

Jesus began to model the new society for his followers and critics. For Jesus, the beginning of community was the sharing of food. But Jesus emphasized that the sharing of meals was intended to go beyond close family and friends. His table fellowship was for the least, the lost, and the lonely. It was to include the outsider and the marginalized, the despised and those who are socially-defined enemies. Since Jesus had no home, no wealth, no banquet table, and no food to offer, he modeled inclusive table fellowship by publicly accepting invitations to dinner from others—often from those considered "sinful" people by virtue of their occupations.

Jesus began to teach others the ways in which the kingdom of God would be radically different from normal society. Love and compassion were at the center of his political reality.

> *I say to you that listen, love your enemies, do good to those who hate you, bless those who curse you, pray for those who abuse you. If anyone strikes you on the cheek, offer the other also; and from anyone who takes away your coat do not withhold even your shirt. Give to everyone who begs from you; and if anyone takes away your goods, do not ask for them again. Do to others as you would have them do to you.*[9]

the march to Jerusalem

According to the synoptic gospels, sometime in his third year of healing and teaching in Galilee, after building the core of his movement, Jesus set his sights on Jerusalem in Judea. He decided to go there to confront the Sadducees—the rich and powerful rulers of the people—at their symbolic seat of power. He would interrupt the operations of the Jerusalem Temple with a popular demonstration for economic justice.

Jesus clearly understood that arrest and death are always potential and likely consequences of the pursuit of justice in an unjust society. He cautioned his followers that in order to follow him, they must be willing to risk public execution on a cross—the penalty for civil disobedience and insurrection by common people. It was a time of decision. Jesus was heading

---

9. Luke 6:27–31

towards a confrontation with power that risked his life and the lives of his followers.

Jesus' entry into the city on the Sunday before Passover was a noisy demonstration that attracted wide attention. According to Mark's story, Jesus was hailed as a charismatic messiah with leafy branches cut from date palm trees and strewn in his path.

> Then those who went ahead and those who followed were shouting, "Hosanna!"[10]

Hosanna was originally a Hebrew cry for help meaning "save us now!" As an exclamation of adoration it became more of an expression of thanks: "our salvation has arrived!"

On Monday morning, Jesus headed straight for the Temple and created a public disturbance in the Court of the Gentiles in full view of the Sadducees and the Roman garrison in the Antonia Fortress. On the surface, Jesus seems angered about commerce in the Temple precincts. Some interpreters think that Jesus disapproved of the Temple's rites of animal sacrifice. Still others believe that his demonstration was against the Temple as a symbol of the Jewish religion itself, as if Jesus was rejecting the religion he was raised in and was replacing it with a new one based on himself as the center of devotion. But most likely, this demonstration at the Temple was a demonstration against the people who managed it and benefited from it—the Sadducees.

The Sadducees were a small group of affluent aristocratic families that formed the ruling upper class in Judea. They were enormously wealthy and lived in great luxury and splendor. Included in their ranks were the high priests of the Jerusalem Temple and a few families of great political influence. The chief priests lived off a Temple tax and the tithes collected from the peasants. By the first century, the lay nobility in Jerusalem had gained ownership of much of the arable land in Judea and other regions.[11] Together with the chief priests, they were in charge of the Temple treasury—essentially the national bank. Thus, they controlled the entire economy. Members of the elite Sadducee party also formed the *Sanhedrin* (san-hee'-drin), the high court and legislative body of the Jewish people. Although Judea was now ruled by a Roman procurator, the day to day operations were entrusted to this wealthy oligarchy (*ruling few*) of the Sadducees.

---

10. Mark 11:9

11. Nolan, *Jesus Before Christianity*, 27. Also Jeremias, *Jerusalem in the Time of Jesus*, 147–232.

The Sadducees were given a free hand to rule the local population as long as they were loyal to Rome, maintained order, and collected the tribute due to the emperor. They cooperated closely with the Roman governor and kept a tight lid on any potential liberation movements in the country that might threaten the status quo and their own privileged positions. There is no question that the Temple was an instrument of the state as was the case in any other ancient temple-state where priest and king are allied.

Peasant indebtedness was the tool by which the wealthy acquired land for their large estates. During times of drought or poor harvests, small farmers were often forced to borrow from the wealthy elites who loaned money to them at interest, which was a clear violation of the traditional Hebraic laws.[12] Their patrimonial land was often given as collateral on these loans. When the farmers could not pay their debts, their property was taken from them. The debt records for all of these transactions were kept by the elites in the Jerusalem Temple, providing us with a clue to Jesus' angry criticism of those who controlled the temple precincts when he entered it.

All of the objects of Jesus' anger in his demonstration were legitimate operations in the huge Court of the Gentiles that surrounded the central areas reserved for Israelite women, men, and priests alone. The Temple required bird and animal sellers on site so that pilgrims would be able to offer sacrifices that were ritually acceptable. Money changers were required to change foreign currencies into the approved coinage for payment of the temple tax. Jesus upset these operations by driving out those who were selling and buying and not allowing "anyone to carry anything through the temple." But the real objects of his protest were not low level functionaries.

We are told that Jesus addressed the crowds in the Temple with these words:

> *Don't the scriptures say, 'My house is to be regarded as a house of prayer for all peoples'? But you have turned it into a hideout for crooks.*[13]

Jesus was not condemning the Temple as a place of robbery, but as a den or hideout for the robbers. A den is not where the robbers rob, it is the place where they count their ill-gotten gains. It was not a few moneychangers or dove sellers who were the target of Jesus anger, but the thieves, robbers, and brigands at the top levels of society who perpetuated a system of economic injustice, who robbed people of their land, their wealth, and their livelihoods. The governing Sadducees understood his message clearly.

12. Exodus 22:25, Leviticus 25:37, Deuteronomy 23:19–20
13. Mark 11:17

The Sadducees had decided that they needed to shut Jesus up before he instigated a rebellion, either violent or nonviolent.

> So the chief priests and the Pharisees called a meeting of the council, and said, "What are we to do? This man is performing many signs. If we let him go on like this, everyone will believe in him, and the Romans will come and destroy both our holy place and our nation." But one of them, Caiaphas, who was high priest that year, said to them, "You know nothing at all! You do not understand that it is better for you to have one man die for the people than to have the whole nation destroyed." . . . So from that day on they planned to put him to death.[14]

When Jesus was arrested late on Thursday night and brought before the chief priest on Friday morning, the Sadducees sought evidence for a capital crime. The chief priest asked Jesus if he was the messiah—a warrior king intending a violent revolution. When brought before Pilate, Jesus was asked if he claimed to be king of the Jews. In both cases, Jesus turned the accusations back on the accusers and never answered directly. He was charged by the Sadducees with blasphemy, but Rome executed him for sedition. On the cross was a sign that listed his anti-government crime—attempting to become king of the Jews. The cruelty of his crucifixion revealed what imperial authorities do to one who attempts to subvert the domination system. For those who witnessed this event, the cross was not a symbol of divine sacrifice or the taking on of unmerited suffering—it was the price of resistance to the social and economic destruction of empire.

Six agonizing hours after his crucifixion began, on a spring afternoon in the year 30 CE, Jesus died. His heart stopped beating and his brainwave activity ceased. The spirit of life that had animated him at birth, left his body. The biblical tradition says that the body was then removed from the cross and placed in a tomb, sealed with a large stone. But, the Roman practice of crucifixion did not usually allow for burial. Instead, the naked bodies of crucified victims were left hanging on the cross, to rot as they were exposed to the elements, and be eaten by carrion, a meal for crows and hungry dogs. In any event—whether he was left on the cross or buried in a tomb—we simply do not know what eventually became of Jesus' corpse. In the gospel accounts, the women who went to the tomb on Easter morning were unable to find it. It was never seen again. The earthly Jesus, the pre-Easter Jesus, was gone from history. But he was not to be forgotten.

---

14. John 11:47–53

the resurrection as an uprising

The resurrection accounts of Jesus in the New Testament are not stories about a resuscitated corpse. What the first disciples of Jesus experienced was far more than a revived earthly body. What they experienced was something completely new and different. The resurrection was a mystical experience of the living presence of Jesus among those who knew him, loved him, and followed him.

The wealthy and powerful thought that the execution of Jesus would eliminate the threat he posed. But the movement he created did not end with his death. In a very real sense, Jesus was resurrected in the people who believed in his message of hope and justice and who followed his example. They felt his presence among them, and this presence gave them the courage to transform their lives with passion, zeal, and courage for the sake of the world. They began a passionate uprising, a conspiracy of love, that gradually spread in the confident hope that they could create a better world. Clarence Jordan (1912–1969), a New Testament scholar and translator of the "Cotton Patch Gospels" once wrote:

> *The proof that God raised Jesus from the dead is not the empty tomb, but the full hearts of his transformed disciples. The crowning evidence that he lives is not a vacant grave, but a spirit-filled fellowship; not a rolled-away stone, but a carried-away church.*[15]

The political nature of the Jesus movement and its threat to the status quo of empire is unmistakable. Blasphemy and sedition were frequent charges aimed at the followers of Jesus in the first three centuries after his death, and capital punishment was the fate of many of the key leaders of the early movement. According to tradition, Peter was crucified in Rome and Paul was beheaded there by the emperor Nero (37–68). The Jewish historian Josephus (37–100) reports that Jesus' brother James (the Just) was stoned to death by Temple authorities in Jerusalem. Legends reported by Christian historians Hippolytus of Rome (170–235) and Eusebius (263–339) say that four of the disciples met similar fates: Andrew and Bartholomew were crucified, Stephen was stoned, and James, the son of Zebedee was beheaded. Something was going on in the early Jesus movement that clearly threatened the religious and political authorities of the domination system.

It is wrong to simply view Jesus as a spiritual savior with a heavenly goal. He was concerned about our lives in the here and now, not in the hereafter. He had a political vision for how society should be structured and what values it should embody. He taught about the coming new reality and

---

15. Jordan and Lee, *The Substance of Faith*, 29.

he modeled it in his own life. He created a movement to carry it on after his death, and the early church continued to live out his vision of communities of sharing and equality for many decades, perhaps even centuries, after his crucifixion.

When Jesus announced the kingdom of God, he was putting forth a vision of a world governed by love—more peaceful, more compassionate, more equitable, and more just. Planted deep in our hearts, this dream defines our mission as followers of Jesus. We are called to transform the hearts, minds, and politics of our cities and towns, our states, our nations, and the entire global community so that children everywhere will be fed, clothed, healed, and educated.

The way of Jesus is a conspiracy of love, compassion, justice, and peace. In the first century, Jesus led his small movement in a concerted action to subvert the prevailing domination system of his society. He called for economic justice, he shared meals with those who were considered outcasts and rabble, he taught creative nonviolent responses to domination, and he publically demonstrated at the seat of political and religious power. He was executed for daring to challenge the status quo that benefitted the top 1 percent of his society.

The way of Jesus led to the cross. That is where Jesus calls us to follow today. This is not some inward spiritual journey. This is a confrontation with the real world of power, violence, poverty, disease, suffering, and death. To follow Jesus means to live faithfully in spite of the consequences. It means a willingness to be ridiculed and mocked, to suffer unjustly and, if necessary, to die for the sake of the reign of love. But we are not alone. The spirit of Jesus walks ahead. His vision leads the way. And he bids us to come and join him in the journey to a better world.

CHAPTER 12

a holy spirit

The fruit of the spirit is love, joy, peace, patience, kindness, generosity, faithfulness, gentleness, and self-control.[1]

—PAUL THE APOSTLE (C. 5–67 CE)

The earliest followers of Jesus were recognized by their dramatic personal and corporate transformation. They embodied the dynamic spirit that they first witnessed in the life of Jesus and that later transformed their own lives. The book of Acts testifies to a dramatic change in the spirits of Jesus' disciples after the crucifixion of Jesus. They went from cowering behind closed doors in Jerusalem to speaking courageously in front of political and religious authorities. Something had changed. They were filled with a "holy spirit."

When the Hebrew word *ruach* (*roo'-akh*) and the Greek word *pneuma* (*nyoo'-mah*) are interpreted as *spirit*—as they often are in biblical texts—they refer to an invisible animating and moving force of God. But in every case, when the combined phrase "holy spirit" is used, it represents an almost radical transformation within a person, a visible uniqueness, and a force for change. People who are filled with a holy spirit act differently. They go well beyond the ordinary, they envision sweeping new possibilities for the future, and they courageously speak truth to power.

A short study of biblical references to the term "holy spirit" may be worthwhile at this point in order to clarify the use of that term in Christianity. The phrase "holy spirit" appears about 89 times throughout the Bible,

---

1. Galatians 5:22

with 86 of those instances in the New Testament.[2] In Hebrew "holy spirit" is *ruach ha-kodesh* (*roo'-akh hah-koh-desh'*) and in Greek it is *pneuma hagion* (*nyoo'-mah hag'-ee-ohn*). The modifiers *ha-kodesh* (*hah-koh-desh'*) and *hagion* (*hag'-ee-ohn*) represent the "holy" part of the phrase. One meaning of *hagion* is something that is set apart for or prepared for God, something blessed or consecrated for a holy purpose, something made sacred or sanctified. So in the New Testament, being filled with a "holy spirit" indicates a dynamic human spirit that marks one who is set apart and dedicated to the work of love in the world.

lost in translation

The problem for understanding what the biblical writers meant in these 86 New Testament texts is that, in most modern English translations, *pneuma hagion* is nearly always translated as "*the* Holy Spirit," with the definite article "the" and with capital letters implying a sacred name for a person-like being—the third person of the Trinity. However, that is simply not what the majority of those texts literally say, nor is it what they most likely mean.

The New Testament texts were written in *koine* (*koy-nay'*) Greek, a common dialect that was spoken and written in eastern Mediterranean countries in the Hellenistic and Roman periods. Because these biblical texts were written entirely in lower case (without space between words and without any punctuation), capitalization is always an interpretation made by the translator. But in many of these texts, the capitalization is not warranted by the context.

Koine Greek had no indefinite articles like "a" or "an" in the English language. In New Testament Greek, if the definite article "the" is not used, the indefinite article "a" is always assumed. Therefore, if any article is required to make better sense of a phrase like "holy Spirit" in these texts, it should always be "a" and never "the," unless that definite article is specified in the original language.

Accordingly, the definite article "the" is found in just 38 (or 44 percent) of the 86 New Testament texts, and 27 of those instances come from a single writer—the author of Luke and Acts. In the other 48 (or 56 percent)

---

2. The gospels have 24 instances of the term "holy spirit," the book of Acts has 39, and the various letters by Paul and other writers have another 23, giving us a total of 86 occurrences. Of the 38 references to "*the* holy spirit," 22 are found in the book of Acts and 5 in Luke's gospel. Therefore, the author/editor of Luke and Acts accounts for 27 of the 38 references to "*the* holy spirit." This means that nearly two-thirds of the occurrences in the New Testament are derived from a single author. Matthew, Mark and John use the term "*the* holy spirit" just five times.

occurrences of "holy spirit," the definite article "the" is simply not found in the earliest Greek versions. Yet, in nearly every instance, the English translation in our modern Bibles is rendered as "*the* Holy Spirit." This is clearly an imposition by a translator based on a theological bias and agenda. And this mistranslation has led to much misunderstanding and misguided theological thinking within the church for centuries.

A case can be made that the 48 references to *pneuma hagion* (*holy spirit*)—without a definite article—were never intended to refer to a person-like being. Instead, for the New Testament writers, *pneuma hagion* referred to a powerful internal driving spirit that fills the lives of people with a special recognizable character, a zeal for a holy or sacred purpose. One can certainly be filled with the spirit of love, the spirit of compassion, or the spirit of courage without relying on the intervention of a supernatural being. These are fully-human qualities that many of us experience. In other words, many of these texts were never intended to be read as "*the* Holy Spirit," but just simply as "*a* holy spirit."

the gift of a holy spirit

In many of the New Testament texts, a holy spirit is something that is "poured out" on people, giving them a new life, a courageous boldness, a gift for speech, and a new vision. Similarly, other texts indicate that people are sometimes "filled" with a holy spirit, meaning that they are overflowing with the spirit of God. The verbs "pouring" and "filling" suggest that in a normal human state, one's spirit is running on low. When one is filled up with a holy spirit, one's life is transformed and the change is evident to others.

In most of these texts, a holy spirit fills people's lives, sometimes suddenly, and marks them for special purpose or role. It inspires some to take on great tasks and causes others to have visions about a revolutionary social change that they loudly announce to the world. In these New Testament stories, we see people who have become filled with *passion, zeal,* and *courage*. Other attributes might apply as well, but those particular characteristics are clearly observable in the characters of the early Jesus movement. As we read the book of Acts, we find the dispirited disciples of Jesus who have been trembling in fear after the crucifixion. Suddenly, with the gift of a holy spirit, they become courageous and bold individuals, willing to speak out and defy authority, at a risk to their lives.

At one point, I re-read all of the 86 biblical texts in question, substituting the words "passion, zeal, and courage" for the phrase "holy spirit." I found that this replacement often worked quite well and it helped me reach a deeper understanding of what a holy spirit might have meant in the early Jesus movement. It certainly helped me refocus my thinking away from a person-like divine being and make a fresh appraisal of "holy spirit" as a dramatic personal transformation. When translators began modifying "*a* holy spirit" to "*the* Holy Spirit," they replaced radical personal transformation with a divine being that brings about consolation, comfort, encouragement, sanctification, and community—the traditional characteristics of the work of the Holy Spirit. Those aspects may be important in the Christian life, but I think something extremely important is lost. When courage is replaced with comfort, it's a different kind of faith.

John's gospel, which is always uniquely different from the synoptic gospels of Matthew, Mark, and Luke, refers to the Holy Spirit with the term *paraclete*—from the Greek *parakletos (par-ak'-lay-tos)*—meaning one who consoles and comforts, one who encourages and uplifts, or one who intercedes and advocates in court.[3] It primarily reflects a spirit that is directed inwardly, not outwardly. The Paraclete or the Holy Spirit may be a personal comforter, but "a holy spirit" is more often an agitator—a force for activism, advocacy on behalf of others, and protest against injustice. A holy spirit drives us from the comfort and security of our homes and sanctuaries into the world to spread the message of the kingdom of God and to work for its implementation. It represents a passion, zeal, and courage about social justice, about concern for the poor, about fighting global hunger, about the care of the earth, and about non-violent resistance to systemic evil. And this transformational passion is what many find lacking in the church today. Rather than being comforted, a holy spirit is a motivation for a conspiracy of love against the normalcy of the world, a subversive challenge to the domination system and its politics of selfishness.

---

3. John 14:16, 14:26, 15:26, and 16:7. *Parakletos* is often translated as "the advocate," with male gender.

PART 4
a new path

CHAPTER 13

a theology of weakness

[God] is weak and powerless in the world, and that is the way, the only way, in which [God] can be with us and help us.[1]

—DIETRICH BONHOEFFER (1906–1945)

As we enter the postmodern world, the age-old omnipotent God is slowly dying in the human imagination. For many, this supernatural being is already dead. The image of a God who acts with power and might in the natural world and in human society is becoming increasingly incredible. To think of God as *love* is radically different. In regards to power, the chief characteristic of God as love is weakness. Love can only act in the world through the relative weakness of human beings. Without an omnipotent cosmic God dwelling somewhere out there, we have only human love, intelligence, and compassion to save us. Singly, each of us can do little. United, we can accomplish much if selfless love, compassion, and justice is our collective guide.

Yet, for many, thinking of God as the embodiment of weak human love is a poor substitute for the old supernatural image. Without a powerful cosmic God to fulfill our psychological needs for safety and security, we have to rely on one another to give us comfort and shelter. Without an omnipotent God who can answer our prayers, we must each pray for the strength, intelligence, and courage to change the world ourselves. The answer, as Jesus said, is to love one another, to care for one another, and to forgive one another. These actions are the manifestation of the God of love in our world.

1. Dietrich Bonhoeffer, *Letters and Papers*, 360.

a God of the margins

In the Hebrew Bible, God is proclaimed as a protector of the poor, especially widows and orphans who had no other male protector in society, and immigrants (resident aliens) who had no social kinship network during pressing situations. In a domination system, the rich and powerful don't need God's protection. They are in charge. The system serves them and benefits them. The Bible says that God chooses sides—the weak over the powerful—and ultimately moves into the margins of society in solidarity with the poor. You will find the presence of God among those who suffer, grieve, and hunger. Jesus said that the kingdom of God promises to reverse the social conditions of those in the margins.

> *Blessed are you who are poor, for yours is the kingdom of God.*
> *Blessed are you who hunger now, for you will be satisfied.*
> *Blessed are you who weep now, for you will laugh.*[2]

Jesus also said that the kingdom of God will not be found among societal elites because they are wedded to the status quo and will not welcome social, political, or economic change.

> *But woe to you who are rich, for you have already received your comfort.*
> *Woe to you who are well fed now, for you will go hungry.*
> *Woe to you who laugh now, for you will mourn and weep.*[3]

In commenting on the blessings and woes announced by Jesus, Paul Tillich said,

> *The situation of the people of Galilee to whom Jesus spoke is still our situation. The Woes are promised today to all of us who are well off, respected, and secure, not simply because we have such security and respect, but because it inevitably binds us, with an almost irresistible power, to this eon, to things as they are. And the Beatitudes are promised today to all of us who are without security and popularity, who are mourning in body and soul. And they are promised not simply because we lack so much, but because the very fact of our lacks and our sorrows may turn our hearts away from things as they are, toward the coming eon. The Beatitudes do not glorify those who are poor and in misery, individuals or classes, because they are poor. The Woes are not promised to those who are rich and secure, classes or individuals, because they are*

2. Luke 6:20–21
3. Luke 6:24–25

rich. If this were so, Jesus could not have promised to the poor the reversal of their situation. He praises the poor in so far as they live in two worlds, the present world and the world to come. And He threatens the rich in so far as they live in one world alone.[4]

Consequently, Jesus lived and ministered in the margins of his peasant society among despised and rejected people: prostitutes, tax collectors, and lepers. It was among those considered immoral and impure that the message of the kingdom of God would be gratefully welcomed. It was here that the kingdom was desperately needed.

> *Jesus said to them* [the religious and social elites], *"Truly I tell you, the tax collectors and the prostitutes are entering the kingdom of God ahead of you."*[5]

Jesus taught in the parable of the Pharisee and the tax collector that God will be found at the margins of the religious and social establishment, not in the central institutions of the pious, proud, and literate elites.

> *Two people went up to the temple to pray, one a Pharisee and the other a tax collector. The Pharisee, standing by himself, was praying thus, "God, I thank you that I am not like other people: thieves, rogues, adulterers, or even like this tax collector. I fast once a week; I give a tenth of all my income." But the tax collector, standing far off, would not even look up to heaven, but was beating his breast and saying, "God, be merciful to me, a sinner!" I tell you, this man went down to his home justified rather than the other.*[6]

According to this parable, God justifies—meaning, God absolves and champions—those who stand at the margins, and rejects those who are privileged to stand in the center. Was God's response to their prayers different because the Pharisee was unbearably proud and the tax collector was humbly penitent? I think there is more going on here than that. It has to do with insiders and outsiders, those who belong and those who don't belong, those who are socially accepted and those who are rejected. The sacred precincts of the temple were only available to those who met specific holiness requirements. The tax collector belongs to a class of people who must stay outside the bounds of the temple as those who are considered ritually unclean. He is judged a "sinner" by virtue of his profession. He stands apart not because he sees himself as unworthy, but because he knows

---

4. Tillich, *The Shaking of the Foundations*, 26–27.
5. Matthew 21:31
6. Luke 18:10–14

this is his proper place as an outsider in Hebrew society. He is not allowed to enter further in and temple guards were ready to enforce this prohibition. Like prostitutes and lepers, the tax collector is ostracized from his society's religious institutions.

In this parable, I believe that Jesus is saying that the ruling activity of God in the world—found in the alternative community of the kingdom of God—has moved from the sacred precincts of the temple (or any religious institution) to the profane arena of secular society. It has moved from the church to the streets. God is more concerned with the damage caused by power politics, economic injustice, and social exclusion of marginalized people than with the pious praise of insiders. God is more likely to be found in the lives of people at the bottom of the ladder where life is messy, than at the top where life is comfortable and secure. These hurting places are the arenas where Jesus lived, worked, and taught, and this is the arena to which his followers are called. After all, Jesus was a marginal person. He was born a peasant in a landless family who were members of the working poor. He spent his life working to create a just and caring community among his fellow peasants—a weak and powerless people.

a God of weakness and suffering

Dietrich Bonhoeffer—who was imprisoned and hanged in Nazi Germany like that young boy at Auschwitz—came to regard God not as omnipotent, but as weak and powerless. In Jesus—as an image and icon of the invisible God—he saw weakness and suffering as the way God operates in the world. He reasoned that if Jesus is the decisive revelation of God's nature, then the weakness and suffering of Jesus on the cross can be viewed as an image of God's weakness in the world. In one of his letters from prison, Bonhoeffer said:

> *[God] is weak and powerless in the world, and that is the way, the only way, in which he can be with us and help us . . . Man's religiosity makes him look in his distress to the power of God in the world; he uses God as a Deus ex machina. The Bible however directs him to the powerlessness and suffering of God; only a suffering God can help.*[7]

The Latin phrase *deus ex machina* (*day'-us eks mack'-in-ah*), meaning "god out of the machine," refers to situations in ancient Greek theater in which a crane was used to lower an actor playing the part of a god onto the

---

7. Bonhoeffer, *Letters and Papers*, 360–361.

stage. Bonhoeffer uses the term to refer to the religious hope that God will miraculously step in to resolve a hopeless situation like a comic book action hero. Bonhoeffer believed that God does not step in and does not intervene in history to save us; God has not, does not, and will not. Bonhoeffer's view of history from the first half of the twentieth century—two world wars, the holocaust, and a global economic depression—was evidence enough that God does not act in this way.

Bonhoeffer, who saw God's presence in Jesus, believed that God is found most definitively in the suffering of Jesus on the cross. But he went further to state that God suffers not just with Jesus, but with *all* the victims of the world. "Our God is a suffering God," he said. But exactly how does God suffer? And what does that mean about the nature of God?

Bonhoeffer was challenging a long-standing doctrine in Christian theology—that of divine impassibility—which holds that the theistic God of Greek philosophy (Theos) is incapable of suffering because this God is without passion or emotion. (The term *impassability* simply means "without passions.") Emotion would imply that an unchangeable God changes. By responding to situations with appropriate emotions such as joy or suffering, God must experience ups and downs as humans do. A God who feels emotion therefore must be a God who changes. For many Christian thinkers influenced by Greek philosophy, this was not possible. God's unchanging impassibility was the dominant view among Christian theologians for nearly two thousand years. But the Hebrew Bible presents a different picture of God.

There is ample evidence in the accounts of the Hebrew Bible that God was capable of great emotion, including compassion. In the book of Exodus, we read that God *compassionately heard the cry* of the Hebrew slaves in Egypt and determined to liberate them.[8] In the books of the Hebrew prophets, we read that God *grieved over the sins* of the people. God was often *distressed by their unfaithfulness*. So disheartened was God by their hardheartedness that God became *angry*. However, the prophet Amos reported the message from God that "my heart recoils within me; my compassion grows warm and tender. I will not execute my fierce anger . . . I will not come in wrath."[9] Thus, each of the Gods of the Hebrew Bible (Yahweh and Elohim) suffers with us, is distressed and angered by our behavior, and feels a deep compassion toward a wayward humanity, but the emotionless God of Hellenistic Christianity (Theos) does not.

8. Exodus 2:23–25
9. Hosea 11:8–9

As Bonhoeffer and others have argued, a theistic God who can look down on the state of the world and not be moved, a God who can see suffering without feeling compassion or pain is inferior to a God who does. For many theologians, it is better for the God of supernatural theism to be vulnerable than unconcerned. As a result, late twentieth-century theology began to realize that divine impassability had become an untenable doctrine. In the wake of Auschwitz and Hiroshima, it seemed impossible to believe in a God who is not sensitive, emotional, and compassionate. Theologian Jürgen Moltmann (b. 1926) wrote, "Were God incapable of suffering in any respect, and therefore in an absolute sense, then He would also be incapable of love."[10] In other words, a dispassionate God cannot be a loving God.

weak theology

In recent years, the term "weak theology" has been put forth to contrast the "strong theology" of the ancient creeds and orthodox Christian doctrine. A strong theology represents the character of a strong God, envisioned as an all-powerful creator and supernatural interventionist in history. In contrast, a weak theology describes a God with limited or weak power. Strong theology argues that the reason that God does not intervene to save the weak and oppressed is because God chooses to withhold power, often in the name of free will. In the same way, strong theology contends that the crucified Jesus chose to withhold his divine power in order to fulfill God's plan for human salvation. But some theologians now see the suffering of Jesus on the cross and God's inaction to save him as evidence that both Jesus and God were powerless to act in a supernatural manner. A weak theology contends that God and Jesus exhibit a weak kind of power in the world—weak forces like love and forgiveness.

Philosopher and theologian John Caputo (b. 1940) writes in *The Weakness of God*, "The strong point about weak theology is that it is a theology of the cross."

> *The divinity of the truly divine God is to be displayed neither in a display of magic by Jesus or his heavenly Father . . . The divinity is rather that [Jesus'] very death and humiliation rise up in protest against the world, rise up above power . . . both Roman power and a God of power who has the power to intervene . . . The call, the cry, the plaint that rises up from the cross is a great divine "no" to injustice, an infinite lamentation over unjust suffering and innocent victims. God is with Jesus on the cross, and*

---

10. Moltmann, *The Crucified God*, 230.

> *in standing with Jesus rather than with the imperial power of Rome, God stands with an innocent persecuted for calling the powers that be to task. The name of God is the name of a divine "no" to persecution, violence, and victimization . . . On this scheme . . . the transcendence of "God" does not mean God towers above being as a hyper-being. Rather, God pitches his tent among beings by identifying with everything the world casts out and leaves behind . . . God withdraws from the world's order of presence, prestige, and sovereignty in order to settle into those pockets of protest and contradiction to the world. God belongs to the air, to the call, to the spirit that inspires and aspires, that breathes justice. God settles into the recesses formed in the world by the little ones, the nothings and nobodies of the world.*[11]

Luther coined the term "theology of the cross," but used it in a different way. He contrasted it with a theology of glory that emphasizes earning divine favor through righteous acts. Luther believed that the cross—the symbol of the crucifixion of Jesus—represents the only way that God reconciles and saves humanity from the power of sin. For Luther, divine power was revealed in the weakness of the crucified Jesus who suffered an apparent defeat at the hands of evil powers. This sacrifice enabled God in Jesus to conquer death and the powers of evil for all time. (The flaw in this argument of course is that death and evil powers are still with us.) Importantly, Luther perceived that divine power can take the apparent form of weakness. Still, traditional theology also envisions God as acting with great power when God chooses. For instance, God will eventually defeat the forces of evil in a consummate bloodbath. Therefore, God is not truly weak, but only appears to be weak for divine purposes. But perhaps this theology is wrong. Perhaps God truly cannot act to save us.

In the gospels of Mark and Matthew, Jesus cries out to God in agony, "My God, my God, why have you forsaken me?"[12] Jesus receives no answer other than the silence of God, the absence of God, a complete abandonment by God. Mark may have placed these dying words on the lips of Jesus from the text of Psalm 22:

> *My God, my God, why have you forsaken me?*
> *Why are you so far from helping me, from the words of my groaning?*
> *O my God, I cry by day, but you do not answer;*
> *and by night, but find no rest.*[13]

11. Caputo, *The Weakness of God*, 42–45.
12. Mark 15:34, Matthew 27:46
13. Psalm 22:1–2

However, the words in Mark's gospel are quoted in Aramaic—"*Eloi, Eloi, lema sabachthani?*" (*el-o-ee', el-o-ee', la'-ma, sa-bakh-tha'-nee*)—giving them more authenticity as the actual words of Jesus. Although inspired by the ancient psalm, these words represent the tragic situation of the crucifixion—a heartfelt cry of agony and loss. For Jesus, there would be no divine intervention. Just like that Jewish child on the gallows in the concentration camp, God did not step in. Just like millions of other innocent victims of disease, hunger, and violence, God does not alter the tragic situations of their lives.

God did not save the six million Jews who were murdered in the Holocaust. God did not save the 160 million people who perished in the many wars of the twentieth century. Even today, God does not miraculously feed the 800 million people in our world who do not have enough nutrition to lead healthy, productive lives. Nor does God save the seven million hungry people—including three million children under the age of five—who die every year due to malnutrition. The omnipotent God of traditional theology does not and will not save us, but an incarnate God of love within humanity powerfully draws us into compassion for and solidarity with the people who experience pain, hunger, violence, and oppression. Love rouses us to action on behalf of those innocents who suffer unjustly. Love calls us to create a more just society that will put an end to the grief, misery, and distress that we encounter daily.

Theologian Peter Rollins (b. 1973) believes that the crucifixion experience of Jesus is the trauma we all personally experience when we feel the absence of God in our lives. Ultimately, it calls us to give up the most treasured images of a God who will rescue us in times of need.

> *What is lost here is a way of relating to God as deus ex machina, as some being "out there" who ensures life makes sense. On the cross, Christ becomes the absolute outsider. Everything that has supported him thus far is stripped away. The religious system of the day sought his execution, the political system happily provided it, and his social circle quickly abandoned him. All that would ground him had been fundamentally shaken apart. There is no support here for Christ. On the cross, he is left naked, alone, dying.*[14]

For Rollins, to participate in Christ's death is to personally experience the radical doubt, suffering, and the sense of divine forsakenness that Jesus experienced on the cross. But let us be clear, the God we are speaking of, who abandons us to suffering, is the ancient supernatural theistic God of

---

14. Rollins, *Insurrection*, 27.

the human imagination, the all-powerful transcendent God that dwells "out there." On the other hand, the incarnate God of love is neither dead nor absent, but is found among us in the form of a friend, a neighbor, or an enemy. The crucifixion is the profound experience that brings an end to a traditional way of thinking about God and opens up new possibilities of theological reasoning.

Look at it this way: if Jesus was the human incarnation of a supernatural theistic God, then God died on the cross with him; if Jesus was not the theistic God in human flesh, then God simply abandoned him. In other words, in the crucifixion of Jesus and the unjust suffering of millions of others, the supernatural God of traditional religion has either left the scene or has died.

Rollins believes that the loss of the theistic God, while traumatic, can open up a new experience of God dwelling in our midst. The God revealed in Jesus is present in the work of human love. The resurrection experience is finding God anew at the depth of our lives, expressed in love toward others.

> *It is not difficult to find the intellectual affirmation of doubt and unknowing within the church today. Many believers explicitly reject the use of God as a solution to some problem. They affirm that a life of faith transcends mere dogmatic affirmations and that it involves an ongoing transformation by love, in love, toward love. They view doubt, ambiguity, and complexity as important aspects of a mature Christianity, they see the experience of God's absence as part of the faith, they talk openly about the importance of doubt, and they reclaim parts of their Jewish heritage, a tradition that has always understood faith to be deeper than some intellectual assent.*[15]

a weak force for justice

Because God is love, God is also justice, because justice is the social form of love. We might amend the words of John's first epistle to say that "God is love/justice." God takes the side of the poor, because we are told that "Yahweh is a God of justice."[16] Justice is always about helping those in the margins obtain dignity, equity, and the necessities of life. If God is found in the pursuit of justice, God is the divine "No!" to systems of oppression, persecution, repression, and violence.

15. Ibid, 42–43.
16. Isaiah 30:18

So how does a God of love/justice create a just society? Justice for the oppressed rarely comes from the top of society, from the center of power. God works through people at the bottom and on the margins to achieve change. God uses weak people who employ the weak tactics of love and nonviolent resistance. Paul wrote:

> God chose the weak things of the world to shame the strong. God chose the lowly things of this world and the despised things—and the things that are not—to nullify the things that are.[17]

Jesus did not choose the way of traditional power. He chose not to pursue political and military power in his efforts to change the world, consistently rejecting the role of messiah and son of God. He refused any and all efforts to make him a king. The "weak power" of Jesus negated the use of violence toward others.

Commenting on Caputo's *The Weakness of God*, professor Richard Beck (b. 1967) concludes:

> You add all that up and what you have is a radically different view of God's power. God does not exercise top-down power and control from on high. God doesn't "lord over" the world. The power of God works in the opposite direction, from the bottom-up. God's power is the power of the cross, the power of weakness and powerlessness, the power of loving servanthood and self-giving. This is why we must become like little children—become weak, lowly and despised as those described in 1 Corinthians—if we are to enter the Kingdom of God, a Kingdom not characterized by top-down power but by being the one in the "last place." And when we step into this loving and powerless way of living we become born of God, we come to know God, and God comes to live in us.[18]

As writer and theologian Henri Nouwen (1932–1996) has written,

> Surrounded by so much power, it is very difficult to avoid surrendering to the temptation to seek power like everyone else. But the mystery of our ministry is that we are called to serve not with our power but with our powerlessness. It is through powerlessness that we can enter into solidarity with our fellow human beings, form a community with the weak, and thus reveal the healing, guiding, and sustaining mercy of God . . . As followers of Christ,

---

17. 1 Corinthians 1.27–28

18. Richard Beck, "On Warfare and Weakness: Part 5, The Weakness of God," Experimental Theology blog, June 24, 2013, Online: http://experimentaltheology.blogspot.com/2013/06/on-warfare-and-weakness-part-5-weakness.html

a theology of weakness

we are sent into the world naked, vulnerable, and weak, and thus we can reach our fellow human beings in their pain and agony and reveal to them the power of God's love and empower them with the power of God's Spirit.[19]

Global domination systems exploit and oppress the vast majority of people on earth, especially women, children, ethnic and religious minorities, the working poor, and undocumented immigrants. This has been true for nearly every human society since the rise of civilization. Wealthy and powerful elites employ unjust laws and armed violence to maintain the status quo of the domination system that is structured for their benefit only.

Those living under the oppression of a domination system sometimes choose one of two responses when conditions get too bad: fight or flight—revolution or exodus. Mostly, however, they choose to simply survive with silent, grudging, passive resistance. Jesus taught another response to the victims of domination—active nonviolent resistance to the principalities and powers that govern our world.

Jesus did not look to God to magically transform the suffering and pain of human existence. Instead, he taught people to form communities of active resistance—communities that live together in active opposition to the domination system—communities of sharing and mutual support; communities of inclusion for the marginalized, the despised, and the stranger; and communities that compassionately care for the imprisoned, the sick, and the hungry in their midst. He called these societies of resistance "the kingdom of God."

Because domination systems are human social creations, Jesus believed that it is up to human beings to transform them into fair and just societies. If we can create communities of political inequality, social injustice, and economic suffering, we can deconstruct them and reform them.

Jesus taught a weak kind of power in the eyes of the world—love, compassion, forgiveness, generosity—traits and practices that the mighty scorn. For rich and powerful people like Donald Trump, these are the attributes of "losers." Jesus taught and modeled these "weak power" behaviors as a way to effect change without violent coercion. Because he was committed to the power of love and nonviolence, he did not violently resist when arrested, beaten, and executed. John Caputo sums it up:

The perverse core of Christianity lies in being a weak force. The weak force of God is embodied in the broken body on the cross.[20]

---

19. Nouwen, *The Selfless Way of Christ*, 62–64.
20. Caputo, *The Weakness of God*, 43.

The weak people of the world do not possess weapons of violence equal to that of the domination system. They cannot compete with the brutality of entrenched power and are quickly and mercilessly defeated if they take up arms. The successful weapons of the weak have always been resilient defiance, active resistance, nonviolent protest, and enduring struggle in the face of insurmountable odds.

Nonviolence is an unarmed form of resistance, scoffed at by those in power. Yet nonviolence rooted in the power of love has shown that it can overcome the hatred, injustice, and violence of the rich and mighty, for oppressors can only dominate if the oppressed masses allow it. When people refuse to cooperate, when they resist in large numbers, systems of oppression crumble and fall. Nonviolence demonstrates the potential power of disarmed weakness over the revealed weakness of unjust power.

Again, more wisdom from John Caputo:

> *The power of God is not pagan violence, brute power, vulgar magic; it is the power of powerlessness, the power of the call, the power of protest that rises up from innocent suffering and calls out against it, the power that says no to unjust suffering, and finally the power to suffer-with (sym-pathos) innocent suffering, which is perhaps the central Christian symbol.*[21]

living in the margins

For the last half-century, a variety of new theological expressions have arisen under the umbrella term "contextual theology" as an alternative approach to the "received theology" of ancient church doctrines. Contextual theology is a way of thinking about God, Jesus, the Bible, and the Christian life from cultural perspectives that differ from the experience of white middle class Christians in the United States. Black theology, feminist theology, queer theology, and liberation theology are all expressions of this contextual approach. These are theologies that spring from the underside and the margins of society. They reflect the realities of people who are often beleaguered, broken, and demoralized by mainstream culture. Contextual theologies frequently deal with the issue of justice by seriously considering biblical responses to the unjust conditions that often confront the victims of prejudice, oppression, and violence.

In response to the often inflexible, unchanging approach of traditional received Christian theology, contextual theologies are supple and responsive

---

21. Ibid, 43.

to new realities. Rather than the exclusivity of orthodox dogma, contextual theologies seek to find a loving, inclusive, and generous path. They seek to be relevant to the ever-changing conditions of the despised, rejected, and abandoned people of the world. Contextual theologies are often unsettling and frequently controversial to those who are advantaged by the status quo.

These new theological approaches are fundamentally a method of understanding the profound human experience of the least, the lost, and the lonely people of our world. The process begins by listening to, learning from, and living in deep solidarity with those in society's margins to whom few pay attention and even fewer care. It is rooted in the stories of their pain and struggles. Many of us are people of privilege who simply find it difficult to identify with people whom our culture forces to their knees in shame, sorrow, and despair. Yet, this marginal world is where we are called to dwell as followers of Jesus—living in solidarity with marginal people, rejecting cultural conformity, and transforming our self-centered values of exclusivity, power, privilege, success, and security.

In Christianity, like many other religious traditions, orthodox beliefs and morality are used to create boundaries, borders, and delineations that define the differences between insiders and outsiders, good and bad, righteous and unrighteous, holy and profane, clean and unclean, acceptable and unacceptable. These boundaries serve the purposes of the powerful and privileged. It was into the borderland between these two polarities that Jesus was born, lived, taught, and died. He embraced the excluded people at the margins, particularly those who were rejected by the privileged and powerful insiders of the religious, social, and political establishments of his day. As followers of Jesus, we are called to follow him into these borderlands as our new spiritual home. This is to be our place of mission and service, our place of conspiracy and resistance.

Pastor and educator Shanta Premawardhana has said:

> *The borderland is not to be tolerated as a temporary inconvenience, or a condition to be transcended, wrote theologian Paul Tillich, rather, it is to be claimed as home. We are called to hold out at the boundary and to resist the temptation to flee this condition of pressure by settling down on one side of the boundary or the other, he said.*
>
> *In that borderland we find fellow travelers, wearied by the journey, oppressed by the system, and lacking in organized power, unable to act for our own liberation. Those of us in the margins are a varied bunch. We come from different places, are colorful,*

have a variety of beliefs, cultures and life-styles. We are misfits to the dominant culture.[22]

Like Paul's description of Jesus in his letter to the church at Philippi, we are called to empty ourselves from positions of privilege and power to take the form of servants, even at the risk of denigration, persecution, arrest, and death.[23] Learning to live out Jesus' command to love our neighbor (which is common to many religious traditions) requires us to dispense with artificial religious barriers and to identify with those who live daily in the margins of a society still dominated in the United States by conservative white males who often claim to be Christian. As followers of Jesus, we are called to engage with those who are different from us ethnically and religiously through the practices of radical hospitality, interreligious collaboration, and political solidarity. But the important thing is that we are to engage not as well-meaning superiors who stoop to help the inferior poor, but as equals. We are to engage as brothers and sisters. We are to connect in such a way that we can share the experience and pain of those who society disdains. It is there we encounter the weakness of the God of love/justice.

---

22. Premawardhana, "A Demonstration of Contextual Theology."
23. Philippians 2:5–8

CHAPTER 14

a religionless Christianity

If religion is only a garment of Christianity—and even this garment has looked very different at different times—then what is a religionless Christianity?[1]

Jesus does not call us to a new religion, but to life.[2]

—DIETRICH BONHOEFFER (1906–1945)

Postmodern people seem to be heading away from traditional "church Christianity" to some new mode of being a Christian in the world—Christianity developing outside of the walls of a church building. Nearly 70 years ago, Dietrich Bonhoeffer (1906–1945) first conjectured on the possibility of this happening. Bonhoeffer was a German Lutheran pastor and theologian who opposed the state-controlled German Evangelical Church formed under Adolf Hitler. In my earlier book, *A Conspiracy of Love*, I told the story of Bonhoeffer's activities with the dissenting pastors of the Confessing Church in Germany who stood in opposition to the Nazi takeover of the German Evangelical Church.

Initially, the resistance was focused on theological matters alone. About 25 percent of Protestant clergy opposed attempts by the state to conform Christian teaching and worship to Nazi ideology. Gradually, Bonhoeffer began to see that the church could not continue to be concerned simply with the purity of its own life and practice. He believed the church was the

1. Bonhoeffer, *Letters and Papers*, 280.
2. Ibid, 362.

church only when it lived for others. Bonhoeffer realized that the church needed to do more and become active in the resistance to systemic evil.

> *We are not to simply bandage the wounds of victims beneath the wheels of injustice, we are to drive a spoke into the wheel itself.*[3]

Bonhoeffer's resistance

Bonhoeffer became increasingly engaged in the work of a conspiracy committed to the overthrow of the Nazi government, especially within the *Abwehr* (the German Military Intelligence Office), that planned to assassinate Adolf Hitler and take over the government in order to broker a surrender to the Allies before Germany's destruction was complete. In March 1943, Bonhoeffer was arrested and imprisoned by the Gestapo because documents found in the Abwehr offices linked him to various subversive activities, specifically to his participation in "Operation 7," an undercover activity that spirited fourteen German Jews across the border to neutral Switzerland under the pretext that they were Abwehr agents.

In July 1944, an attempt was made to assassinate Hitler. It failed disastrously, and hundreds of political prisoners were executed afterwards. Bonhoeffer was eventually hanged at the Nazi concentration camp at Flossenbürg on April 9, 1945 only a month before the end of the war in Europe. He was 39 years old and had spent the last two years of his life as a prisoner.

can we be religious anymore?

Nearly a year after his imprisonment, in a letter written on April 30, 1944 from cell 92 in Berlin's Tegel penitentiary, Dietrich Bonhoeffer described his thoughts about the state of Christianity to his good friend Eberhard Bethge (1909–2000), who later edited Bonhoeffer's writings.

> *You would be surprised, and perhaps even worried, by my theological thoughts and the conclusions that they lead to . . . What is bothering me incessantly is the question what Christianity really is, for us today.*[4]

In light of the depravity of the Nazi state and the horrific violence of the Second World War, perpetrated by religious people on all sides, Bonhoeffer

---

3. Bonhoeffer, No *Rusty Swords*, "The Church and the Jewish Question," 225.
4. Bonhoeffer, *Letters and Papers*, 279.

questioned what Christianity represented any more. Why are Christians so unquestioningly captive to their culture? Why did German Christians not protest the persecution of the Jews? Why were they so unwilling to stand up to evil authorities and unjust laws? Bonhoeffer began struggling with what it means to claim to be religious in any real sense. And he saw a time coming in which religion would prove to be fundamentally irrelevant.

> *We are moving towards a completely religionless time; people as they are now simply cannot be religious anymore. Even those who honestly describe themselves as "religious" do not in the least act up to it, and so they presumably mean something quite different by "religious"...*
>
> *And if therefore man becomes radically religionless—and I think that is already more or less the case (else, how is it, for example, that this war, in contrast to all previous ones, is not calling forth any "religious" reaction?)—what does that mean for "Christianity"?*[5]

Bonhoeffer was disappointed that religious people—lay and clergy alike—were not speaking out or taking a stand, and their social and political struggles were conducted without drawing on their faith—or more likely, that their faith had become so disjointed from social and political conditions that they saw no connection.

If religious institutions in every nation were willingly transforming themselves into servants of the state, and were not raising a prophetic voice for peace and justice, was there another possibility for Christianity in the world? In his prison cell Bonhoeffer questioned:

> *Are there religionless Christians? If religion is only a garment of Christianity—and even this garment has looked very different at different times—then what is a religionless Christianity?*[6]

What would Christianity look like when it is stripped bare? Bonhoeffer began to struggle with what remains when the typical traits of a religion—clergy, religious institutions, sacred rites, orthodox beliefs, and an absolute morality—are eliminated. How would that redefine Christianity? What would be left?

What bothered Bonhoeffer was that a person could confess doctrinally correct beliefs, observe its moral codes, and follow the accepted behaviors and practices of the church, while simultaneously hating and oppressing other human beings. The question thus becomes: how is it possible that the practice

5. Ibid, 279–280.
6. Ibid, 280.

of Christianity can become divorced from loving our neighbors in any real sense? How is it that religious practice—including word and sacrament—can leave a person ultimately unchanged at the core of his or her being?

a life of contemplation and action

Dietrich Bonhoeffer believed that, in the future, a new form of Christianity, stripped of its religious garments, would be limited to two things: contemplative prayer and righteous action in the world. He described his thoughts in a letter to the infant son of his good friend Eberhard Bethge on the occasion of the child's baptism in May 1944. Bonhoeffer had been asked to be godfather for his namesake Dietrich Bethge, a duty he could perform only from a jail cell.

> Today, you will be baptized a Christian . . . By the time you have grown up, the church's form will have changed greatly . . . Our church, which has been fighting in these years only for its own self-preservation, as though that were an end in itself, is incapable of taking the word of reconciliation and redemption to [humankind] and the world . . . Our being Christian today will be limited to two things: prayer and righteous action among [humanity]. All Christian thinking, speaking, and organizing must be born anew out of this prayer and action.[7]

I often look at Bonhoeffer's letter as one that could have been addressed to me. I was born less than three years after Dietrich Bethge. With others of my Baby Boomer generation, I have witnessed the increasing decline of "church Christianity" in Europe and North America. Seventy years later, the new form of Christianity is struggling to be born in a secular world.

> To be a Christian does not mean to be religious in a particular way, to cultivate some particular form of asceticism (as a sinner, a penitent, or a saint), but to be a [human being]. It is not some religious act which makes a Christian what he [or she] is, but participation in the suffering of God in the life of the world.[8]

> The religious act is always something partial; "faith" is something whole, involving the whole of one's life. Jesus calls men [and women], not to a new religion, but to life.[9]

---

7. Ibid, 299–300.
8. Ibid, 361. (This translation was taken from Robinson, *Honest to God*, 83.)
9. Ibid, 362.

Bonhoeffer believed that through contemplation and action, the Christian would learn a new way of thinking and seeing: to view the world from the perspective of those at the bottom of society.

> *It remains an experience of incomparable value that we have for once learnt to see the great events of world history from below, from the perspective of the outcasts, the suspects, the maltreated, the powerless, the oppressed and reviled, in short from the perspective of the suffering. If only bitterness and envy have during this time not corroded the heart; that we come to see matters great and small, happiness and misfortune, strength and weakness with new eyes; that our sense for greatness, humanness, justice and mercy has grown clearer, freer, more incorruptible; that we learn, indeed, that personal suffering is a more useful key, a more fruitful principle than personal happiness for exploring the meaning of the world in contemplation and action.*[10]

In the life of Jesus, we can clearly see the two dimensions of religionless Christianity—contemplative prayer and righteous action. The gospels describe Jesus continually moving between these two polarities. He often withdraws to the wilderness or to a quiet, lonely place to meditate and pray alone. And then he jumps back into the life of the world with healing actions and a bold prophetic voice. Prayer and righteous action were the key features of the life of Jesus. This is where Bonhoeffer believed that Christianity was heading in the future. Religionless Christianity is a life of caring for people and responding in concrete ways to heal wounds and alleviate the causes that lead to hurting people. That has been part of the church's mission over the centuries, but sometimes it seems to forget that it is central, not just a peripheral activity.

It will perhaps surprise many to say that the model for a religionless Christianity is Jesus himself. Jesus did not intend to found a new religion. Christianity as we know it was not his objective. His life, teachings and actions were focused on creating a new kind of personal and community life in the midst of the old. He set out to transform human life in the midst of a great empire and to challenge those forces that oppress and divide people in every society. This is the journey he invites us to take. This is where the example of Jesus leads today.

---

10. Ibid, 17.

CHAPTER 15

the way of love

Life's most persistent and urgent question is: "What are you doing for others?"[1]

—MARTIN LUTHER KING, JR (1929–1968)

Love will guide us, peace has tried us,
Hope inside us will lead the way.
On the road from greed to giving,
Love will guide us through the dark night.[2]

—SALLY ROGERS (B. 1956)

All you need is love.[3]

—JOHN LENNON (1940–1980) AND PAUL McCARTNEY (B. 1942)

L ove should be understood as an active verb, not an emotional feeling. Love becomes a reality in the midst of human life only when we embody it, share it, and live it. Therefore, that which we call "God"

---

1. Dr. King made this comment to an audience in Montgomery, Alabama on August 11, 1957. "An individual has not begun to live until he can rise above the narrow horizons of his particular individualistic concerns to the broader concerns of all humanity. Every person must decide, at some point, whether they will walk in the light of creative altruism or in the darkness of destructive selfishness. This is the judgment. Life's most persistent and urgent question is, 'What are you doing for others?'"

2. Sally Rogers, "Love Will Guide Us," 1985.

3. Lennon and McCartney, "All You Need Is Love," 1967.

is compassionate love expressed in action through human hands and voices.

For Dietrich Bonhoeffer, participation in the being of God was centered in a life for others. He believed that it is expressed in two key elements: 1) identifying with those who suffer (through contemplative prayer) and 2) acting in solidarity with them, or on their behalf, to achieve justice in an unjust world.

contemplative prayer

Bonhoeffer believed that regular contemplative prayer focused on the needs of others was important because it draws forth empathy and concern toward those whom we envision. Commonly known as intercessory prayer, this mental process brings individuals into our conscious mind and helps us identify with the situations they face—their joys and their sorrows, their trials and successes, their fears and their failures—making us more sensitive to their circumstances. Thinking deeply about other peoples' suffering—and not just solely our own particular problems helps put everything into a larger perspective.

Today, contemplative prayer is often defined as centering prayer. In contemporary terms, contemplative prayer is a listening process—opening the mind and heart to God that involves rhythmic deep breathing while focusing on a single word or mantra. But that is not how Bonhoeffer used the term. For him, it was not about achieving a state of consciousness focused on inner peace and tranquility; it was about moving beyond ourselves into the lives of others. In contemplative prayer, Bonhoeffer said, "I move into the other person's place. I enter their life . . . their guilt and distress. I am afflicted by their sins and their infirmity."[4] Bonhoeffer believed that this sense of identity with the situations of others was the necessary motivating force that would lead us to "act upon and affect the lives of men and women throughout the world."[5] Contemplation is a matter of opening one's heart and letting one's self be moved with compassion. One scientific study showed that motor circuits in the brain lit up when people were feeling compassionate, as if they were getting ready to do something about the suffering they were sensing.

---

4. Bonhoeffer, *Sanctorum Communio*, 133. I have taken the liberty to replace his male-oriented terms "man" and "his" with the words "person" and "their."

5. Spinner, *A Book of Prayers*, 227. Spinner does not cite the original Bonhoeffer source.

The importance of contemplative intercession is that it can move us to act in real and tangible ways, rather than calling upon an omnipotent God to act in a supernatural way while we sit idly by. Countless people typically pray daily for God to change conditions in the world. Their prayers may often sound as if they are reminding God what God's job is (to bring peace among warring nations, to bring healing to the sick, to be with those who suffer, etc.). They want to put everything in God's hands and let God deal with the mess we have created here below. This kind of prayer allows the petitioner to sit passively aside, waiting for God to act, ignoring the reality that the God of love can *only* work through us in the world. Since the human Jesus no longer dwells among us, it is now our duty as his followers to act on his behalf. A familiar prose poem commonly (but mistakenly) attributed to Saint Teresa of Ávila (1515–1582), a Spanish mystic, reformer, and writer states:

> *Christ has no body now but yours, no hands, no feet on earth but yours. Yours are the eyes through which He looks with compassion on this world. Christ has no body now on earth but yours.*[6]

Bonhoeffer likewise realized that the power we call God can *only* work through us in the world. It is not appropriate, nor is it realistic, to ask God to do things in the world independent of us. Contemplative prayer doesn't ask God to act; it is instead a motivating force for each of us to take action in concrete ways.

Bonhoeffer prayed so that he—acting as one of God's agents—would be motivated to change those things in the world that he could impact personally. He realized that instead of waiting for God to intervene, the God of love waits for us to act. Prayer on behalf of others stirs up the compassionate response that drives us to take the necessary action.

Because a God of love acts *through* us and *as* us, we are called to solidarity with those who suffer, empathizing with them, and sharing their suffering with them. Bonhoeffer wrote: "[We are] summoned to share in God's suffering at the hands of a godless world."[7] Solidarity with the suffering of the world is the essential Christian stance. Service to the suffering of the world is the essential Christian act.

---

6. A number of scholars have stated that these words are not found in the writings of Teresa of Ávila, therefore she is not the source. Instead, they seem to have originated in England around 1890 from the ideas of a Methodist minister Mark Guy Pearse (1842–1930) and later modified to its current form by Quaker medical missionary Sarah Elizabeth Rowntree (dates unknown). The current quote is an abbreviation of Rowntree's writings.

7. Bonhoeffer, *Letters and Papers*, 361.

Contemplative prayer that Bonhoeffer describes begins by bringing to mind those for whom we easily feel compassion—friends and family. It should then begin to expand in ever larger concentric circles to include others, not only those we are fondest of, but also those with whom we have difficulty.

Contemplative intercessory prayer is not just a practice for religious people. Atheists and agnostics can and should pray for others. This is a compassionate process that works for everyone, whether or not one believes in God's existence. "You can pray for someone even if you don't think God exists," said Gordon Atkinson, a Baptist preacher.

Going beyond friends, family, and acquaintances, our contemplation should bring to mind those who are in need and are suffering in our towns, our nation, and the world. This expanded form of contemplation is really a meditation on the issues and crises of daily life, reflecting the news of the world. It is important to look deeply at current events from one's theological perspective and see how that might inform a compassionate response. Karl Barth reportedly said, "We must hold the Bible in one hand and the newspaper in the other." He later clarified that one should interpret the news from the Bible's perspective. For me, the teachings of Jesus and the prophets of the Hebrew Bible provide a unique lens on the problems of the day.

Prayer can be an instrument of insurrection and transformation. If it doesn't lead us to begin the task of fundamentally changing the conditions of the domination system that cause massive suffering, then we do not really understand the purpose of prayer. Karl Barth is also reported to have said, "To clasp the hands in prayer is the beginning of an uprising against the disorder of the world."[8] Reformer Mohandas Gandhi (1869–1948) once said something similar: "Prayer is not an old woman's idle amusement. Properly understood and applied, it is the most potent instrument of action."

compassion

Compassion is a feeling of empathy with the suffering of others, the capacity to feel how others feel. The Latin root of the word *compassion* is a compound of *com* (with) and *passio* (suffer), which gives us the meaning *to suffer with*. Compassion is entering into the pain of another and feeling their suffering—experiencing it, sharing it, tasting it. It is identifying with the sufferer, being in solidarity with the sufferer.

True compassion is being so moved at a gut level that we are moved to the point of action. We are told that Jesus was moved by compassion for

---

8. This comment by Karl Barth is frequently quoted, but its source is not cited.

the poor. "He had compassion on them because they were harassed and helpless, like sheep without a shepherd."[9] And in the parable of the Good Samaritan he demonstrated that the one who loves the neighbor is the one who shows compassion on the one who suffers, even if that person is culturally defined as the "enemy."

Marcus Borg has said that, "For Jesus, compassion was the central quality of God and the central moral quality of a life centered in God." The Pharisees represented a theology of holiness, according to Borg, which was based on the holiness as a defining characteristic of God: "Be holy for I, Yahweh, am holy."[10] Jesus proclaimed a theology of compassion based on an alternative characterization of God's essence: "Be compassionate as your Father in heaven is compassionate."[11] Their differing theologies led them to different religious practices and different ways of living.

righteous action

The word *righteous* may need some clarification because the common understanding of righteousness is 1) being morally right, or 2) being right with God. These moralistic and relational understandings can sometimes lead the Christian to a sense of superior self-righteousness, inconsistent with the stance of Jesus. When he used the term *righteous*, Bonhoeffer was not talking about the moral quality of the doer; he is talking about the nature of the deed. Bonhoeffer was referring to a more holistic biblical understanding of righteousness—standing up for what is right, doing what is right and just. Righteousness means seeking justice in human society.

The terms *righteousness* and *justice* are often linked in biblical texts. That is because they are synonymous, redundant terms. In the original languages of the Bible, the word for justice also means righteousness. The Greek word *dikaios* (*dik'-ah-yos*) in the New Testament and the word *tzedakah* (*tze-dah-kah'*) in the Hebrew Bible have this dual meaning. Righteousness implies a personal and individual dimension, while justice implies a social dimension, but they both have the same objectives—acting on behalf of those suffering from injustice.

Compassionate action usually takes three forms: charity, service, and justice. Although some would also include servanthood under the first category, charity more specifically involves gifts of money, clothing, food, or other material goods, but does not necessarily involve an investment of time and

9. Matthew 9:36
10. Leviticus 11:44
11. Luke 6:36

talents. Charity is very important, but writing a check to a worthy cause does not necessarily transform our lives. We can remain distant from those we seek to help. Service, however, involves us face-to-face with those in need. It can be an immensely transformative experience that can change us from our natural state of self-centeredness into increasingly selfless people. Perhaps it is the only thing that can. Although generosity sometimes leads to self-satisfaction, service often becomes a very humbling and deeply moving experience.

Charity and service are both personal forms of compassionate action. Their objective is to alleviate the effects of suffering in the world. Justice, on the other hand, seeks to eliminate the root causes of suffering. Martin Luther King, Jr. said:

> We are called to play the Good Samaritan on life's roadside; but that will be only an initial act. One day the whole Jericho road must be transformed so that men and women will not be beaten and robbed as they make their journey through life. True compassion is more than flinging a coin to a beggar; it understands that an edifice that produces beggars needs restructuring.[12]

Justice is the social form of compassionate action, focused on transforming the social structures and systems that produce poverty and suffering. It is the political form of caring for the least of these. The difference between charity and service on the one hand and justice on the other is this: charity and service seek to heal wounds, while justice seeks to end the social structures that create wounded people in the first place. William Sloane Coffin has said: "The bible is less concerned with alleviating the effects of injustice, than in eliminating the causes of it."[13] Still, all three of these compassionate practices are necessary components of what Bonhoeffer describes as righteous action among humanity.

charity

Jesus was a radical. And nowhere else is this more evident than in his call for radical charity and generosity. His words are a significant challenge.

> *Give to everyone who begs from you.*[14]
>
> *Do not refuse anyone who wants to borrow from you.*[15]

---

12. King, *Where Do We Go from Here?*, 198.
13. Coffin, *Credo*, 50.
14. Luke 6:30
15. Matthew 5:42

> *Lend, expecting nothing in return.*[16]
> *Sell your possessions, and give alms.*[17]

Jesus challenged his followers to give up everything to follow him. He invited them to step out in a journey of faith with no material security as a safety net. As far as we know, Jesus was homeless and possessionless himself, depending on the charity of others for food and shelter. We are told that he sent his followers out to the villages of Galilee with no money or food, telling them to depend on the kindness of the strangers they met along the way to provide sustenance and shelter.

Matthew, Mark, and Luke all describe a rich young man who came to Jesus to discover what more he could do with his life. He was trying hard to love God and his neighbor. Mark's gospel says that "Jesus looked at him and loved him" for his sincerity and effort. When the young man asked Jesus if there was anything more he could do, Jesus responded:

> *Go, sell what you own, and give the money to the poor, and you will be spiritually rich; then come, follow me.*[18]

We are told the young man "walked away sad, because he had great wealth." Jesus was trying to get those who sought to follow him to understand that there are two ways to achieve security in life. The first is to take care of ourselves by accumulating personal wealth. This is what the rich young man had done. The second is to create a community in which we care for each other by sharing our wealth. This is what loving one's neighbor means. And this is what the rich young man could not do. Maintaining his personal wealth was too important. Giving it away was too great a risk. To live this way requires an enormous act of faith.

Following Jesus can be costly, but we are not required to emulate Jesus by abandoning all our possessions and financial security. Instead, the idea that we should pool our resources to help one another is central to the communities that gathered around him. This was how the Jerusalem community of his disciples structured themselves after the death of Jesus. They maintained their own homes while generously contributing to a common fund in order to care for others as needs arose. This small effort by Jesus' followers represents the beginning of a social safety net in society. It became the most distinctive characteristic of early Christianity for nearly three hundred years. There are still models of this radical approach in small monastic communities and house churches today. But more importantly,

16. Luke 6:35
17. Luke 12:32
18. Mark 10:21

the way of Jesus involves using our pooled resources on local, national, and global scales to care for those afflicted by poverty and war.

The kind of radical personal charity that Jesus recommended is rare. Regardless of our generosity, most of us are cautious in how we use our funds. We know we can do more, yet we hold back, not wanting to be taken advantage of by undeserving people. But, no matter how generous we are, in the end, charity is only a Band-Aid. It fills the gaps left by an unjust society. Charity is important, but it is not enough.

service

Serving the needs of others is the path of transformation from ego-centrism to humility and self-giving love. Our captivity to our ego in the context of the present domination system causes us to value success, importance, and praise. But Jesus calls us to deny ourselves—our self-importance, our self-centeredness, our innate selfishness—and by humbling ourselves, serve others in need.

Matthew's gospel recounts the story of two of Jesus' disciples—brothers James and John—and their mother who misunderstood the political nature of the kingdom of God, who desired greatness and acclaim.

> *Then the mother of the sons of Zebedee came to him with her sons, and kneeling before him, she asked a favor of him. And he said to her, "What do you want?" She said to him, "Declare that these two sons of mine will sit, one at your right hand and one at your left, in your kingdom."*

When the other disciples heard this, they became angry with the two brothers.

> *But Jesus called them to him and said, "You know that the rulers of the Gentiles lord it over them, and their great ones are tyrants over them. It will not be so among you; but whoever wishes to be great among you must be your servant, and whoever wishes to be first among you must be your slave."*[19]

Luke's gospel has a parallel account:

> *A dispute also arose among them as to which one of them was to be regarded as the greatest. But he said to them, "The kings of the Gentiles lord it over them; and those in authority over them are called benefactors. But not so with you; rather the greatest among*

---

19. Matthew 20:20–28

you must become like the youngest, and the leader like one who serves. For who is greater, the one who is at the table or the one who serves? Is it not the one at the table? But I am among you as one who serves."[20]

We all have an inborn desire to be noticed, to be affirmed, and to feel significant. But a servant is one who quietly and humbly serves the needs of others regardless of personal recognition. So, if we're striving to be like Jesus, no task should be beneath us, no person below us, and no appropriate sacrifice too great.

There are many ways to serve, but we should be aware of some pitfalls. Professor Rachel Remen (b. 1938) identifies our natural inclination to help others and to fix them as impediments to real service.

Service is not the same as helping. Helping is based on inequality; it's not a relationship between equals. When you help, you use your own strength to help someone with less strength. It's a one up, one down relationship, and people feel this inequality. When we help, we may inadvertently take away more than we give, diminishing the person's sense of self-worth and self-esteem . . . Helping incurs debt: when you help someone, they owe you. But service is mutual. When I help I have a feeling of satisfaction, but when I serve I have a feeling of gratitude.

Serving is also different to fixing. We fix broken pipes, we don't fix people. When I set about fixing another person, it's because I see them as broken. Fixing is a form of judgement that separates us from one another; it creates a distance.

We may help or fix many things in our lives, but when we serve, we are always in the service of wholeness.[21]

Theologian Jean Vanier (b. 1928) is the founder of L'Arche, a group of communities in 35 countries for people with developmental disabilities and those who assist them. He describes service chiefly as being present with and accompanying another. The word *accompany*, like the word *companion*, comes from the Latin words *cum pane* (*cum pahn'-ay*), which mean "with bread." Accompaniment implies sharing together, eating together, nourishing each other, and walking together.

Accompaniment is necessary at every stage of our lives, but particularly in moments of crisis when we feel lost, engulfed in grief or in feelings of inadequacy. The accompanier is there to give support, to reassure, to confirm, and to open new doors. The accompanier

20. Luke 22:24–27
21. Remen, "Helping, Fixing, Serving."

is not there to judge us or to tell us what to do, but to reveal what is most beautiful and valuable in us.[22]

Anyone can serve another in this way. A true servant is one who has answered an inner call to show up and be present to what is right before them, and who asks the question, "What can I contribute?" Three simple steps can guide you.

- First, observe. Look around to see what the needs are. Identify where people are hurting and suffering. Ask yourself where your heart is drawn.
- Second, reflect. Pray, read, think, talk, journal. Do you have a sense of call or mission? Can you visualize what your heart is calling you to do?
- Third, act. Start small. Do what you can. Your actions may not change the world, but they will impact those you serve and may transform your life in remarkable ways.

The following quote has been often attributed to Mother Teresa. Regardless of who said it, it is an important thought.

If you can't do great things, do little things with great love. If you can't do them with great love, do them with a little love. If you can't do them with a little love, do them anyway.[23]

justice

Loving one's neighbor calls us to much more than charity and service; it means working for a just and equitable society. Justice is ultimately the most important factor in loving our neighbors. Philosopher and activist Cornell West (b. 1953) once said, "Justice is what love looks like in public. You can't talk about loving folk and not fight for justice"[24]

The word *justice* means different things to different people. For many people, it brings to mind *retributive* justice, which seeks to punish lawbreakers. Some of us think of *procedural* justice, which makes sure that everyone gets fair treatment under the law. However, the biblical meaning of justice is *distributive* justice, which promises a fair share of the necessities of life. The Bible teaches that justice is economic sharing. Those who have more,

---

22. Vanier, *Becoming Human*, 129.

23. Attributed to Mother Teresa by Ortberg, *The Me I Want to Be*, 141. No original source cited.

24. This comment by West is frequently quoted, but not cited.

help those who have less. Biblical scholar John Dominic Crossan reacted to the suggestion by some conservatives that the equitable sharing of our resources is nothing more that liberalism, socialism, or communism by suggesting that if we need to give biblical justice an "ism," the best label would be "enoughism."

The pursuit of justice leads us directly into politics. We cannot avoid it. Therefore the command to love our neighbor is always a political command. To follow Jesus and to proclaim the God of justice leads us to a distinctly political stance of looking out for the welfare of the poor and disadvantaged. To avoid proclaiming God's call to distributive justice is to support the status quo of the domination system—which is also a political stance.

Charity, service, and justice are all needed in a suffering world. The question is why Christians nearly always favor the personal forms of charity and service over social justice. In an unjust world, only the first and more limited responses—charity and service—are acceptable to those in power. The work of faith-based charities is often lauded by government until they try to influence government policies to change the status quo. Television journalist Bill Moyers (b. 1934) has said:

> *Charity is commendable; everyone should be charitable. But justice aims to create a social order in which, if individuals choose not to be charitable, people still don't go hungry, unschooled, or sick without care. Charity depends on the vicissitudes of whim and personal wealth; justice depends on commitment instead of circumstance. Faith-based charity provides crumbs from the table; faith-based justice offers a place at the table.*[25]

Dom Helder Camara (1909–1999), a Roman Catholic bishop from the poor Brazilian region of Recife said in the 1960s, "When I feed the poor, they call me a saint. When I ask why they are poor, they call me a Communist."[26] And John Dominic Crossan once said, "Charity gets you canonized; justice gets you crucified."[27] In the church, it is easier to talk about charity than justice. This is because justice gets us squarely into politics where we come face-to-face with the institutional selfishness of the domination system that we have created and supported. More importantly, it gets us into questions of how to achieve justice.

---

25. Moyers' Foreword to Wallis, *Faith Works*, xvii.
26. Rocha, *Helder*, 53.
27. I heard Crossan say this at a retreat at Kirkridge in Bangor, Pennsylvania in 2003. It is found in a slightly different form in *The Birth of Christianity*, 586: "Those who live by compassion are often canonized. Those who live by justice are often crucified."

In the current political realm, conservatives tend to favor charity, while liberals look to justice to deal with issues of suffering. We face a political divide on how to help the poor most effectively. One position holds that it is the role of individuals to voluntarily help the poor to whatever extent an individual feels called to provide from their resources. The other position maintains that as a society we have an obligation to deal with hunger, homelessness, and poverty together through governmental programs wherever possible. The first approach would use free-will offerings, while the other believes that our national treasure allows us to better accomplish societal needs as a people. Ask any major charity in the United States and they will tell you that without government help, charitable contributions fall significantly short of the pressing needs.

In response to suffering, a weak and powerless God of love moves us to action, urging us to transform the human conditions that cause suffering. From Deuteronomy to Micah to Matthew, the call is clear:

> *Justice, and only justice, you shall pursue.*[28]
> *What does the Lord require of you but to do justice?*[29]
> *Strive first for the kingdom of God and God's justice.*[30]

In spite of the seeming immensity of the task, there is hope that a just society is possible. As Martin Luther King, Jr. said, "The long arc of the universe bends toward justice." But as Barack Obama (b. 1961) added, "The arc of the moral universe may bend towards justice, but it does not bend on its own." We are called to be the shapers of the moral universe.

As followers of Jesus, we are called to pursue justice on behalf of the vast majority of people all around the world who suffer under the present domination system. Nobel Peace Prize winner Rigoberta Menchú (b. 1959) wrote:

> *We feel it is the duty of Christians to create the kingdom of God on Earth among our brothers. This kingdom will exist only when we all have enough to eat, when our children, brothers, parents don't have to die from hunger and malnutrition. That will be the "Glory," a Kingdom for we who have never known it.*[31]

The reign of God is about doing for the entire human family what we do within our individual families. Loving the whole human family means

---

28. Deuteronomy 16:20
29. Micah 6:8
30. Matthew 6:33
31. Menchú, *I, Rigoberta Menchú*, 158.

insuring that everyone gets a fair and equitable access to the necessary means of life: food, clean water, clothing, shelter, education, health care, meaningful employment, safety, and protection from violence. As followers of Jesus, it is up to us to figure out how to live together as a human community, how to love one another, and how to care for the earth and all its creatures.

Acts of compassion, charity, service, and justice not only help others, they also transform us into better people. In becoming better people, we have a chance to create a better world. If we live our lives as followers of Jesus, if we engage in his mustard seed conspiracy of love and justice, his vision of the inbreaking reign of love will be fulfilled within us and around us one small sacred act at a time. And all we need is love.

CHAPTER 16

a conspiracy of love

The decisive time has arrived, for the conspiracy of love is rising up to challenge the unjust systems of the world. Change your whole way of thinking and living, and risk everything for this radical message of hope.[1]

—JESUS OF NAZARETH

Join the conspiracy, and love with all your heart and all of your courage. Let your love be defiant. Let your love be rebellious. Join the conspiracy and make change in your life because change will not roll in on the wheels of inevitability, it must be carried in on the backs of lovers.[2]

—SENATOR CORY BOOKER (B.1969)

At the heart of the gospel of Jesus is the *kingdom of God*. This one phrase sums up the entire ministry of Jesus and his whole life's work. As we read the gospels of Matthew, Mark, and Luke, we see that every thought and saying of Jesus was directed and subordinated to one single thing: the realization of the reign of God's love, compassion, and peace within human society. Jesus spoke of the kingdom of God more than any other subject. His number two topic was the danger of personal wealth and a call to radical generosity with those in need.

---

1. My paraphrase of Mark 1:14–15: "Jesus came into Galilee, proclaiming the gospel of God, and saying, 'The time has come, the kingdom of God is at hand; repent and believe in the good news.'" See also Matthew 4:17: "From that time Jesus began to preach, saying, 'Repent, for the kingdom of heaven is at hand.'"

2. Booker, "Conspiracy of Love."

The Greek word which we have translated into English as *kingdom* is *basileia* (*bas-il-eh'-ah*), which means kingdom, realm, reign, or rule. The expression *kingdom of God—basileia tou theou* (*bas-il-eh'-ah too theh'-oo*)—points to the ruling activity of God over human social relationships. Herod the Great had the title of *basileus* (*bas-il-yooce'*) or king. So *basileia* has to do with *who* governs the common life and *what kind* of government they establish. When Jesus used the term *kingdom of God* it was a vision of the kind of government or social contract that God desired within human societies. The kingdom of God stands in direct contrast to the domination systems that govern our world.

Throughout history, nearly every society has favored an elite group of individuals and families at the expense of the majority of less-fortunate inhabitants. For thousands of years, economic elites have rigged society in their favor by crafting systems that would benefit their prosperity and ensure their control over the nation's political and economic affairs. Historically, they have used unjust economic systems to extract wealth from the sweat of slaves, peasants, and laborers, while contributing little to the common welfare. Social control has been maintained with violence and military might, often supported by religious institutions. These societies have invariably been patriarchies where the authority and desires of men have dominated the lives of women and children. The system has frequently favored one race, tribe, or ethnic group over others.

Biblical scholar Walter Wink has referred to these societies as manifestations of an enduring *domination system* that has been part of the human story since the rise of civilization in the ancient near east. Wink describes the domination system in this way:

> *It is characterized by unjust economic relations, oppressive political relations, biased race relations, patriarchal gender relations, hierarchical power relations, and the use of violence to maintain them all. No matter what shape the dominating system of the moment might take (from the ancient Near Eastern states to the Pax Romana to feudal Europe to communist state capitalism to modern market capitalism), the basic structure has persisted now for at least five thousand years, since the rise of the great conquest states of Mesopotamia around 3000 BCE.*[3]

We easily observe the domination system in the structure of kingdoms, empires, and dictatorships. It has been embodied in traditional customs and religious teachings throughout history. But when democratic systems in a largely secular culture are controlled by wealthy and powerful forces, the

---

3. Wink, *Powers That Be*, 39–40.

same results occur. Massive tax cuts for the wealthiest, bloated military budgets, welfare for giant corporations, vast prison systems, and cuts to social services for the poorest Americans are all signs of a domination system.

Jesus declared that a new form of common life was rapidly coming into being. He urgently announced to his contemporaries, "The kingdom of God is at hand!"[4]

Over the centuries, the church has rarely understood the true nature of the kingdom of God as proclaimed by Jesus, and for many people in the church it is not even on their radar screen. In my previous book, *A Conspiracy of Love*, I devoted an entire chapter to clarifying the meaning of the kingdom in Jesus' teachings. I challenged the six most prevalent interpretations of what he meant by the term: heaven, an inner spiritual experience, the church, a separate society, a new state, and a new world. If we read the gospels closely, none of these traditional interpretations fit with the visionary images in the proclamation of Jesus. In fact, most are an attempt to domesticate the vision of Jesus—to control it, to water it down, to render it harmless. Instead, the kingdom of God was the metaphor Jesus used to describe his vision of the way things were meant to be in human society—how things could be dramatically different within us and among us if we embrace a life of love, compassion, service, generosity, and justice.

The power of a vision is that while it describes the future state to be achieved, it begins to immediately shape the present. A community or organization doesn't wait for a vision to magically happen, they work together to make it a reality. Jesus chose to take the long awaited dream of a just and compassionate society, and by articulating and acting on it, made it a vision that would lead to the transformation of the world.

The reigning of God in any society is about a radical shift in human life that stirs the political wind. It is the understanding that a new regime is about to change everything. This is not the old style of change in which one despot is replaced with another. This is about the end of despotic rule entirely, replaced by new social relationships based on equality, compassion, and liberation. This is an announcement that something dramatic is happening in the world. Ancient dreams are becoming reality. A movement is forming, and people are joining. Freedom is coming. Justice is arriving. It is chaotic, but it is exciting.

The leader of this movement is not visible, but the people who join it are—seen here and there engaged in work for change. Some actions are small, under the radar. At other times the results of the individual and

---

4. Mark 1:15. English translations vary: "The kingdom of God has come near" or "The kingdom of God is at hand."

collective work for change becomes readily apparent. There isn't any central coordination, just a common vision guiding the work of many people. Occasionally, a prophetic voice is raised and the powerful take heed.

Yet the challenge is huge. The rule of the rich and mighty is the normal state of civilization, and the old systems refuse to change. Many people benefit from the current situation and the status quo. The purveyors of self-interest and greed are frightened that a different world may no longer favor them. And the economic powers who rule the world's nations are not about to give up their power and privilege and wealth without a fight. They have laws and police forces and armies at their disposal. They show little hesitation to use armed violence, imprisonment, torture, and capital punishment to maintain control. The powerful dominate our information through news media that are controlled by wealthy corporations. For the people of Jesus' revolutionary new movement in any time or place, it is always a season of challenge and danger and risk, which calls for great personal courage, sacrifice, and faith.

When trying to convey the nature of this vision, sometimes the metaphor gets in the way. As a metaphor, the *kingdom of God* does not work very well in present circumstances, nor will it conceivably work any better in the future. Kingdoms are diminishing around the world. Democracies are rising. But no matter what form governments take, domination systems abound. So it would be helpful to find a new metaphor that people can better understand and connect with in the twenty-first century. We need a fresh language that will better describe the vision of Jesus and our role as his followers in a postmodern world.

I believe that *the conspiracy of God* can be an intriguing new metaphor for what Jesus was describing, especially in light of his parables of the mustard seed and the leaven. Brian McLaren has suggested a series of new metaphors including the *dream of God* (the vision), the *revolution of God* (the activity), and the *network of God* (the people). These three come together for me in the *conspiracy of God*. I see the pursuit of the kingdom of God as the subversive activity of a people who are focused on Jesus' vision of a better world—a world governed by love.

The word *conspiracy* derives from the same root as *spirit*. The Latin root *spirare* (*spee'-rah-reh*) means *to breathe*. For example, the word *respiration* is *to breathe again* and *inspiration* means *to breathe in*—to be filled with the spirit. To *conspire* normally connotes agreement or unity in an activity, but it literally means *to breathe together*. Those engaged in a conspiracy are so united around an idea or action that they are seen to breathe as one.

I believe that Jesus called his followers to engage in a conspiracy of profound personal and social transformation that will undermine the global domination system in every family, town, and nation. And when a handful of people engage in this conspiracy, they become co-conspirators in a subversive counter-cultural network inaugurated and led by Jesus. He said, "Where two or three are gathered in my name, I am there among them."[5] Jesus suggested that this kind of conspiracy would become a manifestation of his ongoing presence—a sign of resurrection, a sign of new life, a sign of dramatic change in the world.

I want to take this conspiracy metaphor another step further. I don't believe that one has to be a Christian to be engaged in the work of the conspiracy of God. After all, the peasants Jesus spoke to in Galilee, Judea, and Samaria were not Christians, and they were the first ones called to the task. The Jewish concept of *tikkun olam*, a Hebrew phrase that means repairing or healing the world, likewise suggests that as humans we have a shared responsibility to transform the world through social action in the pursuit of social justice. Many other faiths have similar calls to work for a better world. The vision of Jesus requires the involvement of people everywhere—people of every faith and people of no faith at all. The role of the Christian church should be to point toward this great vision and to bear witness to it, but if the church refuses to respond to the kingdom, or tries to domesticate it, or continues to mislead people about its centrality in the message of Jesus, then the conspiracy of God will still move forward without the involvement of the church.

So, now, I'll push the metaphor even further. In my opinion, one does not even have to believe in God—at least not in the traditional sense of a supernatural being—to be part of the conspiracy of God. When we imagine selfless love as the manifestation of God in human life, this equation of God and love opens up the conspiracy of God to everyone, no matter what their image or their understanding or their definition of God, because it can be understood as the kingdom of love, or the reigning of love, or the ruling style of love, or the governing mode of love that stands in opposition to an unjust domination system. It answers the question "What would the world be like if an unselfish love ruled our families, societies, and nations?" The reign of love involves love for the victims of oppression and love toward the perpetrators of injustice. It is a movement of love that wants not only transformation of the system itself, but a transformation of those who control the system. If justice is what love looks like in public, if justice is the social form of love, then a conspiracy of love is a conspiracy for justice.

So, I have now begun to favor the phrase *the conspiracy of love* as a contemporary metaphor for the reign or reigning style of God that

---

5. Matthew 18:19

comprehends a *vision*, a *transforming activity*, and a *people committed to change*. It suggests that a governing style of love is the vision that guides us, but that the daily work toward that vision is in the form of conspiratorial action. The conspiracy of love is a movement to disturb and confound the domination system and its rampant politics of selfishness with a new possibility—a domination-free society based on love, compassion, equality, and community. That was the message and mission *of* Jesus.

entering the conspiracy of love

The gospel of John begins and ends with the call of Jesus, "Follow me."[6] The disciples followed Jesus through the villages and towns of Galilee and eventually to a cross outside the city of Jerusalem. It was a journey of challenge, excitement, wonder, and terror. The act of following Jesus no matter where it leads is the essence of a life of discipleship. It is a journey that begins with a radical change in the direction of one's life. It takes the followers of Jesus beyond familiar places toward situations far outside their comfort zones. On the way, disciples discover that they have capabilities and talents that were previously unrealized. It is always a process of learning and doing on the move.

To follow Jesus means listening to his teaching; digging into his words and learning their meaning in the context of empire and domination, and like his disciples, sometimes understanding it, sometimes not quite getting it. However, discipleship is based upon the fundamental concept that lessons are to be put into practice as they are learned. The learning and the doing are a lifelong process. To follow Jesus is to embark on a lifelong journey of transformation—moving from a life of self-centered concern to a commitment to the common good of all; moving from cultural captivity to a life of counter-cultural opposition to all forms of domination, oppression, injustice, violence, and ecological degradation.[7]

Rather than standing in contrast to the predominant culture, Christianity is often shaped by the enveloping culture in subtle and profound ways. All of these cultural layers contribute to a life of conformity to social and religious conventions. It was to people such as us—who are shaped by a pervasive cultural conformity—that Jesus proclaimed a new way of thinking and living. The process of transformation that Jesus proposed requires

---

6. John 1:43 and John 21:19

7. In *Meeting Jesus Again for the First Time*, Marcus Borg describes discipleship as journeying with Jesus. The following thoughts are an elaboration of his work.

a questioning of all of our deeply held assumptions and inherited beliefs—political, economic, and religious.

We are called to follow Jesus in the real world—in a nation where guns are considered sacred, where violence is glorified, where military expenditures account for over half of our tax dollars, where market capitalism is deified, where consumerism is celebrated, where racism, sexism, and homophobia are rampant, and where selfishness is the dominant political value. We are called to be a different kind of people. As theologian Jacques Ellul said:

> *Christians were never meant to be normal. We've always been holy troublemakers, we've always been creators of uncertainty, agents of a dimension that's incompatible with the status quo; we do not accept the world as it is, but we insist on the world becoming the way that God wants it to be. And the Kingdom of God is different from the patterns of this world.*[8]

Following Jesus is a response to his call to establish justice and peace in the world. It makes one a troublemaker, a revolutionary, a seeker of change. It calls on one to be an agent of transformation, or as Jesus said, to be like a mustard seed in a tidy garden, a pinch of yeast in a large bowl of bread dough, a dash of salt in a pot of soup, or a small lamp in a darkened room. It is to add your light to the sum of lights so that little by little a violent, hungry, and suffering world can be renewed for the sake of its children.

the way of Jesus

As I read the deeds and words of Jesus in the gospels, I find nine key characteristics of the Way he taught others to follow. There may be more, but these nine themes run throughout his teachings and are obvious to a casual reader. They are radical actions, revolutionary ways of living that threaten the domination system, because they provide prescriptive remedies to the pervasive violence, oppression, suffering, and inequality that is epitomized by the status quo in nearly every society.

To follow Jesus means to embrace and manifest these qualities:

- radical love
- lavish generosity
- extravagant forgiveness

---

8. Jacques Ellul, *Meaning of the City*.

- inclusive hospitality
- compassionate action
- selfless service
- a passion for justice
- creative nonviolence
- simple living

These nine characteristics are the building blocks for a lifestyle of discipleship that can lead to the transformation of the world. Following Jesus means trusting that the Way of Jesus leads to a different quality of life—a fuller, more authentic human life lived for others and for the earth we inhabit. These are clear examples of the "weak force" of Jesus. They do not demand or compel or coerce; they invite.

1) To follow Jesus is to incarnate *radical love*—not love as a feeling, but love in action. Love is extending oneself to help one's neighbors—working for their spiritual, emotional, and physical growth. Love in our homes means that we work to make sure that our family members are cared for. Love in our community, nation and world means the same thing. Everyone is fed and clothed. Everyone receives adequate health care and opportunities for education. Furthermore, Jesus calls us to love our enemies, seeking their transformation instead of seeking to do them ill. Radical love means always expanding our boundaries. It involves working toward reconciliation with good and bad alike.

> *Love your neighbor as yourself.*[9]

> *I give you a new commandment, that you love one another. Just as I have loved you, you also should love one another. By this everyone will know that you are my disciples, if you have love for one another.*[10]

> *Love your enemies. Do good to those that hate you. Bless those who curse you. Pray for your abusers.*[11]

2) To follow Jesus is to share what we have with others. It calls us to a *lavish generosity*—graciously sharing our lives and resources. It means giving freely without thought of return. It also means generosity in many

---

9. Matthew 22:39
10. John 13:34–35
11. Q14 / Luke 6:27–28 / Matthew 5:44, 46

different contexts and at different societal levels: to individuals in need, including friends and family; to charities and nonprofits doing compassionate work for all people, both locally and globally; and through taxes paid to our local, state, and national governments to support education, health care, social programs, and emergency responses to people in need, here and around the world.

> *Give to everyone who begs from you, and do not refuse anyone who wants to borrow from you.*[12]

> *Lend, expecting nothing in return.*[13]

3) To follow Jesus is to forgive each other. It is a life of *extravagant forgiveness*—reconciling with those we have hurt and those who have hurt us, forgiving again and again and again.

> *Then Peter came and said to him, 'Lord, if my brother sins against me, how often should I forgive? As many as seven times?' Jesus said to him, 'Not seven times, but, I tell you, seventy times seven.*[14]

4) To follow Jesus is to welcome and accept others. It is the practice of *inclusive hospitality*—breaking down the barriers that divide us and accepting others without judgment. It means mixing with the unloved and undesirable. To follow Jesus is to welcome and accept everyone into our common life, inviting all to join us in community—the stranger, the alien, the immigrant, the refugee, and people of all races, faiths, and sexual orientations. It means affirming their rights in our society.

> *When you give a banquet, invite the poor, the crippled, the lame, and the blind. And you will be blessed for they cannot repay you.*[15]

> *It's not the healthy people who need the doctor, but the sick. I have come not to invite the respectable, but the undesirable.*[16]

5) To follow Jesus is to embrace a life of *compassionate action*. It begins with empathy with the situations of those who suffer and compassion toward their plight. It means opening our eyes to the needs around us and being moved to the point of action—caring for the stranger at the side of the

---

12. Matthew 5:42
13. Luke 6:35
14. Matthew 18:21–22
15. Luke 14:13
16. Mark 2:17 (My paraphrase)

road, the least, the lost, and the lonely. To follow Jesus means finding meaning and purpose in a compassionate love that binds us to the welfare of all.

> *Be compassionate as your Father is compassionate.*[17]

> *Blessed are the compassionate, for they shall receive compassion.*[18]

6) To follow Jesus means *selfless service*. It means engaging in personal service to people in need—meeting fundamental human needs of food, clothing, and shelter. It means giving up our need for importance in order to serve the least among us as an equal, not as a superior.

> *The greatest among you must become like the youngest* [or behave like a beginner], *and the leader like one who serves.*[19]

> *Whoever wants to be first must be the last of all and servant of all.*[20]

> *The greatest among you will be your servant.*[21]

7) To follow Jesus is to have *a passion for justice*. It means becoming an agent of change for a world in which everyone gets a fair share of resources and opportunities. It means speaking out on behalf of those who have no voice. It means challenging the politics of selfishness and pursuing an alternative politics of compassion. To follow Jesus means working for change from the bottom of society and not the top; from the margins and not the center. To follow Jesus means making the reign of love—societies governed with compassion, equality, and justice—a priority in our lives.

> *Strive first for the kingdom of God and its justice, and all these things will be given to you as well.*[22]

> *Blessed are those who hunger and thirst for justice! They will be satisfied.*[23]

---

17. Luke 6:36
18. Matthew 5:7
19. Luke 22:26
20. Mark 9:35
21. Matthew 23:11
22. Matthew 6:33
23. Matthew 5:6

8) To follow Jesus means using *creative nonviolence* in situations of conflict. It means seeking change without resorting to violence and absorbing hostility with nonviolent defiant action.

> *If anyone strikes you on the cheek, offer the other also; and from anyone who takes away your coat do not withhold even your shirt.*[24]

> *Blessed are those who work for peace, for they shall be called God's children.*[25]

9) To follow Jesus means *living simply* on the earth, living lightly like an itinerant or sojourner. It means not being bound by possessions and a lifestyle of wasteful consumption.

Today, our earth is threatened. Climate change is transforming life on Earth. Around the globe, seasons are shifting, temperatures are climbing, and sea levels are rising. Longer, more intense droughts threaten crops, wildlife and freshwater supplies. And meanwhile, our planet must still supply us—and all living things—with air, water, food, and safe places to live. To adequately address this crisis we must urgently reduce carbon pollution and that will mean changes in the way we live and consume.

I haven't found any particular emphasis on the care and protection of the earth, its resources, and its creatures in the first-century gospel accounts and the teachings of Jesus. It was essentially a non-issue when the global population was no more than 300 million people. But in the twenty-first century, with a population of over seven billion—increasing to eight billion within ten years—it is a vital concern. However, Jesus *did* teach a lifestyle that opposed the mad accumulation of wealth and material possessions. The followers of Jesus were taught to live simply, not because simplicity is a virtue in itself, but because the resources we do not consume may be used to benefit others. Saint Elizabeth Anne Seton (1774–1821), a formerly wealthy New York socialite, summed up the necessary message for our time when she said, "Live simply so that others may simply live."

The way of Jesus is a path toward a vision of the way the world ought to be, the way it is meant to be. It is a freely chosen path, but not without risk. There is never any assurance of success; only a promise of continuing challenge. It is a matter of trying and failing, and sometimes succeeding, but always continuing. Guided by the vision, the journey itself is the most important thing.

24. Luke 6:29
25. Matthew 5:9

a new (and old) theology

In the end, a postmodern theology about the nature of God and the Christian life does not have to be complicated. It is simply this: God is love/justice. God is encountered in two arena of life: in our personal relationships and in the pursuit of social justice. When God is conceived as human love, God's power is necessarily weak. Love does not force or compel us. It calls, entices, and invites us. Justice likewise is a weak power. Unlike civil law that requires compliance under force of punishment, justice is simply a vision of how things should be, of how love can be manifested in public. Justice also calls to us, pulling at us to do more and be more. It lures us toward a better world.

Love and justice are clearly "weak forces." But they are not powerless. They are the only forces that are capable of changing the world. Activist Marian Wright Edelman (b. 1939) once said,

> *You just need to be a flea against injustice. Enough committed fleas biting strategically can make even the biggest dog uncomfortable and transform even the biggest nation.*

Jesus described this approach in the parable of the unjust judge, or perhaps titled more accurately as the parable of the persistent widow.

> *In a certain city there was a judge who neither feared God nor had respect for people. In that city there was a widow who kept coming to him and saying, "Grant me justice against my opponent." For a while he refused; but later he said to himself, "Though I have no fear of God and no respect for anyone, yet because this widow keeps bothering me, I will grant her justice, so that she may not wear me out by continually coming."*[26]

Luke put this parable in the context of prayer, but if we strip away his preamble and conclusion, the parable is really about a flea making a dog uncomfortable. The judge dwells in a city and thus may be a member of the urban elite. Nothing apparently shames him (neither God nor other people) and perhaps he is considered unjust because he willingly accepts bribes to influence his decisions. The widow is a powerless person in her society. Yet she has the audacity to continually harass the judge for justice. And he finally gives in to her persistence. She wears him down. If the parable is about prayer and is considered as an allegory, then God is portrayed as an unjust judge. But what if we see God in the character of the persistent widow, always seeking justice? That is more likely to be where God is found in the struggle between justice and law. Because many of Jesus' parables are

---

26. Luke 18:2–5

about the kingdom of God, this is a story about kingdom tactics. Weak and powerless people keep striving for justice until the system gives in.

worship in a secular world

So if God is a symbol for self-giving love and the pursuit of social justice, how can we worship God in a postmodern world? Doesn't this change everything when there is no longer an all-powerful being to praise and supplicate? Prayer must be considered in a new way, but so must worship. In terms of a secular postmodern religious expression, if you want to demonstrate your love God, love your neighbor. Even more, love your enemies. If you want to praise God or worship God, work for justice. According to the Bible, the worship that God desires is the establishment of a just society. The Hebrew prophets Amos, Isaiah, Hosea, and Micah knew this well. To piously religious people living in an unjust domination system, they said:

> I [Yahweh] *hate, I despise your worship, and I take no delight in your religious gatherings . . . Spare me the din of your praise singing; let me hear none of your strumming on guitars. But let justice roll down like waters, and righteousness like an ever-flowing stream.*[27]

> *Is this not the fast that I* [Yahweh] *choose: to loose the bonds of injustice, to undo the thongs of the yoke, to let the oppressed go free, and to break every yoke? Is it not to share your bread with the hungry, and bring the homeless poor into your house; when you see them naked, to cover them, and not to hide yourself from your own kin?*[28]

> *I* [Yahweh] *desire love and not worship, the knowledge of God rather than sacrificial contributions.*[29]

> *If you oppress poor people, you insult the Creator who made them; but kindness shown to the poor is an act of worship.*[30]

---

27. Amos 5:21, 23–24 (My paraphrase)
28. Isaiah 58:6–7
29. Hosea 6:6
30. Proverbs 14:31

> *To do righteousness and justice is more acceptable to Yahweh than worship.*[31]

> *With what shall I come before Yahweh's presence and bow myself before God on high? Shall I come before him with offerings at the altar . . . with ten thousands of rivers of oil? . . . He has told you, O mortal, what is good; and what does Yahweh require of you but to do justice, and to love kindness, and to walk humbly with your God?*[32]

Can we be faithful to God without corporate worship? In his letter to the Christians at Rome, the Apostle Paul suggested that God wants something entirely different from us—an alternative kind of worship: a life of service to others, an ethic of compassionate action, and the pursuit of peace and justice. For Paul, these acts represent the only form of worship that a God of love deems good, acceptable, and perfect.

> *I appeal to you therefore, brothers and sisters, by the mercies of God, to present your bodies as a living sacrifice, holy and acceptable to God, which is your spiritual worship. Do not be conformed to this world, but be transformed by the renewing of your minds, so that you may discern what is the will of God—what is good and acceptable and perfect.*[33]

In this context Paul's use of the term "spiritual worship" seems to refer to an "active-practical spirituality." In *A Conspiracy of Love*, I described four major forms of spirituality. The first two—*ascetic* spirituality (disciplines of self-denial and abstention from worldly pleasures) and *mystical* spirituality (practices such as meditation, mindfulness, and contemplation)—are inwardly focused, leading to personal spiritual growth. We are most familiar with these forms. But Jesus taught an outwardly-focused spirituality leading to engagement with the world around us. *Active-practical* spirituality promotes service to others as a form of spiritual practice. In addition, Jesus personally modeled a *prophetic-critical* spirituality that goes beyond offering charitable service to challenging the fundamental causes of social inequality and injustice as a spiritual task. This is the spirituality of justice. This is the kind of worship that the Hebrew Bible says that God desires. Typically, a service of worship is found in a sanctuary at a special time, but a life of service as worship can be exhibited in secular society every day of the week.

---

31. Proverbs 21:3
32. Micah 6:6–8
33. Romans 12:1–2

In an unpublished essay, Dr. Lesly Massey, a Disciple of Christ pastor, wrote:

> Paul does not define worship in terms of rituals or ceremonies performed by Christians when assembled together, and therefore segregated from routine life. On the contrary, true worship is offered through the believer's daily life by means of a noble ethos practiced openly in the world. God's will is accomplished through that which is seemingly profane, and with such God is well pleased . . .
>
> True worship, therefore, amounts to an approach to mundane activities that gives evidence of an inner conversion and transformation by the living presence of Christ . . . In order to "worship" God one must offer a "service to God." The interests of God, the will of God, are not "served" by rituals, symbols, gestures, ceremonies, or platitudes. Paul was convinced, from his understanding of the teaching of Jesus, that God cannot be patronized by human lip-service. Rather, God is served by noble and exemplary living, motives, attitudes, perspectives, choices, and actions that demonstrate divine love and goodness in the world.[34]

Therefore, worship is giving one's whole self to the service of others and the pursuit of a just society. Our offering to the God of love/justice is manifested in our persistent agitating for justice, like that of the widow. It is never an easy task. Yet, it is not an impossible one either. So, how do we begin? Here are four steps each of us can implement as we strive to instigate the subversive and transformative vision of Jesus in our specific time and place:

- Be a bearer of the vision of the reign of love. Hold up a vision of how things ought to be.
- Be a conscience for the world. Critically assess how things are today. Point out the distance between the reality and the vision.
- Be a prophetic voice and an advocate. Identify those who are being hurt by the politics of selfishness in our contemporary domination system. Speak out for those who have no voice. Stand beside those who do. Be a moral compass for social leaders and elected officials.
- Be a change agent. Start small. Join with others as co-conspirators in the conspiracy of love.

---

34. Lesly F. Massey, "Perspectives on Christian Worship In Light of Romans 12:1" (2005).

return to plan A

Just before he died, Dietrich Bonhoeffer outlined a small book he intended to write about a religionless Christianity. One section would deal with belief. These were his brief notes:

> What do we really believe? I mean, believe in such a way that we stake our lives on it? The problem with the Apostles' Creed? [These] antiquated controversies . . . are now unreal. The faith of the Bible and Christianity does not stand or fall by these issues. Well then, what do we really believe?[35]

I often wonder how the entire nature of the church would change if we abandoned the Age of Belief embodied in traditional rites and doctrines and returned to an Age of Faith embodied in the lifestyle of the first followers of Jesus. What would a postmodern church be like if the creeds were no longer at the center of religious life, but were instead replaced by pursuing the nine lifestyle changes that Jesus encouraged?

I believe that focusing the church's teaching on these radical practices would dramatically change the content and the character of Christian congregations and, while making many uncomfortable, would draw many others to the Christian community as a place where something important happens not only on Sunday mornings, but more importantly during the rest of the week.

This book has challenged many traditional teachings of the church by questioning and carefully deconstructing accepted ideas about God as an omnipotent supernatural being; the Holy Spirit as a person-like being; the virgin birth and bodily resurrection of Jesus; the return of Jesus as an apocalyptic judge; the kingdom of God as a post-apocalyptic event; the doctrine of original sin; the cross as a symbol of sacrificial atonement; the existence of heaven and hell; and eternal life as a non-ending existence in heaven.

In contrast, I have tried to present a simple postmodern theology that presents God as a symbolic personification of human love; Jesus as a teacher of radical compassion and an outspoken agent of social justice; the kingdom of God as a contemporary "conspiracy of love" that challenges the unjust systems of the world; the Way of Jesus as a journey of transformation from cultural captivity to a counter-cultural life of activism and service; the cross as a symbol of the consequences of defying the authority and power of the domination system; and the resurrection of Jesus as the epiphany of his presence in a vision, in a voice, or in the face of a stranger.

---

35. Bonhoeffer, *Letter and Papers*, 382.

As we said at the outset, what many people do not realize is that the church developed as Plan B. Jesus did not seek to found a new religion centered on rites, rituals, buildings, and clergy. Instead, he proclaimed the inbreaking kingdom of God—a vision of the way the world would be if a God of love/justice governed our common life. Moreover, he taught a way of living consistent with that vision. To be faithful followers of Jesus is to return to Plan A.

As followers of Jesus, let us commit ourselves to a lifestyle of radical love, lavish generosity, extravagant forgiveness, inclusive hospitality, compassionate action, selfless service, a passion for justice, creative nonviolence, and simple living. Let us live with passion, zeal and courage, filled with a holy spirit that transforms our lives so that we might bring good news to the oppressed, bind up the brokenhearted, and proclaim release to the captive. Let us experience a new urgency and a new commitment to feed the hungry, clothe the naked, shelter the homeless, and visit those who live in isolation. Let us reach out to those whom no one else will touch, to accept the unacceptable, and to embrace the enemy. Let us respond to the call of Jesus and join his conspiracy of love.

bibliography

Armstrong, Karen. *A History of God: The 4000-Year Quest of Judaism, Christianity, and Islam.* New York: A.A. Knopf, 1993.

Augustine. *Confessions.* Translated and edited by Albert C. Outler. 1955. No pages. Online: http://www.ling.upenn.edu/courses/hum100/augustinconf.pdf

Baker, Sharon L. *Executing God: Rethinking Everything You've Been Taught about Salvation and the Cross.* Louisville, KY: Westminster John Knox, 2013.

Baylor Institute for Studies of Religion, *American Piety in the 21st Century: New Insights to the Depth and Complexity of Religion in the US* (September 2006). Online: http://www.baylor.edu/content/services/document.php/33304.pdf.

Bonhoeffer, Dietrich. *Letters and Papers from Prison.* New York: Macmillan, 1972.

———. *No Rusty Swords.* New York: Harper & Row, 1965.

———. *Sanctorum Communio.* London: Forgotten Books, Reprint 2013. (This was Bonhoeffer's 1927 doctoral dissertation, first published in 1930. Harper & Row published it in English as *The Communion of Saints* in 1963.)

Booker, Cory. "Conspiracy of Love." (Commencement address, Stanford University, June 17, 2012). No pages. Online: http://news.stanford.edu/news/2012/june/transcript-cory-booker-061912.html.

Borg, Marcus. *The God We Never Knew: Beyond Dogmatic Religion to a More Authentic Contemporary Faith.* HarperSanFrancisco, 1997.

———. *The Heart of Christianity: Rediscovering a Life of Faith.* San Francisco: HarperSanFrancisco, 2003.

———. *Meeting Jesus Again for the First Time.* San Francisco: HarperSanFrancisco, 1994.

Borg, Marcus J. and John Dominic Crossan. *The First Paul: Reclaiming the Radical Visionary Behind the Church's Conservative Icon.* New York: HarperOne, 2009.

Caputo, John D. *The Weakness of God: A Theology of the Event.* Bloomington: Indiana University Press, 2006.

———. *What Would Jesus Deconstruct?* Grand Rapids: Baker Academic, 2007.

Chesnut, Glenn F. "The Ground of Being: God and the Big Bang." Online: http://hindsfoot.org/g06grnd.pdf.

Coffin, William Sloane. *Credo.* Louisville: Westminster John Knox, 2004.

Cox, Harvey. *The Future of Faith.* New York: HarperOne, 2009.

Cupitt, Don. *Reforming Christianity*. Santa Rosa, CA: Polebridge, 2001.
Diels, Hermann Alexander. *Die Fragmente der Vorsokratiker* (The Fragments of the Pre-Socratics). Berlin, 1903.
Ellul, Jacques. *The Subversion of Christianity*. Grand Rapids, MI: Eerdmans, 1986.
Fox, Matthew. *A New Reformation: Creation Spirituality and the Transformation of Christianity*. Rochester, VT: Inner Traditions, 2006.
Freeman, Anthony. *God in Us: A Case for Christian Humanism*. Charlottesville, VA: Imprint Academic, 2001.
Funk, Robert. *Honest to Jesus: Jesus for a New Millennium*. HarperSanFrancisco, 1996.
———. "Twenty-one Theses." *The Fourth R*, Volume 11, Number 4 (July–August 1998).
Gibson, Arthur. *The Silence of God: Creative Response to the Films of Ingmar Bergman*. New York: Harper & Row, 1969.
Gloer, Hulitt. "Love Feast." *Holman Bible Dictionary*. Nashville, TN: Holman Bible Publishers, 1991. Online: http://www.studylight.org/dic/hbd/view.cgi?number=T3930
Holloway, Richard. *Doubts and Loves: What is Left of Christianity*. Edinburgh: Canongate, 2001.
Jeremias, Joachim. *Jerusalem in the Time of Jesus*. Philadelphia: Fortress, 1969.
Jordan, Clarence and Dallas Lee, editor. *The Substance of Faith and Other Cotton Patch Sermons*. New York: Association, 1972.
Kantonen, Taito A. *The Christian Hope*. Philadelphia: Muhlenberg, 1954.
Kaufman, Gordon. *In the Beginning . . . Creativity*. Minneapolis: Fortress, 2004.
———. *Jesus and Creativity*. Minneapolis: Fortress, 2010.
Keen, Sam. *Hymns to an Unknown God: Awakening the Spirit in Everyday Life*. New York: Bantam, 1994.
King, Martin Luther, Jr. *Where Do We Go from Here: Chaos of Community?* Boston: Beacon, 2010.
Kolodiejchuk, Brian. *Mother Teresa: Come Be My Light—The Private Writings of the Saint of Calcutta*. New York: Doubleday, 2007.
Kushner, Harold S. *When Bad Things Happen to Good People*. New York: Schoken, 1981.
Mack, Burton. *Who Wrote the New Testament?* New York: HarperCollins, 1995.
Macleish, Archibald. *J.B., A Play in Verse*. Boston: Houghton Mifflin, 1958.
Massey, Lesly F. "Perspectives on Christian Worship in Light of Romans 12:1." (Unpublished manuscript, 2005).
Menchú, Rigoberta. *I, Rigoberta Menchú: An Indian Woman in Guatemala*. London: Verso, 2009.
Moltmann, Jürgen. *The Crucified God: the Cross of Christ as the Foundation and Criticism of Christian Theology*. New York: Harper & Row, 1974.
Moyers, Bill. Foreword to *Faith Works: How Faith-based Organizations are Changing Lives, Neighborhoods, and America*, by Jim Wallis. Berkeley, CA: PageMill, 2001.
Nolan, Albert. *Jesus Before Christianity*. Maryknoll, NY: Orbis, 1976.
Nouwen, Henri. *The Selfless Way of Christ: Downward Mobility and the Spiritual Life*. Maryknoll, NY: Orbis, 2007.
Ortberg, John. *The Me I Want to Be: Becoming God's Best Version of You*. Grand Rapids: Zondervan, 2010.
Peck, M. Scott. *The Road Less Traveled: a New Psychology of Love, Traditional Values, and Spiritual Growth*. New York: Simon & Schuster, 1978.

Peterson, Eugene H. *The Message: The New Testament, Psalms and Proverbs*. Colorado Springs, CO: Navpress, 1993.
de Porete, Marguerite. *The Mirror of Simple Souls*. c. 1296–1306. Ellen L. Babinski, translator. New York: Paulist, 1993.
Premawardhana, Shanta. "A Demonstration of Contextual Theology." (December 21, 2015). No pages. Online: https://www.scupe.org/a-demonstration-of-contextual-theology/
Rauschenbusch, Walter. *A Theology for the Social Gospel*. Louisville: Westminster John Knox, 1997.
Remen, Rachel Naomi. "Helping, Fixing, Serving." *Shambhala Sun* (September 1999). No pages. Online: https://www.uc.edu/content/dam/uc/honors/docs/communityengagement/HelpingFixingServing.pdf
Robinson, John A. T. *Honest to God*. Philadelphia: Westminster, 1963.
———. *The New Reformation?* Philadelphia: Westminster, 1965.
Rocha, Zildo. *Helder, O Dom: uma vida que marcou os rumos da Igreja no Brasil* (Helder, the Gift: A Life that Marked the Course of the Church in Brazil). Petrópolis: Editora Vozes, 1999.
Rollins, Peter. *Insurrection*. New York: Simon and Schuster, 2011.
Rue, Loyal. *Everybody's Story: Wising Up to the Epic of Evolution*. Albany: SUNY Press, 2000.
Sheehan, Thomas. *The First Coming: How the Kingdom of God Became Christianity*. New York: Vintage, 1988.
Spinner, Chuck. *A Book of Prayers: to the Heavens from the Stars*. Bloomington IN: AuthorHouse, 2008.
Spong, John Shelby. "Twelve Theses." *The Fourth R*. Volume 11, Number 4 (July–August 1998).
———. *Why Christianity Must Change or Die: A Bishop Speaks to Believers in Exile*. HarperSanFrancisco, 1998.
Sussman, Dalia. "See Spot Go to Heaven? The Public's Not So Sure." ABCNews/Beliefnet poll (July 2001). No pages. Online: http://www.beliefnet.com/Inspiration/Angels/2001/05/See-Spot-Go-to-Heaven-The-Publics-Not-So-Sure.aspx.
Taylor, Barbara Brown. *Leaving Church: A Memoir of Faith*. HarperSanFrancisco: 2006.
Tertullian, *Apologeticus* (The Apology), c. 197 CE. No Pages. Online: http://www.tertullian.org/anf/anf03/anf03-05.htm#P253_53158.
Tillich, Paul. *Dynamics of Faith*. New York: Harper, 1958.
———. *The Shaking of the Foundations*. New York: Charles Scribner's Sons, 1948.
Van Biema, David. "Christians Wrong About Heaven, Says Bishop." *Time* (February 7, 2008). Online: http://www.time.com/time/world/article/0,8599,17108444,00.html.
Vanier, Jean. *Becoming Human*. New York: Paulist, 2008.
Wiesel, Elie. *Night*. New York: Bantam, 1982.
Wink, Walter. *The Human Being: Jesus and the Enigma of the Son of the Man*. Minneapolis: Fortress, 2002.
———. *The Powers That Be: Theology for a New Millennium*. New York: Doubleday, 1998.
Woolf, Virginia, Nigel Nicholson and Joanne Trautmann Banks, editors. *The Letters of Virginia Woolf: Volume II: 1912–1922*. New York: Harcourt Brace Jovanovich, 1976.
Wright, N. T. *Surprised by Hope: Rethinking Heaven, the Resurrection, and the Mission of the Church*. New York: HarperOne, 2008.

www.ingramcontent.com/pod-product-compliance
Lightning Source LLC
Chambersburg PA
CBHW050844230426
43667CB00012B/2147